Changing Australian Education

About the author

Alan Reid AM is Professor Emeritus of Education at the University of South Australia. Long recognised as one of Australia's leading educators, he has won many awards for his distinguished contributions to education, including the Gold Medal of the Australian Council of Educational Leaders.

Changing Australian Education:

How policy is taking us backwards and what can be done about it

Professor Emeritus Alan Reid, AM

Routledge
Taylor & Francis Group
LONDON AND NEW YORK

First published 2019 by Allen & Unwin

Published 2020 by Routledge
2 Park Square, Milton Park, Abingdon, Oxon OX14 4RN
605 Third Avenue, New York, NY 10017

Routledge is an imprint of the Taylor & Francis Group, an informa business

Copyright © Alan Reid 2019

All rights reserved. No part of this book may be reprinted or reproduced or utilised in any form or by any electronic, mechanical, or other means, now known or hereafter invented, including photocopying and recording, or in any information storage or retrieval system, without permission in writing from the publishers.

Notice:
Product or corporate names may be trademarks or registered trademarks, and are used only for identification and explanation without intent to infringe.

 A catalogue record for this book is available from the National Library of Australia

Set in 11.5/16 pt Sabon by Midland Typesetters, Australia

ISBN-13: 9781760875206 (pbk)

To the memory of Les Kemp, a great Australian educator.

Contents

Preface		ix
Introduction: A tale of two policy discourses		xv
Part 1	**The current state of Australian education policy, and why it must change**	**1**
Chapter 1	Neoliberalism comes to Australian education	3
Chapter 2	The damaging effects of current education policy directions	27
Part 2	**What are the problems?**	**51**
Chapter 3	Taking the public out of public education	53
Chapter 4	Standardised testing and its problems: A case study of the Programme for International Student Assessment (PISA)	79
Chapter 5	Evidence-based policy: The use and abuse of research	102
Chapter 6	Outside influences on education policy	130

Part 3	**Changing the educational narrative**	**151**
Chapter 7	The perils of ignoring the purposes of education	153
Chapter 8	Towards a process for thinking about futures for Australian education	167
Chapter 9	Using the process: A case study of the fourth industrial revolution	189
Part 4	**New policy directions for Australian education**	**227**
Chapter 10	New curriculum directions	229
Chapter 11	New pedagogical directions	254
Chapter 12	New directions in system-wide and school-based cultures	271
Epilogue:	Towards a new narrative for Australian education	289
Glossary		305
Acknowledgements		308
References		310
Index		334

Preface

The importance of education and educators

It has been my good fortune to have chosen education as a career. It is a field that is crucial to the wellbeing and functioning of Australia as a whole and every local community in it. Through education, individuals are given the opportunity to fulfil their potential, as well as develop the capacities needed to contribute to the economy and be active and productive citizens and members of social and cultural communities. Of course, formal education has always had this role but it has never been so important as it is now, given that we are living at a time when the speed of change is exponential.

The role of educators is central to the educational process and involves having not only knowledge about one or more areas of human endeavour, but expertise in helping people to learn and the capacity to form human relationships to assist that effort. For these reasons alone, being an educator is an incredibly rewarding job. There can be nothing more exhilarating than watching young people realise the power of learning.

But, more than this, one of the attractions for educators is that, unlike many other occupations, there are no absolutes in education, no clear-cut answers. Rather, education is about ideas and values, and so what constitutes a good education often changes from one context to the next. As a result, being an educator means being involved in a continuous process of learning involving discussion and debate, action and reflection, theory and practice and more—or at least it should mean that . . .

Some personal reflections

I remember as though it was yesterday my first appointment as a teacher at a new metropolitan high school in the north of Adelaide over forty years ago. The school had been designed as one of the first 'open space' high schools in the state, and it was alive with educational possibilities. The principal, Les Kemp, to whom this book is dedicated, was a brilliant educator who wanted to exploit the opportunities the new school presented. Les was a democrat who believed that the best leadership did not come from issuing orders from a hierarchical position, but from assisting teachers, students and parents to collaborate, share ideas and make joint decisions. He encouraged curriculum innovation, urging his teaching staff to devise curriculum approaches that best suited the context of the students and helped them to become inquisitive and independent learners with dispositions for caring about others and the wider common good, not just their own self-interest.

Teachers at the school knew that Les trusted their professional expertise, and they grasped the freedom with relish. The Social Science faculty, of which I was a member, spent hours—after school or at weekends—debating, sharing, evaluating and planning. We just loved our work and, as demonstrated by the educational outcomes that were achieved, the students lapped it up too. Driving home from school one night, I remember thinking that there was no other job that I would want to do. This one had more intellectual stimulation and fun than any other occupation I could imagine.

Forty years later, I still believe that education can contain that promise and excitement. But in those intervening years, education policy has slowly and inexorably eroded many of the aspects that made education such a rewarding and stimulating career. Sadly, in the process, it has rendered it more difficult for educators to form the relationships and exercise the pedagogical freedom needed to help learners to soar. At the same time, the joy of grappling with educational ideas and trialling and evaluating new approaches to address dilemmas, problems and challenges has been diminished. In its place has emerged a grey uniformity wherein, under the guise of 'lifting standards', state and federal governments have used their bureaucracies to control educators by means of top-down accountability mechanisms and intrusions into their work.

Certainly, there are many teachers and principals who kick against the traces and work hard to provide stimulating learning environments and experiences for the students in their care. But these efforts are made all the more difficult by the standardising culture, and less enjoyable, as the uncertainty of education gives way to the hubristic certainty of 'best practice' and 'key performance indicators'. Now, collaborative work is individualised and teachers are burdened by the intensification of their work, mostly associated with the increased administrative demands that accompany top-down forms of accountability (McGrath-Champ et al., 2018; Stroud, 2018).

Over the past twenty years I have watched these developments from my position in teacher education at the University of South Australia. During that time, I kept in touch with many of my former school-based colleagues and was saddened by their increasing disillusionment with the lack of trust shown in their professional expertise by policy-makers. Like some others in the academy, much of my research and writing was focused on trying to understand what was happening, writing critiques that described the damage that was being done, and railing against the policy agenda in conference keynotes. But it seemed such a puny response in the face of an ideological juggernaut. I was becoming increasingly despondent about my chosen profession.

However, in the last two years I have started to shake off my despondency, as green shoots of change have begun to appear on the educational landscape. For example, serious questions are now being asked about the place and role of the National Assessment Plan—Literacy and Numeracy (NAPLAN) in the policy assemblage, not just by teacher unions and some academics who have for many years warned about the damage it is doing in its current form, but also by politicians and some ministers for education, parent groups and think tanks. At last it is being conceded that concerns about NAPLAN do not signify a disregard for foundation skills like literacy and numeracy. Rather, they are based on the negative effects of the ways in which the test is being used. It seems that there might be an appetite for different forms of accountability that are richer and more expansive.

There are other signs as well. In 2018, I accepted an invitation from the Australian Secondary Principals' Association (ASPA) to write a monograph about education and the future. During the course of the writing I visited a range of schools, and spoke at conferences about the ideas in the monograph. This gave me the opportunity to talk with hundreds of educators around Australia. I noticed a growing determination by practitioners to win back the curriculum space that had been taken from them over the past thirty years. While they had always found ways around the bureaucratic impediments placed in their way, the associated administrivia was intrusive and time-consuming, and they wanted things to change.

During this period my old principal Les Kemp died in his early 90s, after a wonderful life. I was given the honour of delivering a eulogy about his contributions to education. Naturally, I described his guiding democratic and curriculum philosophies, and, after the funeral, many former colleagues and currently practising educators gathered at the wake. Old war stories were told, some burnished with age, but what came through—after forty years—was the excitement we all felt about being educators at that school, at that moment in time, when our expertise was trusted and we experienced genuine professional collaboration.

Of course, talk also turned to the current teaching environment, and many of us bemoaned the strictures under which educators are now operating. It was agreed that there was no point in going back to another time—the contemporary context has a different set of challenges, and anyway, there were aspects of that period, such as the lack of women in leadership positions, that must be consigned to history. But it was acknowledged that the spirit of our experience—the collegial relationships, the democratic decision-making, the sense that we were curriculum designers as well as implementers—set within a system of public education that prized its publicness, is timeless.

By this time I had developed the strong feeling that the climate was right for a significant change in the direction of Australian education policy. This was confirmed at a national forum in Canberra in March 2019, organised by principal associations from all education sectors—secondary and primary, Catholic and independent—and attended by representatives of key professional associations and parent groups from across the country. The purpose of the forum was to discuss the ideas in my monograph, and to establish a common voice in response to the proposition that it is time for Australia's educators to be more active in shaping public discussion and influencing policy directions and settings. There was a lot of energy in the room, and the day concluded with the presidents of the four organising associations signing a commitment to work together to ensure that educators' voices and views will make a major contribution to policy-making in the future.

By this time I was convinced that it is not too late to change the direction of Australian education policy, but we will have to act quickly. My sense is that the scale of the change requires a major overhaul, not simply tweaking a few current strategies. Australian education policy needs a new narrative, one that is sturdy enough to replace the pinched discourse that has been so dominant for so long. Such an ambitious project will require ideas from a range of sources, so I decided that my small contribution could be to expand my thoughts into a book that tries to explain how and why the dominant standardising narrative emerged, investigates its consequences, and proposes an alternative, more futures-focused narrative for Australian education. That is the genesis and the purpose of the book. It is written with the belief that Australian education can lead the world in shaping a new educational narrative that better prepares young people to face the challenges of the future.

Alan Reid, May 2019

Introduction

A tale of two policy discourses

The school education debate in Australia at both state and national levels comprises multiple voices, and yet much of it is based on a strange dichotomy. The dominant side of the debate has a standardisation[1] focus. It is represented by what has been described as the global education reform movement (GERM), which has a number of features, including school choice, competition between schools in an education market, high-stakes testing regimes that drive public accountability, narrowing the range of subjects and how they are taught, and publicly naming and shaming schools to drive improvement (Sahlberg, 2012, 2015). These strategies prize competition, regulation, quantification and conformity, and end up making education systems more uniform.

---

1 Standardisation is usually described as meaning the development and implementation of agreed technical standards that apply to all in a particular field. In this book, I argue that standardisation has been taken well beyond any useful purpose in education. Rather its spirit invades all policy areas, making all schools conform to the same narrow, technical standards without considering context. It stifles creativity and critical thinking and largely excludes the professional expertise of teachers from policy-making decisions.

Many countries around the world, including Australia, have been infected by GERM, as governments use the data provided by powerful international groups such as the Organisation for Economic Co-operation and Development (OECD) and the World Bank as the centrepiece of evidence-based policy, and contract private multinational corporations and consultancy companies like Pearson and McKinsey to develop educational strategies.

Running in parallel to standardisation is a less prominent side of the education debate that has a futures focus. It is based on the premise that the rapidity and extent of change in the contemporary world demands a new approach to education, one often referred to in reports as '21st-century learning' (e.g., Trilling & Fadel, 2009; Bellenca & Brandt, 2010; Scott, 2015). These reports cite accelerating globalisation and exponential growth in new technologies as factors that have spawned a number of specific economic, social, political and environmental developments, including digital technologies such as artificial intelligence (AI), machine learning, robotics and bio-technologies; climate change and resource depletion; metadata; diversity, migration and urbanisation; and more. They argue that such changes demand a significant rethink of traditional approaches to education. Strategies include student-centred teaching approaches, integrated and project-based learning, inquiry, more flexible student groupings, a focus on general capabilities, and so on. Rather than uniformity, such strategies prize flexibility, adaptability, collaboration and agility.

The differences between the standardisation and futures approaches are stark. Of course, in practice these often appear more as differences in emphasis, rather than as sharp antonyms; and sometimes both approaches are touted by the same people or groups. For example, the Programme for International Student Assessment (PISA)—a standardised test in the vanguard of GERM, and the justification for the implementation of many of the standardised approaches around the world—is owned and controlled by the OECD. And yet the OECD also promulgates reports that have a futures focus and propose approaches at odds with standardisation (e.g., OECD, 2018a).

This notwithstanding, it is clear that the standardisation focus is holding the upper hand, and has been instantiated in the framing of education policy in many countries, including Australia. This is despite the fact that teachers and educational researchers have demonstrated its negative consequences, arguing that such approaches actually stratify education systems, create educational inequalities, deprofessionalise educators, diminish the quality of education, and fail to address the challenges of the future (e.g., Ball, 2008; Rizvi & Lingard, 2010; Apple, 2013; Reid, 2013a; Ravitch, 2016; Thrupp, 2018).

Even judged by its own measures, the standardising discourse has been a failure. The outcomes of the past three PISA tests—measures that are touted by GERM advocates as indicative of the quality of education systems—are claimed to have recorded a steady decline in Australia's position on the international league tables in mathematics, science and reading. Every three years since 2003, the release of the results has been accompanied by much wailing and gnashing of teeth by politicians and the mainstream media. We are told that things must improve. The answer? More of the same! That's right, despite thirty years of the standardising discourse in education, those who advocate it believe that educational quality continues to decline and that the answer is to ramp up standardisation!

A South Australian case study

Rather than talk in generalities, it might be useful to look at a case study of the standardisation logic in action. In 2017, the Education Department in South Australia engaged the international consultancy firm McKinsey and Company, at a cost of more than a million dollars, to map out a plan to make South Australia a 'world-class' education system. McKinsey has been at the forefront of the standardising agenda in education, having been commissioned by many countries around the world to advise on 'improvement' strategies, and so more of the same was expected.

McKinsey's first task was to establish the meaning of the concept of 'world-class'. This was done using what they called a 'Universal Scale', which was based on the National Assessment Program—Literacy and Numeracy (NAPLAN) results from 2017 mapped back to the Universal Scale via the latest PISA, TIMSS and PIRLS results.[2] This statistical feat produced the number 482, which placed South Australia in the arbitrarily McKinsey-defined 'good' band of schools, but well below countries in the 'great' band above, the highest of which were Canada, Finland and Estonia with a score of 530. This was shown on a graph, with an upward line drawn between 482 and 530 over a ten-year period showing the rate of acceleration needed for South Australia to achieve 'world-class' status. So there it is. The quality of South Australian education is captured in a single number, and its educational aspiration for the future is represented by another number. It is reminiscent of Douglas Adams's *Hitchhiker's Guide to the Galaxy*, where the answer to the meaning of life, as calculated by a supercomputer over the past 7.5 million years, is 42.

Now there are many questions raised by the statistical methodology employed here—including the validity and reliability of the tests themselves—which cast serious doubt about the plausibility of the 'Universal Scale'. But leaving those aside, the number is based primarily on tests in literacy, mathematics and numeracy, and science from Years 3–10. That is, the most that could be claimed is

---

2   These three international tests are the Program for International Student Assessment (PISA) which is conducted every three years by the OECD and tests 15 year old students in mathematic literacy, science literacy and reading literacy; Trends in Mathematics and Science Study (TIMSS) which tests Year 4 and Year 8 students in mathematics and science, and is a project of the International Association for the Evaluation of Educational Achievement (IEA); and the Progress in International Reading Literacy Study (PIRLS) of the IEA, and tests Year 4 students in reading literacy every five years

that the number reflects educational outcomes in a small number of subjects in the compulsory years of schooling. That is very different from claiming that the number represents the quality of an education system. Obviously it says nothing about a huge range of other subjects such as the arts, humanities, social sciences, and technology; nothing about the general capabilities we might want young people to develop; nothing about the quality of the relationships in the system; nothing about the extent of inequalities in educational outcomes; nothing about the senior secondary years; and so on. Basically, it tells us very little. And yet we are informed that South Australia will be a 'world-class' system if it improves its current number by 48 points over ten years—assuming, of course, that those countries at the top on 530 points don't improve at the same rate!

So what was McKinsey's plan to get the South Australian education system from 482 to 530? It won't come as a surprise to learn that this also involves measurement and numbers. South Australian schools have been rated using NAPLAN and South Australian Certificate of Education (SACE) results and then, using those numbers and a 'trajectory of improvement' score based on results in previous years, assigned a number from one to five. The numbers correspond to 'stages of improvement', which, from the lowest to the highest, are described as 'build foundations', 'maintain momentum', 'shift gear', 'stretch' and 'inspire'. Schools have been supplied with literacy and numeracy guides with strategies that correspond to the 'stage' the school has been assigned, and required to develop a three-year plan for improvement almost entirely focusing on literacy and numeracy (Williams, 2018).

This recent development in South Australia is an example of the logical end result of the direction that education policy in Australia has taken over the past thirty years. Indeed, it encapsulates all the signature characteristics of the standardising agenda: educational aspirations are described by banal slogans such as 'world-class'; educators are excluded from discussions about approaches to improvement as an international consultancy firm takes their place; the breadth of education is reduced to literacy and numeracy to improve test scores; there is an unshakeable belief in the certainty and accuracy of numbers and statistical results; strategies for 'improvement' are uniform; and labelling and competition are expected to drive improvement. It is a mechanical and lifeless approach to educational improvement.

At the same time of course, there are many South Australian schools that are involved in highly innovative curriculum work, despite such a policy agenda. The sad thing is that this work is not being done in an environment that promotes and supports innovation in curriculum and pedagogy. Rather, educators are forced to innovate in the policy cracks, as they also grapple with the competing, and often contradictory, demands of the standardising approaches foisted on them. However, the fact that educators maintain the commitment to shape educational programs that will challenge and excite students, as well as equip them for the future, is what makes the fight for a better educational narrative so important.

The origins of the standardising policy discourse

So where did the standardising agenda come from, and why has it been so dominant in Australian education at the level of state as well as national education policy? **Chapter 1** describes the genesis of the standardising agenda, tracing it back to neoliberalism, the political and economic settlement that has dominated the western world for the past forty years, since the collapse of Keynesian economics and the welfare state in the early 1970s. Based on a belief in an unfettered free market, neoliberalism places the individual and 'individual responsibility' at its core, and so marginalises or rejects concepts such as the 'public good' and 'community'.

Areas of social policy such as education have not been immune from neoliberal ideology, and have adopted many of its central tenets and strategies. In education, the standardising narrative is based on a set of core neoliberal purposes, principles and values. Thus, education has become a private commodity to be accessed by individuals trying to maximise their self-interest. Schools are located in an education market competing for custom, and parents and students are customers who are helped to make choices by comparing schools on league tables constructed on the basis of standardised tests.

Chapter 2 argues that the standardising policy setting is causing real damage to Australian education, and is not serving our national interest. Apart from producing inequitable educational outcomes and stratifying schooling, it is having adverse effects on our sense of community. At a time when Australian society needs a more caring, generous, compassionate and respectful community, education policy is based on a suite of policy assumptions that focus on the self-interest of individuals. More than this, although the standardising agenda justifies its strategies on the grounds that they improve educational quality, in fact they make it more difficult for educators to personalise learning and to adapt the curriculum to the needs of a changing society. In short, the standardising approach works against high quality—notwithstanding the claims of its proponents that it will result in a 'world-class' education. It is clear that Australian education policy needs a new education narrative.

Why has the standardising discourse been so dominant?

While the standardising agenda is the dominant policy narrative, it does not have the field to itself. Many educators are using pedagogical approaches that exploit the new technologies, personalise learning programs and integrate learning. However, such approaches rarely become part of the mainstream policy discourse—they are being employed despite the policy regime that bears down on teachers' work, rather than because of it. Educators struggle on a daily basis against the constraints imposed by standardised testing and intrusive accountability mechanisms. Similarly, in the professional literature many education researchers and practitioners are proposing new ways to think about school education, albeit in different ways and with different emphases—again with little policy impact. Why don't these alternative voices get any traction? Why is the standardising policy agenda so difficult to dislodge?

The major reason for the dominance of the standardising discourse is that it is based on an educational narrative that has a coherent core, comprising its purposes and an accompanying set of principles, values and assumptions. These have become so normalised that they are simply taken for granted, as are the strategies that spring from them. **Part 2** provides examples of how the neoliberal education policy discourse plays out in Australia. Each of the chapters takes a different aspect—the interpretation of a key concept like 'public' (**Chapter 3**), the 'truths' revealed by standardised tests (**Chapter 4**), what constitutes educational 'research' (**Chapter 5**), and 'borrowing policy' from other countries (**Chapter 6**)—to show how the standardising discourse not only shapes policy, but puts its ideological stamp on educational language and practice.

All of this means that when educators challenge a strategy but not the assumptions upon which it is based, it can be a Pyrrhic victory. For example, even if the campaign to remove NAPLAN were to be successful, unless the foundations of the standardising discourse are also changed, it simply means that a new approach based on the same principles and assumptions would regrow in its place. In other words, until the core narrative is changed, alternative strategies will simply be drawn into the standardising orbit.

Towards a new educational narrative

It will be no easy task to reverse the process and repair the damage done by the standardising discourse. For a start, given the symbiotic relationship between neoliberalism in the economic sphere and neoliberalism in the social sphere, challenges to the standardising agenda need to go beyond just changing the direction of education policy. Clearly educators will have to be part of the broader project of trying to shift the grip that neoliberalism has on our society. But there are many signs that neoliberalism is unravelling. Indeed, according to Nobel prize-winning economist Joseph Stiglitz, there is a consensus among economists that '[n]eoliberalism is dead in both developing and developed countries' (Martin, 2016). In Australia, there are indications that both major political parties are starting to move away from the dead-hand of the neoliberal policy narrative, towards a more caring and compassionate narrative focused on the common good (Johnson, 2019).

But there is no reason to wait until neoliberalism meets its inevitable demise before acting to address the problems it has caused in education. Indeed, it may be that education is the key to dismantling other aspects of neoliberalism. After all, such a task will require a citizenry with the relevant knowledge, capacities and insights to be able to challenge its basic tenets and to shape an alternative agenda. If we are to turn our back on the selfish individualism of neoliberalism, the dog-eat-dog competition, the lack of care and compassion for others—the stuff that has so manifestly not worked and is propped up now by empty slogans touting the benefits of discredited notions like 'trickle-down economics'—then education is going to have to make an important contribution.

If this is to happen—if the current standardising agenda is to be seriously challenged—then there is need for a new and powerful educational narrative. It is important that the alternative agenda does not simply amount to a yearning for a return to the past. Although there are aspects of Australia's educational past that should be revived—such as the agreement that well-resourced public schools are the benchmark for a quality education system—the past was not an educational golden age. There were many aspects to which we must not return, including imbalances of power relationships in education systems, curricula that privileged the knowledge of particular social groups, and an almost sole diet of didactic pedagogy. The past must be recognised but not fetishised. Clearly, breaking the stranglehold of the standardising approach demands policies and practices that are better suited to the changing environment of the 21st century.

Part 3 of this book proposes the elements of a new and powerful narrative for Australian education. **Chapter 7** starts the process by exploring what the educational literature is saying about the kinds of changes that are needed in education. It concludes by arguing that many of the proposals assume, rather than articulate, the purposes and values of education, and that no educational narrative can survive without being explicit about these.

Chapter 8 then describes three key elements of a new educational narrative. They are:

1. *Purposes:* that are the bedrock of the narrative setting out why education is needed in the contemporary world
2. *Values and principles:* that are consistent with the purposes and that challenge the selfish individualism and standardisation of the neoliberal policy narrative
3. *A process:* that enables educators and policy-makers, in an ongoing way, to understand, monitor, evaluate and assess broad societal trends and the changes they are bringing in the various arenas covered by the purposes of education. This information is used to make decisions about curriculum, pedagogy, school structure and environments.

All three elements of the new educational narrative are interrelated and must be addressed. Thus, the purposes, values and principles must serve as reference points for deciding on the kinds of strategies that are suggested by the process.

Implications for policy and practice

In the face of the incredible speed of change in the contemporary world, the traditional stop–start approach to curriculum development is no longer adequate. Thus, Chapter 8 proposes a six-step process as the third element of a new narrative for Australian education. The process is designed to enable educators and policy-makers to make decisions about curriculum, pedagogy, school structure and environments in an ongoing way, using an investigation of a key societal issue as the starting point. **Chapter 9** trials the process with a case study of a major societal change—the fourth industrial revolution—and explores its impact on the arenas covered by the purposes of education. The rest of the book uses the insights from the case study to iterate a number of curriculum policies/strategies that are suggested by the case study and that are consistent with the identified purpose, values and principles.

The educational implications of the case study are proposed in **Part 4**.

Chapter 10 identifies the key connected elements of a contemporary curriculum—disciplinary learning, interdisciplinary learning, general capabilities and meta-learning—and explores the blockages to some of these ideas and how they can be addressed.

Chapter 11 looks at the implications of the case study for pedagogy and proposes a teaching and learning framework to facilitate the flexibility demanded by a curriculum that meets changing societal demands. The blockages to a more flexible pedagogical approach are investigated and some suggestions made for their removal.

Chapter 12 outlines the environment needed to nurture a culture of research and inquiry at schools and system-wide levels; and to model the characteristics and values that are the bedrock of the new narrative. It argues that approaches that exclude the voices of educators, students and parents must be jettisoned. It is pointless aspiring to develop values such as trust, collaboration, respect and empathy if the top-down decisions of policy-makers treat these groups with disdain.

The **Epilogue** reflects on the case study and its process. In particular it argues that, if used in conjunction with the purposes and principles, the new educational narrative is sturdy enough to present itself as real alternative to the standardising discourse that has such a hold on educational policy-makers. Indeed, in the face of the information from the case study about the effects of technological disruption on work, the economy and social and cultural life, the standardising agenda looks lifeless.

This book is written in the belief that it is time to change. It makes the case that, notwithstanding the many fine ideas and programs educators have developed over the past few years—despite rather than because of the current policy regime—we do not have a powerful narrative that unites these ideas into an approach capable of meeting the challenges of the 21st century rather than the certainties of the 20th century. Education, now and in the future, is too important to be shaped by impoverished policy-making that standardises education, demeans educators, sells students short and fails to meet the challenges of the future.

Part I

The current state of Australian education policy, and why it must change

Overview

Part 1 examines the origin, history and effects of the dominant standardising discourse in education. It identifies its weaknesses and describes the damage it is doing, as the basis for thinking about how it might be challenged.

Chapter 1 explores the development of the philosophy and key features that lie at the heart of the standardising discourse—that of neoliberalism. It then moves to describe the various ways in which neoliberalism has shaped education policy, showing how it is this ideology that has resulted in the standardising discourse that has been, and continues to be, so dominant in Australian education.

Chapter 2 analyses the damaging effects that neoliberal education policy has had on Australian education. It focuses on seven adverse consequences and argues the need for a new educational policy narrative.

Chapter 1

Neoliberalism comes to Australian education

The Introduction to this book argued that a new educational narrative is needed if Australian education is to undo the damage that has been done to it by the standardising discourse that has so dominated education policy over the past thirty years. However, changing an entrenched policy direction is complex, not least because the ideology that shapes it is so embedded in the language, concepts, beliefs and assumptions of policy-makers. It is not just a matter of changing aspects of it or drafting an alternative narrative. Unless the ways in which the standardising discourse maintains its dominance are understood and addressed, alternative strategies are only likely to be colonised by it. Thus, the first task is to understand the origins of the standardising discourse and the various forms it has taken over the years. In the Introduction it was argued that the standardising discourse in education was spawned by the philosophy of neoliberalism, and so that is where the analysis will begin.

The rise of neoliberalism

For the past forty years, a dominant narrative has shaped Australian society. Described as neoliberalism, it comprises a set of ideas and practices that are supported by a foundational philosophy that embraces our cultural, as well as our economic and political, lives. David Harvey explains it as a theory of '. . . political and economic practices that proposes that human well-being can best be advanced by liberating individual entrepreneurial freedoms and skills within an institutional framework characterized by strong private property rights, free markets and free trade' (Harvey, 2005, p. 2). At its heart is the individual, who advances her/his self-interest by competing with others to get ahead. Neoliberalism posits that the best way to organise ourselves is to create the conditions for competition to flourish; and the most efficient way to do that is through the free market. All aspects of society should be run like a business, with the profit motive dominant, and winners and losers created. In this process, the individual becomes a customer or consumer, rather than a citizen (Cahill & Toner, 2018).

Neoliberalism maintains that the path to wealth creation requires governments to get out of the way of the 'wealth creators' by removing regulations that constrain business, and by lessening their tax burden. Rather than governments orchestrating the distribution of wealth, this should be managed by the market, with the rewards to business 'trickling down' to benefit all. In this way, inequality is seen as a social good. Neoliberal governments thus unshackle businesses from government controls and 'red tape', and deregulate economic levers such as banking, currency exchange and capital movement (Monbiot, 2017; Denniss, 2018). At the same time, public services are expected to adopt the structures and processes of business, or are outsourced or privatised. By defining individual freedom as the ability to make choices in a market, neoliberalism commodifies activities such as education, childcare and health by turning their delivery into market exchanges. As Monbiot puts it, neoliberalism defines human society *by* the market, and *as* a market, which is

> run in every respect as if it were a business, its social relations reimagined as commercial transactions; people redesignated as human capital. The aim and purpose of society is to maximise profits. (Monbiot, 2017, p. 30)

So entrenched is neoliberal philosophy that it appears to be a law of nature; so powerful are its ideas that they have shaped our language, and the way we see the world, ourselves and the alternatives that are open to us in the future. So where did it come from?

The origins of neoliberalism

The term neoliberal first appeared in Europe in the late 1930s and the basis of the philosophy was described by the Austrian economist Friedrich Hayek in *The Road to Serfdom*, which was published in 1944. In that book Hayek argued against central government planning, which he claimed crushes individualism and inevitably leads to totalitarian control. At the time his targets were the social democratic projects of Britain's welfare state and Roosevelt's New Deal in America, and his ideas were immediately attractive to those, particularly the wealthy, who felt constrained by high taxation and government controls.

Over the next thirty years, a transatlantic network of journalists, businesspeople and academics worked to spread Hayek's ideas through think tanks such as the Mont Pelerin Society which Hayek co-founded in 1947, universities and the mainstream press (Dunlop, 2018). One particularly influential group of economists at the University of Chicago continued to refine and harden neoliberal theory. Milton Friedman was a key member of this group, and his 1962 book *Capitalism and Freedom* provided a powerful summary of the developing neoliberal narrative. Friedman urged that government should only involve itself in matters related to the survival of its people and the country, and stand aside from all other matters. For Friedman, it is the combination of unfettered free markets and the entrepreneurial spirit that produces successful societies.

By the 1960s the neoliberal narrative had many adherents, but it remained at the edges of economic policy. Since World War 2, the prevailing economic theory of economist John Maynard Keynes had been in the ascendancy. Keynesian economic policy comprised such measures as high tax rates for those with the highest incomes, full employment and the provision of public services and welfare safety nets to support those without adequate means. While postwar economies boomed, Keynesian economics was unassailable. But with the impact of globalisation and the economic crises of the 1970s, it began to founder. Neoliberalism was waiting in the wings and it was not long before its prescriptions entered the mainstream political debate.

Margaret Thatcher, who became Prime Minister of Great Britain in 1979, and Ronald Reagan, who became President of the United States in 1980, were both devotees and immediately after they were elected started to implement the full suite of neoliberal policy offerings. This included deregulation, privatisation, tax cuts for the wealthy and attacks on trade unions. At the same time, international organisations such as the World Bank, the International Monetary Fund and the World Trade Organization imposed neoliberal policies on many other countries (Monbiot, 2017).

Neoliberalism was taken up by the progressive as well as the conservative side of politics. Thus, the Clinton and Obama Democratic administrations in the US and the Blair Labour government in the UK pursued a neoliberal policy agenda, albeit in a diluted form. In this version, the language of markets, competition and deregulation that infused economic policy was leavened by the establishment of safety nets for those who were most adversely affected by laissez-faire economics. In Britain, this watered-down version was referred to as the 'Third Way' (Giddens, 1998), since it purported to offer an alternative to Keynesian economics and neoliberalism—although, with the benefit of hindsight, it is clear that the main tenets of neoliberalism were still at its core.

Neoliberalism and Australia

Australia was not immune from the new dogma. Up until the early 1980s the Australian economy had been regulated through policies such as trade protection, restricted migration and centralised wage fixing through conciliation and arbitration. However, after the election in 1983 of the Hawke Labor Government, these policies began to be dismantled on the grounds that their removal would create the conditions for Australia to trade and compete in the international market. Thus, the Hawke government floated the exchange rate, reformed the labour market, reduced tariff barriers and privatised or commercialised government authorities to enable them to respond more quickly and efficiently to market signals (Shanahan, 2009). Many of these changes bore some similarity to what was happening under neoliberalism in the US and the UK. But there were some significant differences.

The Hawke government attempted to soften the adverse consequences of unleashing market forces on the Australian economy in ways that differed significantly from the hard-line policies adopted by Reagan and Thatcher. Thus, in changing the centralised wage fixation system, it negotiated a Prices and Incomes Accord that broadened the wage debate from one solely focused on take-home pay, to one that proposed a social wage including more funding for education, health, childcare and welfare for those the market had disadvantaged. That is, Labor retained the social welfare part of the Keynesian project (Pocock, 2009).

Swan (2017) argues that such measures mean that it is inaccurate to portray the Hawke/Keating governments as implementing neoliberal policies, preferring instead to describe it as 'Australian Laborism', which predated Blair's Third Way ideology. This is a view that assumes there is only one version of neoliberalism. The form neoliberalism takes does not play out in the same way in different cultures and contexts: it depends on emphasis, previous history and intention. However, there are some fundamental tenets of neoliberal thought that define it anywhere, and these lay at the heart of Labor policy. Undoubtedly, the aim was to shift to a more market-oriented economy with less reliance on government regulation; more competition; and a marketised and trimmed down public sector (Pusey, 1991). Although Thatcher's and Reagan's neoliberalism was much starker and harsher than the Australian Labor government's version in the 1980s and 1990s, the latter nonetheless bore all the hallmarks of neoliberal ideology. More than this, it laid the groundwork for the harder version that followed.

The election of the conservative Howard Liberal/National Party Coalition government in 1996 saw a ramping up of neoliberalism. Over the next twelve years there was an even greater emphasis on the individual and the free market, an increase in privatisation, tax relief for the wealthy, marginalisation of trade unions, reduction in spending on public infrastructure, and downsizing of the public sector. These policies were accompanied by a growing community distrust of government and a greater focus on the individual. Social wage programs were replaced by an emphasis on take-home pay, and small tax cuts were delivered regularly. Now the focus was on individual opportunity and productivity, rather than redistribution of wealth through government programs (Megalogenis, 2012).

During the Coalition's period in government, traditional notions of fairness, egalitarianism and equal opportunity were slowly replaced. Gone was the Keynesian approach to social welfare posited on the belief that it was the duty of any civilised society to support those who are least advantaged. Under the Coalition government's version of neoliberalism, those requiring welfare assistance began to be talked about as failures being supported by those who had the will, ability and motivation to succeed: the leaners relying on the lifters, as the then-Treasurer described it in 2014 (Hockey, 2014).

When the Howard government lost the 2007 federal election, it seemed that the incoming Rudd Labor government would adopt the softer version of neoliberal policy. However, the impact of the Global Financial Crisis (GFC), which began to be felt from August 2008, changed all that. The 2008 crash of the derivatives market and the subprime mortgage lending that had been constructed by a number of American banks and investment companies revealed the manifold weaknesses and internal contradictions of neoliberalism. Driven by greed and profit, and in the absence of regulation, the US housing market bubble burst with a vengeance, leaving thousands of people unable to service loans and without homes and jobs. And the impact was not just felt in the United States. The derivatives market had been globalised and many of the big banks and investment firms in the US had been drawn into the foolhardy schemes. This meant that when the American banks froze credit to deal with the crisis, so too did global credit markets freeze, and stock markets crash.

Ironically, the response to the chaos caused by neoliberal ideology was to resort to government intervention. The United States government pumped US$13 trillion into taxpayer-funded bailouts and guarantees in an effort to unfreeze American and global credit markets. They ran up government debts that were close to 100 per cent of gross domestic product, and they printed money. So much for a free market unfettered by government interference! Under a neoliberal philosophy it seems that business takes the profit while government bears the risk.

While government intervention stabilised the system after a few years, it had generated massive unemployment, and triggered a prolonged recession. More than this, as Mason (2015) observes, governments in America, Britain, Europe and Japan offset their spending through austerity programmes whereby

> they transferred the pain away from people who'd invested money stupidly, punishing instead welfare recipients, public sector workers, pensioners and, above all, future generations. In the worst hit countries, the pension system has been destroyed, the retirement age is being hiked . . . and education is being privatized so that graduates will face a lifetime of high debt. Services are being dismantled and infrastructure projects put on hold. (Mason, 2015, p. 4)

In this way, the businesses that created the GFC were assisted by governments, while the most disadvantaged in the community were further penalised.

Australia escaped the worst of these effects for two important reasons. First, the form neoliberalism had taken in Australia from the time of the Hawke government was not as pure as it had been in countries such as the United States. Thus, Australia had maintained stricter regulatory controls in the banking system, which meant that the derivatives market was not as laissez faire as it had been in the US. The second reason was the Keynesian-like economic stimulus designed by the Rudd government, as part of which taxpayer funds were spent on some nation-building projects, including the Building the Education Revolution (involving the design and construction of school infrastructure, such as halls and gymnasiums for schools) and the Home Insulation Program (involving the installation of pink batts).

At the time it seemed that the GFC was the canary down the mine for neoliberalism. Its central element was a belief in the capacity of the free market to order society and to bring wealth and prosperity to all; and this had been exposed as a sham. One of the first to draw attention to this was the Australian Prime

Minister, Kevin Rudd, who in February 2009 wrote an essay for *The Monthly* titled 'The Global Financial Crisis', arguing that the GFC heralded a paradigmatic shift in the philosophy and ideas that had informed policy-making for the previous thirty years. Indeed, for Rudd it spelt the beginning of the end for neoliberalism, which he defined as 'free market fundamentalism, extreme capitalism and excessive greed' (Rudd, 2009), which had become the orthodoxy of our time. For Rudd, the GFC meant that neoliberalism could no longer justify the extent of inequality or excuse the greed that it generated.

Rudd set out a new social democratic agenda in which there was a balance between the market and the state, and a commitment to social justice, the latter being a word and concept that had been expunged from Howard's policy-making agenda. It seemed that change was afoot, although it must be said that parts of the subsequent Rudd/Gillard philosophy remained firmly rooted in neoliberal philosophy. However, when the Liberal/National Party Coalition regained government in 2013 under the leadership of Tony Abbott, it was as though the GFC had not happened. Neoliberal policies and the language of neoliberalism were back with a vengeance and have shaped government policy ever since—albeit containing the same set of contradictions that have accompanied it since the 1980s, such as supporting the private sector with subsidies when politically advantageous (Denniss, 2018). Indeed, although faith in neoliberalism has been severely dented, and many economists and commentators have pronounced its impending demise, neoliberalism retains its hegemony in policy-making and political discourse. So what has been its impact, and why is it so hard to dislodge?

The effects of neoliberalism

The first thing to say is that the promise of wealth trickling down to benefit all has proven to be an illusion. Monbiot points out that, far from making society more wealthy, neoliberalism has created inequality even while it has put the brakes on economic growth:

> Economic growth has been markedly slower in the neoliberal era (since 1980 in Britain and the US) than it was in the preceding decades; but not for the very rich. Inequality in the distribution of both income and wealth, after 60 years of decline, rose rapidly in this era, due to the smashing of trade unions, tax reductions, rising rents, privatisation and deregulation. (Monbiot, 2016)

In 2017, the International Monetary Fund's (IMF) regular Fiscal Monitor report calculated that income inequality had increased in nearly half of the world's countries over the past three decades (IMF, 2017). One of the drivers of such inequality is the unequal ownership of national wealth, comprising publicly owned assets (e.g., schools, hospitals) and privately owned assets. Since 1980, in nearly all countries there have been very large transfers of public to private wealth. That is, while overall national wealth has increased, public wealth is now negative or zero in rich countries (Savola, 2017). The crucial point is that such a shift severely limits the capacity of national governments to tackle inequality. If, as Wilkinson and Pickett (2009) point out, the greater the inequality the greater the social dysfunction, then neoliberalism may have advantaged the very wealthy, but it has done so at the expense of social harmony, cohesion, well-being, and (ironically) economic growth.

Australia's experience mirrors that of other rich countries. An Australian Council of Social Services (ACOSS) report calculates that in terms of income inequality in Australia, someone in the highest 20 per cent of the income scale lives in a household with five times as much income as someone in the lowest 20 per cent of the income scale. Indeed, someone in the top 1 per cent of income scales receives an average weekly income twenty-six times what someone in the lowest 5 per cent of that scale receives. In terms of wealth inequality, those in the highest 20 per cent of the wealth scale hold nearly two-thirds of all wealth, while those in the lowest 50 per cent hold only 18 per cent of all wealth (ACOSS, 2018). Even those who have been staunch advocates of neoliberal economic reform, such as the head of the Australian Competition and Consumer commission (ACCC) and the OECD, are beginning to document its failures, observing that increasing inequality has actually dampened growth (Cahill & Toner, 2018, introduction).

And yet despite what the GFC exposed as its weaknesses, despite the manifest inequalities it has generated, despite the inefficiencies in economic and social policy it has so clearly produced, neoliberalism is still the dominant ideology in the western world. What accounts for its resilience? The answer can be found in the language and ideas that have accompanied it for so long. These have become so embedded in public discourse that it seems as though they are natural laws, regardless of the contradictions and paradoxes they embody.

Obviously, neoliberal policies play out in different ways in different contexts. Nonetheless, there are some common features that are as much cultural and political as they are economic. These stem from the core belief that the best way to arrange society is through the interrelationship between the free market and the choice-making individual. The correlate of this belief is that governments should get out of the way of individuals and businesses so that they are unimpeded by regulations and taxes. Indeed, it is argued that the best results are achieved when those who have the means are encouraged to spend and invest—that is, when their taxes are cut—and when government expenditure on public services is reduced. These key elements of the neoliberal discourse have changed the tenor of public debate in a number of ways. In his *Quarterly Essay*, Richard Denniss (2018) describes claims about neoliberalism, exposing many of the contradictions between its core beliefs and its practices. For example, and in no particular order, neoliberal rhetoric:

- creates the impression that the interests of the wealthy coincide with the interests of the community at large
- serves to shift the debate about public policy away from questions about what is right or fair, towards a debate about what is affordable and efficient, and in particular that government spending is wasteful
- encourages people to think of themselves as consumers exercising choice in their own self-interest, rather than as citizens with an interest in the common good
- enables governments to cut community programs on the grounds that there is a 'budget emergency' while providing subsidies to big business on the grounds that it creates jobs
- establishes the assumption that marketisation is the best way to drive important public infrastructure and programs, and fans a mistrust of the public service; in so doing, it has created an environment in which reducing the public service is seen as a necessary goal while masking the fact that, when they are privatised, many privately run public facilities are less efficient and do not serve the public interest
- constructs the debate about support for the least advantaged upon questions about their motives, and the need for strategies to ensure that any support does not have 'unintended consequences'; at the extreme end of neoliberalism, inequality is actually seen as desirable because it is claimed to promote individual initiative and so build wealth
- defines freedom in ways that benefit businesses while attacking workers or the environment
- reduces faith in democratic life by, for example, convincing many that a debate about the direction and nature of our society is a distraction from economic matters such as tax cuts and industrial relations reform.

In these and other ways, neoliberalism does not simply function as an economic philosophy, it pervades our social and cultural lives. It has helped to establish the parameters of our public debate by organising that debate around the needs of the market, and masking the interests and power relations it serves. If the GFC heralded the manifold failings of neoliberalism as a way to run the economy, then a public sphere coarsened by narrow self-interest and inequality demonstrates that neoliberalism impoverishes social and cultural life too.

This brief sketch of the history and features of neoliberalism has been provided because it is impossible to understand what is happening to education today without appreciating the broader context within which education policy and practice is shaped. The point is that the basic tenets of neoliberalism have been used to fashion the purposes, strategies and policies that are currently dominant in the educational discourse. The Preface referred to the global education reform movement (GERM) as the catch-all term used to describe the standardising educational agenda that has dictated education policy over the past thirty years. GERM is the educational child of neoliberalism.

However, it would be foolhardy to talk in generalities and assume that GERM is the same all over the world. Just as neoliberalism in the economic sphere has manifested in different ways in different nation-states, so too has neoliberal education policy assumed a variety of forms with a range of effects. It will be argued in this book that neoliberalism in education is having a toxic impact on education while failing to grapple with the challenges of the 21st century. But if we are to develop an alternative educational narrative, the first task is to understand the particular form that GERM has taken in Australia, and to analyse its impact. Only then will we be in a position to suggest approaches that will better suit Australian society now and into the future.

Neoliberalism comes to Australian education
Australian education before neoliberalism

In the second half of the 19th century, public schools in the various Australian colonies were established to cater for working-class children whose families could not afford private education. In the first instance, compulsory public education was confined to basic or elementary schooling, the main aim of which was to 'gentle the masses' for purposes of social control (Miller, 1986). Secondary education, for which one paid fees at private colleges, was primarily for the children of the upper and middle classes, who were seen as the future leaders.

When Australia federated in 1901, education remained the constitutional responsibility of the states. Gradually, through the first half of the 20th century, access to education was broadened by increasing the age of compulsory school attendance and expanding secondary education and making it free to all children. This was justified through a liberal meritocratic ideology that maintained that advancement up the educational ladder, and thus social advancement, should occur on the basis of ability, interest and effort, rather than be determined by birth (Campbell & Proctor, 2014).

However, this emerging ideology did not question the relationship between a child's background and educational outcomes. The structures that were established to offer different pathways for students invariably replicated and reproduced the prevailing social structures and circumstances. By the 1950s, it remained the case that the majority of university students came from private schools that offered an academic curriculum, while students from working-class backgrounds either left school as soon as they reached the compulsory leaving age of fourteen years, or were overwhelmingly represented in technical schools. The few working class students who made it to university were cited as examples of the efficacy of the ideology of meritocracy.

During the 1950s and 1960s, economic growth, the post-World War 2 baby boom, and waves of migration led to increased demands on schools as people, recognising the potential of education, began to insist on the provision of greater opportunities for their children. By the 1960s, the age of compulsion rose to fifteen years and the economy required more skilled workers. Education was seen as a central nation-building project, important not only for economic growth but also for social cohesion as Australian society became more diverse (Campbell & Proctor, 2014).

As an aside, it is relevant to point out here that such developments heightened the interest of the Commonwealth government in school education and, from the 1960s, it began to contribute to school funding—a contribution that was expanded and systematised by 1973. Once that happened it was inevitable that the Commonwealth would want more say in education policy, such as curriculum. Thus, from the 1970s onwards, the tensions between the nation-building aspirations of the Commonwealth government on the one hand, and the constitutional responsibility of the states for school education on the other, became a central feature of Australian education. However, despite specific policy differences, there is a broad bipartisan political agreement about the Commonwealth's role in education. Since this book is about the key ideas that inform the dominant educational narrative, and since the narrative has been adopted by all sides of politics, it will only differentiate between the two levels of government when it is pertinent to the analysis. It will be assumed that the arguments for a new narrative apply equally to state, territory and national governments.

So, by the 1970s Australia was moving to an age of mass secondary education. With more young people staying at school for longer periods, the correlation between school success and such factors as class, gender, ethnicity and 'race' became apparent. It was clear that education was favouring particular groups, and researchers and practitioners began to grapple with the causes of, and reasons for, unequal educational outcomes. There was a growing realisation that equity was not only an individual matter (e.g., providing equal access and opportunities) but also a collective social concern. Educating all young people to acquire the capacities to function as active citizens was not something that could be left to chance or unevenly distributed: it was a common good that was a prerequisite for a vibrant and healthy democracy. Concerns about equity and social justice became an established part of the education landscape, and led to the development of a range of strategies and approaches through the 1970s and 1980s. For example, there were new funding policies based on a commitment to a fairer (re)distribution of resources, and new national curriculum projects, such as the famous Disadvantaged Schools Program, which sought to address the ways in which the official curriculum had tended to embody the cultural capital of dominant groups.

While some inroads were made into the manifest inequalities, it was clear that this was difficult and complex work, and that sustainable long-term change was going to take many years to achieve. Inequalities of educational outcomes were persistent and by the mid-1980s it was recognised that approaches and strategies seeking to address equity needed to be grounded in research and inquiry, and be systematic and appreciative of the contexts in which education is practised. It was also apparent that the structure and processes of education systems needed to address such matters as gender imbalances in leadership positions within state education systems and schools.

Despite these challenges, the period of the late 1960s through to the mid-1980s had been one of educational expansion, innovation and experimentation. Ministers for education relied on the advice of education experts in the states' public services; teachers were trusted as professionals who had the school-based knowledge to tailor programs to suit the students in their care; and there was a general consensus that the official curriculum should be broad and comprehensive. Public schools were understood as the major educational provider in the country, located in every local community, attended by nearly 80 per cent of students, and widely seen as serving the public good.

All of that changed from the late 1980s onwards, as the shadow of neoliberalism fell upon education.

The emergence of a standardising discourse

As described earlier, when the Hawke Labor government was elected in 1983, it moved quickly to put in place neoliberal economic strategies designed to address the challenges of globalisation, while maintaining a commitment to the welfare state. For the first few years education was not touched by neoliberalism; indeed, Labor maintained its traditional commitment to equity in education. For example, it kept the national Disadvantaged Schools Program (DSP) and introduced the famous Participation and Equity Program (PEP), which had a special focus on access and participation. It also tried to apply some needs-based principles to federal funding to schools, which was becoming a running sore in the education debate.

However, by the second term of the Hawke Labor government (1985-1987) neoliberalism began to spread to areas of social policy, and education was a prime target. The government argued that since education was the most important way Australia developed its human capital, it was central to the development of an internationally competitive economy. The economic purposes of education were now paramount, and for this reason the Labor government insisted that the national government should be a major player in the formation of school education policy, rather than a bit player supporting the states and territories by funding curriculum projects.

From that time on there were numerous signs of neoliberal philosophy being applied to education. In 1988, the new federal Minister for Education, John Dawkins, released a major policy statement, *Strengthening Australia's Schools*, which made it clear that education was a major tool of microeconomic reform. Statutory bodies, such as the Schools Commission which had been formed by the Whitlam government, were deemed not to be sufficiently under government direction and were abolished. A new federal Department of Employment, Education and Training was established to take their place, the title underlining the strong mutual relationship between education and human capital formation, and the privileging of an instrumentalist approach to education policy.

The instrumentalist approach was accompanied by new models of corporate managerialism designed to reform the public service by introducing the approaches of private corporations and by placing it under greater ministerial control (Knight & Lingard, 1997). It was not long before education departments at the state and territory levels, as well as the federal department, were swamped with vision and mission statements, performance indicators, strategic plans, and intrusive accountability mechanisms to control teachers and schools. As the education agenda became more instrumentalist, so the need for expertise in education was seen as unnecessary. After all, with the 'ministerialisation' of education, the role of departments of education had shifted from one of providing the minister with 'frank and fearless' advice, to one of managing the minister's political and policy agenda.

The new lingua franca was corporate-speak, and so public servants without education backgrounds but with generic skills in 'management' increasingly populated departments of education, right up to those leading the departments. Previously, there were sections of education departments that had been based on the idea that since education was complex, policy should emerge from ongoing research and evaluation about educational ideas. In the new environment, such tasks were deemed to be superfluous. Thus, research and curriculum sections were either slimmed down or abolished, and in their place sprang up sections rejoicing under such titles as 'People and Culture' and 'System Performance'. When 'expertise' was needed, external consultants could be commissioned from the private sector. Neoliberalism had arrived!

After its election in 1996, the Howard Coalition government retained the strong emphasis on the economic purposes of education, the desire for a strong federal hand in education policy, and the corporatisation of the public service. But it introduced an additional element of the neoliberal philosophy—markets, choice and competition—that had been largely missing from the Labor agenda. The logic was that, in education, parents and students are understood to be consumers making choices in an education market. This in turn fosters competition between schools as they vie for custom. And all of this, it is claimed, will promote educational quality. From a neoliberal perspective, education is constructed as a positional good to be used for the benefit of individuals, rather than as a social good. In the presence of such a philosophy, the discourse of equity is pushed to the background and replaced by the concepts of choice and competition.

Once the Howard government added this element, the central features of the neoliberal education agenda were in place, and although there have been shifts in emphasis during the periods of successive Labor and Liberal/National Party governments, they have remained intact ever since. As a result, Australian education has changed irrevocably. So, what policies have been developed and implemented on the back of these neoliberal assumptions?

First, in the name of providing choice in an education market, the Howard government sought to expand the private sector. One of its first acts was to abolish the Hawke government's 'New Schools Policy', which had placed a check on unrestrained growth in the number of private schools by ensuring that new schools could only be set up in localities where there was a clear demographic need. Without this regulatory control, many low-fee private schools were able to access federal funds and establish themselves in areas already adequately serviced by public schools. This encouraged some parents to leave public education, and fanned the aspirations of others. Of course, making more private schools available on the grounds of parental choice was always an illusion. It is a choice for some. The elite high-fee private schools are well out of the reach of most families; and even the low-fee schools can only be accessed by a certain percentage of the population. For most, the capacity to choose does not exist.

Second, in the name of creating competition between schools in the public system, successive state and federal governments advocated for 'devolution', a policy that purports to hand over power to schools to manage themselves in ways that best suit the needs and context of the school community. In some systems, the increased flexibility brought about by devolution in areas like staffing is beneficial, but for most it turns out that systems are simply using 'devolution' as a way to cut costs and shift responsibility while maintaining control, or 'steer from a distance' (Whitty et al., 1998). This creates frustration in school communities, which are promised greater freedom but find not only that the 'freedoms' are limited, but that they are a mask for increased control.

Third, to support the education market and 'consumer' choice, and to drive quality improvement, neoliberal education policy has promoted standardised testing. At the national level the Rudd Labor government, with Julia Gillard as education minister, introduced the National Assessment Program—Literacy and Numeracy (NAPLAN) in 2008. NAPLAN involves testing students every year at Years 3, 5, 7 and 9; and placing the results for each school on the My School website, which was established to give parents information about schools. As Rudd said at the time, making the results of the tests publicly available gives parents the information upon which school choices can be made, thus enabling parents to 'vote with their feet'. This would, in turn, ensure that schools strive to meet the demands of the market.

At the global level, every three years since 2000, the OECD has run PISA, testing samples of fifteen-year-old students in over seventy countries in mathematics, science and reading. The results are used to compare countries on league tables, with those countries lower down being exhorted to copy the educational strategies of the 'successful' countries. PISA will be examined again in more depth in Chapter 4, but for the moment it is sufficient to point out that it is a part of the neoliberal arsenal performing, at the international level, the same function as NAPLAN performs at the national level.

Fourth, consistent with neoliberal ideology, there have been various attempts to privatise and commercialise education. In places like the United States, attempts are well advanced to privatise public education systems through charter schools, which involve outsourcing public schools to be run by private organisations. In Australia, the privatisation of public education has been more subtle, involving strategies to encourage public schools to be run more like private schools. This might include marketing, branding and advertising—as private schools have always done—in a more competitive public system. Clearly such strategies diminish collaboration, which is a fundamental characteristic deriving from being part of a public education system.

In addition, there has been a trend towards commercialisation within education. This involves multinational companies like Pearson becoming very influential in the making of education policy. Thus, Pearson is not only producing education texts as traditional textbooks, but also developing and selling resources that have traditionally been the province of teachers, such as lesson planning and teaching strategies (Hogan et al., 2015). More than this, in the United States Pearson is now developing, implementing and marking standardised tests in a number of states, conducting teacher certification, and promulgating 'evidence-based' research on what constitutes good teaching practice. Pearson has moved into Australia, and has been engaged by the Australian Curriculum and Assessment Authority (ACARA) to play a role in the NAPLAN tests. There are surely dangers associated with a private company, established to make profits for its shareholders, having so much say about key aspects of education.

The policy examples described above demonstrate the extent to which the neoliberal philosophy has permeated Australian education. It is intriguing that, despite the evidence of the damage it is doing, neoliberalism remains the dominant policy narrative. What are the mechanisms that are being used to hold the neoliberal education agenda in place?

Sustaining the neoliberal educational discourse

Over the past thirty years, neoliberalism has become and remained the dominant educational narrative largely because it is sustained by a number of subtle but powerful strategies and techniques. One of these is the use of language that can naturalise the status quo. Neoliberalism is replete with the language associated with markets, choice, customers, competition and efficiency—words that are not value-neutral. They embody an ideology that includes and excludes certain ways of thinking about education.

Let's take the use of the word 'customer'. Once parents or students are understood to be customers, education becomes primarily an actual or perceived economic exchange or commercial transaction. As soon as that is accepted, a number of other assumptions follow, including the need for a market where choice is exercised by customers and competition is engaged in by providers. In this way, the collective social and common good purposes of education are neglected; relationships between teachers, students and parents are narrowly defined; inequalities produced by market relations are ignored; and education is reduced to satisfying the individual needs of individual customers.

The assumptions of neoliberalism also dictate the ways in which decisions are made and the information base that is used to make them. Market relations demand certainty, and so approaches to decision-making based on educational research and inquiry that recognise complexity, and explore nuances and shades of grey, are unsuitable. Their place is taken by technicised research approaches that tend to rely mainly on the results of national and international standardised tests. These are correlated with variables that are claimed to produce the test results. There are no questions asked about the extent to which such tests—usually conducted in a limited range of areas such as literacy and numeracy, but used to make generalisations about entire education systems—are as objective or as scientific as they are assumed to be. The point is that such research is very acceptable to policy-makers, since it does not question the neoliberal philosophy they are using to shape policy, or expose the interests they are representing. Such knowledge is further embedded in education systems through the device of setting up 'evidence-based' collections of 'best practice' to inform 'evidence-based' policy and teaching practice.

The neoliberal environment has also spawned a panoply of consultants and think tanks to consolidate its 'knowledge base'. These are often people with limited research expertise or background in education. They are commissioned by governments to produce 'research' reports, which invariably either recycle research based on standardised tests, or comprise their own 'research' which almost solely references other consultants and think tanks to substantiate their 'findings' (Barber & Mourshed, 2007; Mourshed, Chijioke & Barber, 2010). In this way, the neoliberal policy regime creates a closed loop of knowledge that justifies and reaffirms the logic upon which it is based (Coffield, 2012).

An appreciation of how neoliberal policy in education is sustained and protected is important if an alternative educational narrative is to have any chance of challenging its dominance.

But just as crucial is the task of understanding the effects neoliberalism is having on Australian education. It will be argued in Chapter 2 that the damage is so extensive that Australia has no option but to change policy direction.

Chapter 2

The damaging effects of current education policy directions

The damaging effects of neoliberalism in education

In Chapter 1 it was argued that neoliberalism has been the dominant narrative in Australian education for the past thirty years. It has been led at the national level by successive Australian governments, who have been able to use their financial strength to insist on certain policy initiatives in school education; but it has also been the favoured ideology of governments at state and territory levels. It has been dominant for so long that it is difficult to do anything other than ascribe to it the educational outcomes that have been achieved on its watch. That is, the position in which Australian education currently finds itself has been shaped and influenced, if not determined, by the neoliberal policy regime described in Chapter 1. So, what have been the effects? It will be argued that there are many negative consequences on educational practices, educational outcomes, and social relations in education. Indeed, such is the damage being done to Australian education that there is no option but to change policy direction.

Consequence 1: Inequitable educational outcomes

A large achievement gap between rich and poor blights Australian education—and the gap appears to be widening (Shepherd, 2014; Bonnor, 2019). The irony is that the mechanisms favoured by the standardising discourse to improve education quality—mainly NAPLAN and PISA— consistently reveal the extent of the inequity produced on its watch. For example, the Public Education Foundation uses PISA[3] data to show that from 2009–2015, students in the bottom socioeconomic scale (SES) quartile are falling further behind their more advantaged peers, and faster; and that Indigenous children and children of newly arrived migrants are disproportionately represented in the groups that are near the bottom of test results (Hetherington, 2018). Indeed, a United Nations Children's Emergency Fund (UNICEF) report found that Australia ranks in the bottom third of countries for ensuring equity at the preschool, primary and secondary stages of schooling (UNICEF, 2018). When PISA results for Australia are disaggregated, they reveal that students in the lowest socioeconomic quartile perform much worse than all other students, and those in the highest quartile perform much better (OECD, 2016a).

These international test results are replicated nationally. Every year, Australia's NAPLAN scores show that the percentage of low-SES, Indigenous and remote area students below the standards in reading, writing and numeracy is between five and nine times the percentage of high-SES students. By Year 9 these

---

3   This book is critical of the simplistic ways in which standardised tests like PISA and NAPLAN are used in the public arena to make judgements about education quality. One of the reasons for this is the narrowness of their focus, and their use in comparing schools and/or countries on league tables. However, currently they are the major system-wide measures of educational outcomes available.

gaps represent a difference of up to four to five years of learning (Goss et al., 2016).

Such results are confirmed by other data which is drawn from different learning areas or year levels. Thus, every three years the National Assessment Program (NAP) conducts sample assessment studies around Australia of student achievement in science literacy, civics and citizenship education, and information and communication technology, and these also highlight the difference between Indigenous and non-Indigenous student outcomes, as well as differences based on socioeconomic status (Ainley & Gebhardt, 2013). Further, a number of studies have demonstrated that at Year 12, socioeconomic status remains a key determinant of educational outcomes. For example, research conducted by the Mitchell Institute at Victoria University found that across Australia in 2015 only 61 per cent of the most disadvantaged students attained Year 12 or equivalent, compared to 89 per cent of the most advantaged; and that only 44 per cent of Indigenous students completed Year 12 versus 75 per cent of non-Indigenous students (Mitchell Institute, 2015).

It is more than coincidental that there are significant differentials between high-SES and low-SES schools in funding, learning resources, facilities and class sizes. The OECD estimates that Australia has the fifth-largest resource disparity between socioeconomically advantaged and disadvantaged schools (OECD, 2013, 2016b). It is hard to believe that we have reached a stage in Australian education where the schools with the greatest challenges are given the least amount of resources to deal with them. These disparities in turn exacerbate achievement gaps.

The consequences of educational inequality do not stop at the school gate. There is now overwhelming evidence showing the deleterious effects of educational inequality on social and economic outcomes and political participation. Productivity falls, participation in civic life is diminished, and social dislocation is greater (Wilkinson & Pickett, 2009; Blanden & McNally,

2014; Janmaat, 2014; Abdullah, Doucouliagas & Manning, 2015; Li & Powdthavee, 2015). Since education is one of the most important determinants of levels of inequality in a society, it is clear that there is need for urgent action to improve equity in Australian schooling.

Consequence 2: A socially segregated schooling system

A dominant characteristic of the Australian schooling system today is that it is highly socially segregated by class and ethnicity. The proportion of students who attend a socially mixed school is lower in Australia than in most other comparable countries, including Canada, New Zealand and the UK (OECD, 2010 & 2018b). Consistent with overseas research (e.g., Fiel, 2015), the extent of social segregation is the direct result of neoliberal policies promoting education markets, choice and competition, buttressed by the increasing amount of federal government funds going to private schools. These policies have encouraged many middle class parents with the capacity to pay private school fees to desert the public system, taking with them their powerful social and financial resources and so weakening their local public schools (Teese, 2011). Thus, in the past forty years, the percentage of Australian students attending private schools has risen from 22 per cent to 35 per cent (Connors & McMorrow, 2015).

The international research confirms that the social stratification of schooling adversely affects educational experiences and outcomes; confirms and maintains inequalities that stem from family background; and has a significant educational and social impact (Fiel, 2015; OECD, 2018b & 2019). It is no different in Australia. Using end of school achievement outcomes, Chris Bonnor (2017, 2019) has shown that high-achieving students tend to be concentrated in high-SES schools, and low-achieving students in low-SES schools. Students from low-SES backgrounds increase their performance as they access schools in higher and higher bands of SES (Teese, 2011; Bonnor, 2019). Conversely, the lower the school is in the aggregate SES range, the lower the overall student outcomes (Perry, 2018). As Perry and McConney (2010) point out,

> the segregation of schools according to SES provides further benefits for students whose economic circumstances allow attendance at high SES schools, and also further handicaps students who lack this advantage. That is, schooling that is segregated by SES is most likely to benefit students who are already educationally privileged, but harm students who find themselves at educational disadvantage associated with low SES backgrounds. Rather than mitigating or mediating educational inequality, school segregation exacerbates it. (Perry and McConney, 2010, p. 81)

This means that 'the burden of lifting up the most disadvantaged is not evenly spread across schools, sectors or locations' (Bonnor, 2019, p. 2). Significantly, the gap has widened over the past decade, with achievement outcomes being increasingly connected to levels of advantage. An OECD report shows that Australia now has the equal fourth-most segregated school system of the 36 countries in the OECD (2018b).

Segregation along ethnic lines is also evident in Australian schooling and has a significant social and academic impact. Christina Ho uses data from the My School website to show that, at the time of her study, high achieving students from language backgrounds other than English (LBOTE) make up 83 per cent of enrolments in selective public schools in New South Wales. At the other end of the scale, students from migrant backgrounds in lower socioeconomic areas of western and south-western Sydney are disproportionately represented in schools—125 schools in Sydney have over 90 per cent of students from a LBOTE— and are more likely to be below average in terms of academic performance (Ho, 2019, p. 4). At the same time, Ho found that there are some schools with hardly any LBOTE students, and others with large majorities—in both cases in proportions which do not reflect the cultural diversity of their communities:

> There are also striking divisions between government and non-government schools in their enrolment of LBOTE students. Sydney, for example, has 99 schools with a student LBOTE population of less than 10 per cent, and they are largely non-government schools and clustered in the North Shore and Eastern suburbs. These schools are much less culturally diverse than the suburbs in which they are located. (Ho, 2019, p. 4)

Such variations and divides are caused by the neoliberal policies of school choice which encourage those with the financial capacity to select what they perceive to be a 'good' school, often outside their local community. Segregation such as this means that students miss out on the cognitive, social and emotional benefits that many researchers have shown derive from young people mixing with others from diverse backgrounds and cultures (e.g., Noble 2009; Harris, 2013; Wells, Fox & Cordova-Cabo, 2016). The more homogeneous schools become, the less possible it is to use the school experience to learn that difference is not a barrier to engagement. Socially-mixed schools can use their diversity to enrich students' lives, and promote social cohesion.

Since school segregation has negative social and cognitive effects, equity policy must focus not only on individuals but also on the social make-up of schools. If better educational outcomes are to be achieved for all students, rather than just those from privileged backgrounds, then it is crucial that the segregation of schools based on SES and ethnic background is reduced. It is all the more urgent given that the gap between the educational outcomes of students from high- and low-SES backgrounds has increased.

Of course, ensuring a greater social mix across schools in Australia is not of itself sufficient to redress disadvantage. Obviously there are other crucial influences, such as the quality of teaching and the calibre of the school environment. But the mantra that the quality of teaching is the most important in-school factor affecting student learning—a truism frequently asserted by commentators and politicians from a neoliberal perspective—fails to recognise that the concept of 'good teaching' cannot be understood in isolation from the many other variables that influence quality student learning. Stratification of schools in Australia is one of these.

Consequence 3: An emaciated view of equity

The fact that inequitable educational outcomes are a characteristic of Australian schooling has not gone unnoticed by policy-makers, and often policy is justified in the name of 'equity'. However, the neoliberal mantra of choice, competition and markets has given equity a very individualistic policy framing in education. Standardised tests such as PISA and NAPLAN are the major source of data used to assess educational achievement and to identify where there are inequitable educational outcomes. This information highlights educational progress made over time, and pinpoints what is called the 'achievement gap' between students. However, that is where it stops. Having identified which students are not achieving, the neoliberal policy agenda focuses its 'improvement' strategies solely on the teacher and student in an attempt to close the 'gap'.

Leaving aside questions about the accuracy of the standardised tests and their narrow focus, closing the 'achievement gap' is an admirable aspiration when there has been an attempt to understand the causes of the gap. That is, identifying the 'gap' should be the starting point for, not the end to, strategies to promote equity in education. An understanding of the contributory causes of differential outcomes demands an appreciation not only of curriculum and pedagogy, but also of the range of social and cultural factors that may have influenced the results (Laing et al., 2019). Such an understanding may show, for example, that the problem is instead caused by an 'opportunity gap' involving the absence of the kinds of resources or learning opportunities that are available to students from affluent backgrounds (Darling-Hammond, 2006). Redistributing material and cultural resources, however, is a necessary but insufficient condition for justice in education. For a start, if 'opportunity' is thought of in terms of enablement, and not just possession, then there is need to ensure that students are not constrained in any way, even when they have the same resources (Young, 2011).

But, more than this, there are other aspects to consider. Using Nancy Fraser's three key principles for 'robust justice', Brennan and Zipin (2018) argue that redistribution must be accompanied by recognition and representation. Thus the cultures, experiences and worldviews of the least advantaged must be recognised and incorporated into the official curriculum and pedagogical practices, just as those groups must be represented in key decision-making processes at all levels. These are matters that must be understood and addressed if the 'achievement gap' is to be closed. A central equity question is how to ensure that those who are regularly represented in the 'low-achieving' groups, are not marginalised or excluded by dominant educational policies or practices.

Unfortunately, neoliberal education policy refuses to recognise these factors. Instead, the focus is on blaming and then 'improving' teachers and students. No questions are asked about the adequacy of the curriculum being taught, or the mechanisms used to assess learning. In the neoliberal policy world, these matters are beyond reproach. Instead, once the results are in and the 'problems' identified, the solutions are immediately devised and implemented. Typically, principals are exhorted to improve their school's standing through strategies that range from 'naming and shaming' schools by comparing results on standardised tests and encouraging competition between schools, to imposing teaching strategies and materials that have 'worked' with 'successful' schools and suggesting schemes of reward and punishment based on test results, such as performance pay (Netolicky, 2016).

If these strategies resulted in improved equity outcomes, they might be defensible. But ignoring the complexities involved in the concept of 'equity' has resulted in policy 'solutions' that are simplistic and, therefore, counterproductive to equity outcomes. They fail to appreciate that learning outcomes are influenced by a range of social and cultural, as well as educational, factors, all of which have to be surfaced, understood and worked on over time. Instead, they force a 'teaching to the test' approach under which the horizons of education are limited to test results. It is a narrow, emaciated and individualistic version of equity.

The key to improving equity does not lie in providing more 'choice', 'competition' and standardisation. These are the policies that have created the problem, and continue to make the situation worse. A new educational narrative would recognise the complexity of achieving equity in education. Such an approach would take on board all that has been learned about equity in education over the past few decades and would be founded on a developed and articulated view of equity and social justice.

Greater equity in education demands hard work over a long period, not quick fixes. The voices of all educators and members of the community are needed to reassert a more sophisticated view of equity. Neoliberal policies have failed the most educationally disadvantaged students.

Consequence 4: The residualisation and privatisation of public education

Over the past forty years, the combined effect of neoliberalism in education in Australia has been to residualise and privatise our systems of public education. Public schools have been residualised in the sense that they have gone from being understood as the major educational providers, which some parents opt out of for reasons of religion and status, to being seen by some policy-makers and members of the community as a 'safety net' for those who cannot afford private schools (Bonnor & Caro, 2007). Although public schools continue to do a magnificent job in their local communities, this is despite government support, rather than because of it. How has it come to this?

In the early 1970s public schools carried nearly 80 per cent of school students, with a consequent high degree of social mix. Thus, public schools were the major educational providers and were described as being free, compulsory, secular and open to all in every local community. Since that time there has been a dramatic change, largely brought about by the introduction of federal involvement in funding school education, and the subsequent neoliberal shift to a discourse of markets, competition and choice. Together, these factors produced a drift to private schools of nearly 14 per cent, resulting in them accounting for 35 per cent of school enrolments (Connors & McMorrow, 2015).

The story of how the Commonwealth government became involved in providing funding for both public and private schools from the 1960s onwards is told in more detail in Chapter 3. At this point it is sufficient to know that after combining income from all funding sources, the income divide between public and private schools is greater now than it has ever been, in favour of private schools. Indeed, the proportion of public money being spent on private schooling in Australia is higher than in any other advanced economy, and has increased significantly over the past decade (McGowan, 2018).

The increased funding to private schools enabled them to improve their position in the education market by making them attractive relative to public schools by improving teacher/student ratios and building state-of-the-art facilities. Aspirational parents with the means to do so moved their children out of the public system, looking for market advantage in a competitive schooling system. The drift of enrolments has had a dramatic impact on the social mix of Australian schools, with an associated negative impact on educational outcomes (OECD, 2018b, 2019). It has resulted in public schools shouldering the challenge of having 82 per cent of low-SES students; 84 per cent of Indigenous students; and 76 per cent of students with disability—with fewer resources! (Cobbold, 2015).

At the same time, the drift to private schools has generated a privatising dynamic in public education. Policy-makers assume that the market appeal of private schools means that they are the gold standard of high educational quality. This judgement completely disregards the resource differentials between public and private schools that result from the government's school funding model, and ignores the evidence showing that when SES is taken into account, public schools do as well, if not better, than private schools in academic results (e.g., Ryan, 2013; Nghiem et al., 2015; Zygnier, 2019). Instead, policy-makers assume that if standards are to lift, then public schools must become more like private schools (Mannix, 2013). Thus, policies that foster choice and competition in the public system are promoted.

In some countries, direct privatisation has been achieved by opening up public schools to be run by private individuals, corporate companies, and for-profit or not-for-profit organisations. In Australia the process has been more indirect, involving the transfer of ideas, techniques and practices from the private sector to make the public sector more business-like and 'independent' of systems. A flagship of this approach is the policy of independent public schools (IPS), which has been taken up in Western Australia, Queensland, and the Northern Territory, and in some other states through an eponymous federal government-sponsored program launched in 2014 (Savage, 2014).

It is important to note that some of the current versions of IPS, such as those in Western Australia and Queensland, amount to little more than increased flexibility for schools in the area of finances and decision-making, and schools have used the 'autonomy' in different ways (Gobby, 2019; Heffernan, 2019). However, it is the language which accompanies the policy that signals the intention, and sounds warning bells for those concerned about the privatisation of public education. Already there are calls for the introduction of 'for-profit schools (to) boost public education' (Jha & Buckingham, 2015).

If parents and students are understood to be consumers making educational choices in a free market; if principals and school boards are charged with the task of maintaining and increasing market share; and if schools are expected to compete for 'custom'—then the essence of public education is stripped away. Apart from there being scant evidence that such versions of 'school autonomy' enhance student learning outcomes, the negative consequences are as follows.

- It establishes public schools as businesses that compete against one another. The most successful are rewarded, and the least successful—invariably those with the least cultural and financial resources—go to the wall. In this way, the privatisation agenda confirms and exacerbates inequalities between schools.
- A lot of time and money is spent on publicity and marketing at the expense of educational outcomes. This sets up principals as surrogate employers, marketers and business managers, rather than as educational leaders seeking to involve teachers and the wider school community in curriculum discussions.
- It destroys the sense of local community engagement with each school, where the school uses the community as a learning resource, and the community uses the school for community activities. When parents choose schools far away from the local community in which they reside, two things happen. It weakens the link between public schools

and their local communities. And it encourages parents to simply leave a school when there are perceived issues, rather than stay, work through the issues and help to build the school.
- It promotes each school as a stand-alone entity rather than as belonging to a system. This then allows governments to escape accountability by giving schools greater responsibility and to reduce resources while setting performance targets, then blame schools if those targets are not met.

The fact is that true public schools aren't independent; they are networked, and they cooperate to build a quality public system overall, rather than competing to create a system where there are shining beacons of success sitting alongside schools that are struggling or failing. True public schools are fuelled by a sense of mutual obligation, not self-interest. In this sense, the term 'independent public school' is an oxymoron.

Our system of public education is not only about individual advancement: it has an important public purpose, which is to enrich and advance our society as a whole. A central part of this role relates to the integrative function of public schools, which bring together children and young people from a wide range of backgrounds, cultures and experiences. The trend to diminish and privatise public schools neglects this fundamental purpose by increasing social segregation. Just as it is important to focus on the issue of increased and fairer funding to address the residualisation of public schools, so too is it important to focus on the dangers of privatising public education.

Consequence 5: An impoverished understanding of educational accountability

Accountability in education is important for at least two reasons. First, in a democracy, there must be public accountability for how taxpayer dollars are spent. Citizens need to be assured that the agreed purposes and goals of education are being achieved at the highest standard possible. Second, educators need quantitative and qualitative data that offers comparable information across an education system. Such information can flag possible problems or issues that can become the starting point for further investigation and analysis. These two reasons for accountability enjoy widespread acceptance. Disagreement arises over the nature of the accountability strategies used, and usually centres on the question of whether or not they add value to educational endeavour.

In the neoliberal policy environment in Australia there are two key sources of information that contribute to the neoliberal approach to accountability: the NAPLAN tests conducted annually across the country and the PISA tests conducted every three years by the OECD at an international level. It will be argued that these two approaches constitute an impoverished form of accountability and are damaging to Australian education. The example of NAPLAN will be used in this section to substantiate that claim.

NAPLAN tests are conducted once a year over a three-day period at Years 3, 5, 7 and 9 in literacy and numeracy. About three months later, the results are fed back to each education system and each school in them; each student receives an individual report of her/his performance; and the schools' results are recorded on the My School website. The release of NAPLAN results each year triggers a feeding frenzy that engulfs school administrations, the press and politicians. Any small shift in 'position' relative to other states and territories is used to praise or berate governments or schools on their education policies; results are placed on the My School website and used by parents to guide school choice; and the media constructs league tables, thus serving to reward the 'winners' and shame the 'losers'.

The extent of this focus has made NAPLAN a high-stakes test for both education systems and individual schools. Not surprisingly, therefore, it becomes the educational focus, even the educational raison d'être, for the following year. It is the basis of the performance targets set, the resources provided, the professional development programs and school reviews instituted, and the incentive schemes proposed. It has even spawned a NAPLAN preparation industry for wealthy parents wanting to assist their child's application to some private schools (Macmillan, 2013; Tovey, 2013).

In these ways, NAPLAN is being used far beyond its original purposes (Johnston, 2017). There is no way that a single test can pretend to be diagnostic, inform teachers, judge and compare the quality of teachers and schools, provide data for marketing purposes, and provide 'evidence' for policy. In trying to meet so many ends, it is satisfying none. Rather, by being stretched in many directions, it has moved from being a mechanism to check the pulse of one part of the education system, to being the reason that schools exist. Improved NAPLAN results have become the purpose of education. In the process, as more NAPLAN-based targets are set, the curriculum is narrowed further and teachers teach to the test. There is no escaping its clutches.

More than this, questions stop being asked about the nature of the tests themselves, and professional discussion is stifled. Despite the different understandings of what a person's literacy actually means in different contexts, a single approach has been adopted and imposed by the Australian Curriculum, Assessment and Reporting Authority (ACARA)—the body that designs and administers NAPLAN—and it has become the only 'truth'. In addition, the serious concerns raised about the methodology used to construct and interpret the tests, the validity of the tests, and the error margins that make year-to-year comparisons of schools and individuals highly problematic, are rarely acknowledged or discussed (e.g., Wilson, 1997; Wu & Hornsby, 2014). Instead, NAPLAN results are treated as scientifically objective truths about educational standards. They suit the neoliberal thirst for certainty.

The evidence showing the damage that NAPLAN is doing to Australian education is mounting, including the negative impacts it is having on learning and student wellbeing (e.g., Wyn, Turnbull & Grimshaw, 2014). And there are some policy-makers, such as the former NSW Liberal party Minister for Education, Rob Stokes, who are speaking up against the use and abuse of NAPLAN, pointing to the damage it is doing to children and Australian education.

> Anaesthetised by the data around us—and hypnotised by the neo-liberal fixation with quantification—we place inordinate emphasis on tests such as PISA and NAPLAN that reduce a student's educational journey to a number, and a school system to a line in a league table. (Stokes, 2018)

But if these voices are to get traction, a new approach to educational accountability must be built into a new narrative for Australian education.

Consequence 6: Dividing and deprofessionalising educators

Over the past thirty years, the neoliberal educational policy agenda has gradually reshaped the relationship between educators and the nature of their work. Chapter 1 described how the 'ministerialisation' of education has diminished the power of state education departments, and how the orthodoxy of corporate management has introduced a new form of educational governance in which generic managerial skills have replaced educational expertise in education bureaucracies. This section will describe the impact neoliberal policies have had on principals and teachers.

The neoliberal mantra of education markets, choice and competition positions principals as entrepreneurs whose job it is to manage the school as a business and to maximise the school's market advantage. Of course, this has long been the job of principals in private schools, but it was not the tradition in public education until the 1990s. Although the effects of this entrepreuneurial discourse are not uniform across a single system, let alone the country, it is clear that its intent is having an impact. Thus, it establishes—sometimes subtly, sometimes overtly—principals and their schools as competitors, which diminishes professional partnerships and collaboration. In addition, principals are expected to spend an inordinate amount of time marketing their school and writing mission statements and strategic plans to meet the demands of central office. In such an environment, it is difficult for principals to find the time to do the reading and research necessary to keep abreast of new curriculum developments, and to engage in the process of curriculum review and development (Ball, 2016).

Such pressures construct principals as managers rather than curriculum leaders, and as education departments' representatives in the school rather than as school leaders working with staff and the community to achieve collectively determined goals. The whole edifice is supported by the fact that principals now have fixed-term tenure. Once their contract comes to an end, they must either win the position back, or win a position at another school. If they can't do that, they are placed elsewhere in the system at the level of their 'substantive' position. Limited-term contracts inevitably produce a climate of fear and compliance. Knowing that the person to whom one reports in central office is instrumental in one's reappointment can focus the mind!

Teachers are similarly pitted against one another, with internal promotion positions limited to finite periods of time and a far greater number of casual contract positions. This has tended to create an environment of permanent competition, with those wanting to hold on to positions constantly looking over their shoulder at colleagues who may aspire to the same position. In such an atmosphere, collegiality and collaboration are difficult to sustain. It has also opened up a divide between principals—who play the role of surrogate employer—and teacher; not to mention the increased workload for the school leadership involved in the endless round of advertising, shortlisting and interviewing.

In a neoliberal policy environment, there is a constant stream of curriculum 'reforms' and accountability processes raining down on schools. The irony is that these occur at the same time that policy-makers are urging greater autonomy for schools through 'devolution'. Such policies are generally a strategy to transfer responsibility, but not authority, to schools; and schools are expected to pick up the increased workload without additional resources, as governments and education departments 'steer from a distance' through a range of policy impositions. Apart from not resulting in improved learning outcomes, the approach intensifies the work of educators.

Numerous studies over the years have documented the material effects on individual teachers (e.g., McGrath-Champ et al., 2018). These have come about through such factors as increased administrative demands and paperwork associated with accountability requirements, including data- and record-keeping; increased class sizes; less time for meeting with colleagues to plan; and a regular stream of new curriculum initiatives.

Work intensification has led to rising rates of teacher stress, burn out, cynicism, disillusionment and resignations, as has been so brilliantly and heartbreakingly described by former teacher Gabbie Stroud in her book *Teacher* (2018). It has also begun the process of de-professionalising teachers by confirming the separation of conception and execution. That is, in the system of remote control, 'experts' from outside the school establish the goals of schooling, the specific policy interventions to achieve them, and the ways to assess them; while school-based educators are charged with the task of implementing it all, and are held responsible for the outcomes.

Through such processes, teachers and principals are cast as technicians who have the technical skills to implement the ideas of others but not the professional expertise to engage in the exciting task of theorising and designing curriculum. Workload intensification also makes it even more difficult for the intellectual work of teaching to take place, and so the life, fun, challenge and enjoyment of teaching is gradually extinguished. Is it any wonder that nearly half of new entrants to the profession leave teaching within five years (Gallant & Riley, 2017)?

Consequence 7: Impoverishment of education knowledge base and growth of pseudo-scientific knowledge

Educators and education policy-makers draw from a professional knowledge base that includes research-based knowledge about education, and knowledge derived from action. The former usually refers to formal research conducted according to accepted research methods and methodologies and spanning quantitative and qualitative methods. The latter usually refers to inquiry in education conducted by practitioners and involving a systematic, but informal, investigation of issues, problems and dilemmas confronted in the course of teaching. Both are important constituents of the knowledge system in education, and they have a symbiotic relationship (Campbell & Groundwater-Smith 2010; Nichols & Cormack, 2017).

There has always been a healthy debate in education about the efficacy of different research and inquiry approaches, with the debate focusing on such matters as the rigour of the methods and methodologies used, the limits and possibilities of knowledge transfer and generalisation, and the limitations of different disciplinary perspectives. This debate reflects the fact that education is a human endeavour, which eschews certainty and dogmatism. A healthy system of education involves an ongoing attempt to understand what is happening and why in order to inform future planning and action at the level of policy-making, practice and anything in between. That being the case, these debates have been an important feature of educational policy-making and practice, and have helped to ensure that policy and practice are informed by a multiplicity of approaches to developing educational knowledge.

Unfortunately, one of the damaging effects of neoliberalism in education has been to contribute to the construction of a knowledge base that is commodified, simplified and technicised. The richness of what had been increasingly recognised as education's knowledge base has been lost and replaced by an approach based on certainty, which rejects anything that can't be quantified or measured (Muller, 2018, Chapter 8). The centrepiece of this approach to knowledge in education is standardised testing in a narrow range of areas. The limits and limitations of standardised tests are ignored, and the results stand as immutable truths about learning and educational outcomes (Koretz, 2017). Not only do they purport to reveal the problems and successes associated with teaching and learning, they are used to assign praise or blame, establish examples of good and bad practice, provide the basis for solutions and set targets. All other knowledge is dismissed as 'soft' or subjective. For neoliberal education policy, what can be measured counts, and what can't be counted is irrelevant.

In this way, neoliberal policy has narrowed the possibilities of and for education. It has turned education into a technical exercise and stripped away its complexity and richness. The literature exposing the shallowness of this approach to education is ignored or rejected by policy-makers in the thrall of the scientific certainty represented by numbers (Ravitch, 2016). No longer is there a symbiotic relationship between educational researchers and practitioners. Instead, the neoliberal knowledge system has spawned three new developments.

The first is the emergence of a coterie of consultants—a consultocracy (Gunter et al., 2014)—who not only do not question the standardised knowledge base, but also use it as the sole evidential base for their own 'research' reports commissioned by governments (Lingard, 2015). Often this involves making pronouncements about the reasons for specific test results, and proposing solutions that will address the perceived problems. Invariably these reports reference other consultants' reports, and in this way, they develop a closed loop of knowledge that justifies and reaffirms the logic upon which it is based.

Second, policy-makers have conceded the importance of evidence in making decisions about education by proposing what they call 'evidence-based' policy. This sounds like a rigorous approach to policy-making, and yet often it is no more than a cover for cherry-picking research in order to legitimate or confirm already determined policies (Whitty, 2016; Ladwig, 2018). Invariably 'evidence' is drawn from research using the medical-based model of randomised trials with standardised test results as the basic ingredient. This model makes it almost impossible to investigate the complexity of education, which is context-dependent and value-laden. It ignores the fact that research involving synthetic meta-analyses or randomised control trials should not be transplanted directly and unproblematically to different contexts (Biesta, 2010). In such ways, evidence-based policy becomes a means by which to consolidate the standardised approach to the knowledge system that characterises neoliberal education.

Finally, the marginalisation of research and practitioner knowledge has left educators exposed to pseudo-science as a substitute for discourse about educational problems. Thus, a cavalcade of consultants with a bag of tricks masked by fancy neologisms has emerged in the neoliberal era. They propose and market ideas and products that offer quick fixes to complex problems, and clever maxims to explain the intricacies of educational practice. Raewyn Connell describes it colourfully:

> [T]here has grown up a gaudy arena of pseudo-science, fads and fakery about education, much of it promoted by entrepreneurial consultants who have multiplied in the neoliberal world. Different consultants market brain science, boys' special

learning styles, parent training, computer solutions, gifted-and-talented programmes, boot camps for troublesome kids, direct instruction, tough love, patent reading schemes, zero tolerance, charter schools and many, many more slogans, programmes and devices. Since Australia is a small market, much of this is copied from the USA, or directly imported. (Connell, 2013, p. 109)

This pseudo-scientific approach to knowledge in education has been allowed to flourish in the neoliberal policy environment. It diverts attention away from the impoverished knowledge base that has become the standard-bearer of a standardised education system. A new educational narrative must grapple with the question of how to return to an educational knowledge system that recognises the complexity of education and turns its back on certainty and dogmatism.

The need for a new educational narrative

In our society, education is the major means by which to meet the challenges of the future, by developing the capacities of people as individuals, citizens in a democracy, workers, and members of social and cultural communities. This is a formidable and yet exciting task, and demands an education system that recognises and understands not only contemporary society, but also the possibilities of the future. In the 21st century, such a system must be open and available to all, be equitable in its provision and practice, promote a respect for the importance of diversity and cohesion, and be accountable to the community. It must value and trust its educators and ensure that education policy and practice is based on the best available knowledge. Each of the seven consequences identified in this chapter work against such a view of the role of Australian education.

This chapter has described the damaging consequences of thirty years of Australian education policy being dominated by neoliberal ideology. It has been argued that neoliberalism offers a narrow, instrumental, regressive, dull and lifeless educational policy regime that does not and cannot meet the demands of the future. Judged by its own miserable measures of educational outcomes it has failed, if the outcry—by the very people who promote the current agenda—following the release of each round of NAPLAN and PISA results is any guide. The irony is that, even as the same people complain that standards of Australian education are declining, they not only fail to recognise their role in this outcome, but offer more of the same to solve the problems for which they are responsible. There has to be a better way than this.

The bright spot is that, despite all the obstacles placed in their way by policy-makers, Australian educators are making valiant efforts to work around the policy impositions on them, to develop programs and practices that suit the needs and the contexts of the students in their care. There are many fine examples of innovative and challenging educational experiences in so many Australian schools. And yet these are ignored by policy-makers who hold to the now discredited neoliberal educational line. So what can be done?

It is difficult to dislodge neoliberalism in education, even at a time when the damage it is doing is now clear, because there is no well-developed and coherent alternative to it. The many fine teaching practices that are happening are often site- or region-specific, and are typically stand-alone initiatives that are not integrated into a coherent educational narrative for the future. In contrast, neoliberalism is based on a narrative that contains a connected set of assumptions and assertions about the nature of society. These have been woven into an ideological story that, having been told and retold so many times, has become the 'way things are'. It is difficult to contest something which appears to rest on natural societal law.

This book is based on the conviction that a progressive, futures-focused educational agenda can only challenge the dominant neoliberal paradigm if it is founded on an alternative and coherent narrative. There are enough progressive educational ideas around that could constitute some of the elements and practices of a new narrative, so there will be no need to start from scratch. But these ideas are disparate and disconnected. What is needed is a process for constructing a new narrative, for identifying its foundation values and concepts, and for shaping the key elements of an alternative educational agenda. That job will be undertaken in Parts 3 and 4 of the book. Before that happens, however, the first task is to explore in more depth the contours of some entrenched neoliberal policies and practices.

One of the problems with new change agendas is that they often ignore the embedded grammars (Tyack & Tobin, 1994) of the practices they are designed to replace. As a result, the new policies are subsumed by established practice whereby, although they might carry a new name, nothing really changes. Thus, before investigating a new narrative, **Part 2** will look in more detail at some case studies of neoliberal strategies in action. This will enable a better appreciation of the landscape into which alternative approaches will be introduced, and provide some ideas about ways to diminish or remove the destructive elements of the neoliberal educational project.

Part 2

What are the problems?

Overview

In Part 1 it was argued that in the 21st century, at a time when humans are facing significant challenges, the dominant official educational policy response has been to standardise education. The purpose of this book is to suggest an alternative narrative. However, given what is known about the nature of educational change, it is not just a matter of coming up with some new approaches and implementing them. No matter how powerful the new ideas might be, if entrenched beliefs and practices are ignored, the new agenda will be subsumed by them.

This points to the need to remove some obstacles and modify others. Some obstacles are obvious; others can be difficult to detect because they have become so much a part of the 'dominant grammars' of an organisation, embedded in its culture and taken-for-granted practices (Tyack & Tobin, 1994). They can be present in classrooms, schools and education systems as a whole. Only when they are identified and understood will systems and schools be in a position to promote an alternative narrative.

Part 2 analyses four ways in which the key tenets of neo-liberal philosophy harness and shape the nature of education policy.

Chapter 3 looks at why and how the great system of Australian public education has been diminished by the neoliberal policy approach to schools' funding.

Chapter 4 explores the Programme for International Student Assessment (PISA) as an example of how standardising testing can damage education.

Chapter 5 uses two case studies to critically scrutinise how educational research is used and abused to serve the neoliberal agenda in the name of evidence-based policy.

Finally, **Chapter 6** interrogates the ways in which non-educators are influencing the neoliberal policy regime and analyses what happens when governments transfer policy directly from other countries without due regard to context and history.

Chapter 3

Taking the public out of public education

Although public education still provides the majority of schooling in Australia, since the 1970s neoliberal education policies have destabilised public systems. In particular there has been a significant decline in the percentage of students attending public schools, and change in the ways in which the nature and purposes of public education are understood. Successive governments have followed the logic of neoliberalism by privileging the private sector. Many policy-makers now see the public system as residual—a safety net provision for those who cannot afford to send their children to private schools, rather than as the bulwark of our education system (Marginson, 1993). How and why has this happened?

Australian education and the funding debate

In the post-World War 2 years, as people began to recognise the importance of education to an individual's chances in life, there was a growth in the number of students staying at school for longer. This led to a burgeoning of public secondary schools as state governments tried to meet the demand. Education was now seen as a right for all, rather than an opportunity to be provided to some on the basis of wealth or ability. Private[4] schools continued to operate but, whereas earlier in the century they had been the main providers of upper secondary education, now public schools had assumed that role, and the enrolment share of private schools decreased (Campbell & Proctor, 2014).

By the early 1970s, public schools, which were funded entirely by state and territory governments, carried nearly 80 per cent of school students, with a consequent high degree of social mix. All local communities—city, rural and remote—had public schools, which were described as being free, compulsory and secular. By contrast, student numbers in the private sector were declining and reached their lowest ebb—of 21.1 per cent—in 1977 (Watson & Ryan, 2010).

However, there was a dramatic change from the late 1970s when the decline in private school numbers began to reverse. From that time on, the Australian schooling system gradually returned to a path of greater social segregation and inequity between schools in terms of resources and educational outcomes. Indeed, the gap between advantaged and disadvantaged schools in Australia is now among the largest in the world. These disparities have hit public schools the hardest (Cobbold, 2017b).

How and why did this happen? It will be argued that the attack on public education over the past forty years has been built and sustained by neoliberal ideology; and the issue of school funding has been central to that. Indeed, it has been the dominant issue in Australian education policy for a number of decades.

---

[4] In this book, the term 'private' is used in relation to all non-government schools, including Catholic, elite Independent, low fee independent, and other systemic religious schools. Of course, in Australia these schools are not genuinely private given the amount of public subsidy they receive. For this reason, they are usually referred to as 'non-government' schools. In the book they are referred to as 'private' schools to make the point that they still operate largely as private institutions (e.g., there are no limits to the fees they can charge, they can dictate which students are allowed entrance to them); and to contrast this with the important public characteristics of public (government) schools.

A new educational narrative must therefore come to grips with the funding issue if the policies that have so distorted our educational landscape are to be reshaped. This means starting with an historical understanding of what has happened and why, which is the focus of the next section. Since the purpose is to understand how neoliberal policy operates to shape the form of a specific policy approach, the emphasis will be more on the philosophy upon which funding strategies have been and are based, than the intricacies of funding arrangements.

The genesis of the schools funding debate

In post-World War 2 Australia, the increase in the numbers of students staying on well into the secondary school years placed pressure on facilities and resources in both the public and private sectors. The private school lobby began to argue stridently for public funds, prompting a decision by the Menzies government in 1964 to put Commonwealth money, for the first time, into private as well as public schools. At first such funding targeted science laboratories and libraries, but in the ensuing decade private schools argued for an increased share of Commonwealth funds (Campbell & Proctor, 2014).

Following the Karmel Committee's report (1973), the Whitlam government decided to place Commonwealth funding for school education on a systematic footing, with recurrent funding grants directed at private as well as public schools. This decision changed the face of Australian education. It has resulted in a stratified education system as a whole, and an increasingly residualised public schooling sector (Marginson, 1993, p. 213). However, it did not have to be that way. It is not the funding of private schools per se that has produced these outcomes, but rather the funding strategies that have been adopted and the values that have shaped them. Together, these have resulted in one of the most inequitable, opaque and dysfunctional education funding regimes in the world.

Today, people from other countries are amazed at the complexity of the hybrid funding and governance models of our schooling system. States and territories have responsibility for schools and largely fund public schools, with a small but growing outlay on private schools; the Commonwealth government largely funds private schools, with a smaller outlay on public schools; and private school income is supplemented by fees, with a generally much smaller fee income in public schools.

This funding complexity has created a fertile terrain for disagreement and debate. Not surprisingly, therefore, it has been seen by the various sectors as the 'main game' and has consequently narrowed the public–private debate to one about the funding of sectors, rather than the purposes they are serving. Within the confines of the funding debate, it is possible to discern two competing discourses at work—funding according to need, and funding according to entitlement. The funding[5] approaches that have been shaped by these discourses over the past forty-plus years will be briefly described, before the consequences of the dominant approach are examined.

From public good to safety net: Entitlement trumps equity
The merging of universalism and need

As public education expanded in the 20th century, the broad settlement that emerged was based on the principle of universalism, meaning that in relation to public education it is the state's

---

[5] Since the Commonwealth became involved in school education, funding for schools has comprised three broad payments to states and territories: general recurrent grants, capital grants and grants for targeted programs for government and private schools. Since the bulk of money is tied up in recurrent funding, this chapter will focus mainly on that component. The purpose is to examine some of the philosophies informing funding approaches, not to give a detailed history of Commonwealth funding of schools. For a detailed history of schools funding see Connors and McMorrow (2015).

responsibility to provide free, compulsory and secular public schools in every community in Australia. There was broad agreement that the primary responsibility of government is to direct taxpayers' money to public schools, not to private institutions. Private schools were seen as an alternative for those parents who might have a specific reason for opting out of public education and could afford the fees.

When the state-aid debate began in earnest in the 1960s, the principle of universalism was invoked by many who opposed taxpayers' money going to private schools. However, as the debate wore on and funding of private schools became a fixture, it was apparent that the major political parties were not prepared to suffer the political pain that would follow the withdrawal of that funding. This caused many public school advocates to modify their stance and concede that public money might be used to assist the poorest private schools. It was assumed, however, that such funding would not compromise public schools which, as public goods, would remain the main focus of funding policy.

The Whitlam government's decision to fund private as well as public schools merged the principle of universalism with the principle of 'need'. From this perspective, all students—public and private—are entitled to a decent standard of education and, therefore, a decent standard of resources, however these might be defined. The argument went that public money should be used to ensure that all public schools achieve the agreed resource standard; and should be combined with private contributions to ensure that all private schools also achieve that resource level. The corollary of this argument is that public money should be used to support private schools on the basis of 'need' to enable them to achieve the standard; but not be provided to those private schools that function well above it (Marginson, 1993).

Having set the philosophy for Commonwealth funding of schools, the next challenge was to construct funding mechanisms that would suit a federal system of divided responsibilities and deliver on the goal of providing a decent standard of education for all Australian students. This included setting a baseline for funding public and private schools; indexing the baseline, and allocating money within the private system.

The Whitlam government proposed a funding model that had an educational and an equity rationale. It used current resource use in schools to establish an index to assess funding needs, with average recurrent resource use in public schools expressed as the benchmark. The government then set four-year funding targets for public and private schools that would reduce and eventually eliminate inequality of resources and educational outcomes between schools. The idea was that money would be distributed differentially to private schools according to need, as assessed against the index of resource standards.

Whitlam's model ran into trouble right from the start. In 1974, a conservative Senate bowed to the demands of the powerful private school lobby and refused to pass the initial funding legislation, which excluded the wealthiest private schools—that is, those schools operating well above the resource standard—until the legislation applied to all private schools. In the end the government conceded, the legislation passed and the new model commenced.

The combination of needs-based general recurrent funding and a number of specific purpose equity programs, resulted in an expansion of the Commonwealth contribution to schools by more than $2.3 billion at 2011 price levels (Connors & McMorrow, 2015, p. 20)—with sixty-five percent of the share of the total amount going to public schools. But it was short-lived. The position of the Senate in 1974 had been a harbinger of what was to come.

In 1976, the Fraser government abandoned Whitlam's resource standards for both sectors by introducing a basic grant for all private schools irrespective of need, with a smaller baseline grant for public schools. Fraser scrapped Whitlam's targets and, instead, indexed future increases in Commonwealth funding to the level of spending on public schools by state and territory governments. The result was that by the end of the Fraser years, the share of Commonwealth funds for private schools had grown by 17 per cent, with a commensurate decrease for public schools. What had brought about this dramatic shift in less than a decade?

The principle of entitlement

It did not take long for Whitlam's equity-based rationale for Commonwealth government funding of schools to be challenged, and eventually overturned, by a new discourse based on the principle of entitlement. The consequences of this philosophical shift, which can now be seen as a harbinger of the neoliberal discourse in education policy, have been profound.

The principle of entitlement in education is based on the idea that since people who opt to send their children to private schools are taxpayers, private schools are as entitled to receive money from the government as are public schools. The argument runs that rather than being an opt-out alternative to public schools, private schools stand alongside public schools as a choice for parents, and therefore public schools should not get preferential treatment. It is choice that should form the basis of public policy, not the universal provision of public education.

The rationale for school choice has changed in emphasis over time, particularly as the neoliberal narrative gained prominence during the 1980s. At first, it was a matter of individual freedom to choose. But before too long it was being justified on the grounds that consumer choice in an education market will produce competition within and between sectors and that this, in turn, will lift education standards as well as save the government money. As this rationale took hold, the locus of policy-making and public discussion gradually shifted from the old state-aid question—should private schools receive any government money?—to questions about the amount of public money to which private schools are entitled. Indeed, the provision of government funds to private schools became so normalised that, over the years, private school advocates have even begun to use per capita arguments—maintaining that the combined level of state and Commonwealth funding per student going to many private schools is less than that of public schools.

The process of normalising funding to private schools has challenged the idea of public education being an essential public good to which private schools are an opt-out alternative. There is now a strong element in public discourse and policy-making that views public schools as a safety net provision for those who cannot afford to send their children to private schools. To understand the effects of this significant change, it is necessary to examine how the principle of entitlement was represented in funding strategies.

How entitlement trumped equity

The logic of Whitlam's needs-based resource standards for funding schools was at odds with the entitlement discourse. The former was premised on the idea that, on the basis of need, some schools should get more than other schools and that wealthy schools with resources well above the standard should get nothing. By contrast, the principle of entitlement insists on the rights of all private schools, no matter how wealthy, to receive government funding.

From Whitlam's legislation in 1974 to the present time, whenever the entitlement principle has been challenged, it has triumphed. For example, in 1984 the Hawke government proposed a 25 per cent reduction in funds to the 41 wealthiest private schools in Australia, but was forced to back down in the face of their fierce opposition. And when the Labor Party took to the 2004 election a policy to increase the overall level of funding to both sectors, but redistribute funds within the private sector in favour of those schools with the most need, the wealthiest schools (who would have received a funding reduction) successfully opposed the proposal on the grounds that it represented class warfare (Smart et al., 1986).

Overall, the principle of entitlement has resulted in a significant increase in the amount of Commonwealth money going to private schools. Thus, once the baseline funding going to private schools was substantially increased by the Fraser government, it was almost impossible for future governments to cut it back. Instead, mechanisms developed to index funding have not only protected but increased the amount of public monies going to private schools. For example, under the Keating government, per-student funding to private schools was distributed as a percentage of a resource standard known as the Average Government School Recurrent Costs (AGSRC) (Connors and McMorrow, 2015). The percentage-linked AGSRC formula, which remained in place for the next twenty years, favoured the private sector because it ignored the fact that public schools carry the majority of students with significant educational disadvantage. Cohorts of students in the public and private systems were treated as though they had the same resource needs. Thus, when state governments decided to spend extra on public schools to address a specific issue such as class size, private schools also benefited, even if it was not an issue for them. That is, funding approaches moved from being based on a known standard with an education and equity rationale, to being percentage-linked to variations in state budget allocations. All the while, the percentage share of public money going to private schools increased (Connors and McMorrow, 2015).

Certainly there have been mechanisms used to ensure a fairer distribution of money within the private sector, such as the Education Resources Index (ERI) introduced by the Hawke government. This involved ranking private schools on the basis of the private income each school received from all sources, and then distributing public funds proportionate to the category into which the school fell (Harrington, 2011). It was an attempt, albeit unsuccessful, to equalise resource differentials within the private sector—but it did nothing to reduce the growing gap in resources between public and private schools. And it did not last.

By the turn of the century, entitlement was trumping equity in education policy. But it was nothing compared to what was to come. The individualistic ideologies of choice and competition were taken to another level by the Howard government, which stated its intention to expand the private school sector. One of its first acts was to abolish the Hawke government's 'New Schools Policy', which had placed a check on unrestrained parental choice of schools by ensuring that new schools could only proceed in localities where there was a clear demographic need (Harrington, 2011). Now the way was clear for low-fee private schools to spring up in areas already adequately serviced by public schools, and encourage parents to leave public education.

Then, in 2001, the Howard government changed the way in which money was distributed within the private sector. Instead of using the level of private resources available to private schools as calculated by the ERI, schools were ranked according to the socioeconomic status of the individual families they served, and money was then distributed across a number of categories, each representing a percentage of AGSRC. In other words, rather than being based on the actual resources and income a school received, assessment of need was now to be calculated on an estimate of parents' capacity to pay.

The SES scheme benefited wealthy private schools in a number of ways. It gave large sums of taxpayers' money to those schools that drew students from socially mixed or low-SES areas. For example, wealthy boarding schools that enrolled students from affluent families living in depressed rural areas benefited from the funding associated with the low-SES area; or private schools could accept high-performing students from less affluent areas and so claim the low-SES rating. In these ways, private schools gained extra funding from the SES model, but did not have to spend money on any of the challenges that educational disadvantage brings with it.

More than this, where private schools would have received less money as a result of the application of the SES formula, the new policy enabled them to maintain their existing funding levels. The Catholic system even signed a separate agreement that not only maintained but increased funding to Catholic schools. In other words, the Howard government ensured that no private school would lose a dollar under the new scheme.

Commonwealth funding for schools doubled in real terms over the period of the Howard government—and three-quarters of that growth was directed to the private sector (Connors & McMorrow, 2015, p. 27). This accelerated the drift from public to private schools and confirmed the status of public schools as a safety net. Entitlement had trumped equity.

The period of the Rudd–Gillard governments from 2007–2013 brought a lull in this development rather than a reversal. Certainly equity returned to policy centre stage through the introduction of national education agreements that rolled together recurrent funding to public schools and targeted programs supporting low-SES schools. But there was no change to the principles of schools' funding as it had developed to that time. The Howard government's SES formula was retained for much of the period of the Rudd–Gillard governments, along with all of the inequities it produced.

The Gonski review and its aftermath

In April 2010, then-Education Minister Julia Gillard announced the long-promised review of schools funding, headed by influential businessman David Gonski. It did not take the review panel long to recognise that the funding model was totally broken and largely responsible for the gross inequities in Australia's education system. As a result, the Gonski Review brought equity back to the centre stage of considerations about funding. However it couldn't shake the entitlement philosophy that by now was so dominant.

Echoing Whitlam's short-lived policy in the 1970s, Gonski proposed a needs-based approach to funding schools. It comprised a common schooling resource standard (SRS) that set a minimum level of funding for every primary and secondary student, based on the resourcing level of consistently successful schools. And it added loadings for students with specific educational disadvantage, such as students from low socioeconomic backgrounds, students with disabilities, Indigenous students, remote and isolated students, and students with English as a second language (Gonski, 2011).

This model would have resulted in the public sector getting a larger increase because it carries the bulk of students with educational disadvantage. Upon the release of the report, there appeared to be broad support from the three education sectors. Indeed, for a time it seemed that the old-style, public/private debate had been consigned to history, and that Australia had found a way to reconcile the demands associated with funding different systems of education inside a cumbersome federal arrangement.

After sitting on the report for an inordinately long time, in April 2013 the then-Gillard government eventually responded with a policy that purported to be based on Gonski. There was to be an SRS of about $9000 per primary student, and $12,000 per secondary student, plus loadings for disadvantage. The plan represented an increase in the overall expenditure on education over a six-year period from 2014 to 2019 of $7.3 billion in real terms over 2013 prices, with a 69 per cent increase for public schools, and a 42 per cent increase to the private sector (Connors & McMorrow, 2015). Annual amounts were to be indexed, with the bulk of the additional money scheduled to appear in the fifth and sixth years, by which time all schools should be operating at the school-resource standard.

Gillard's plan involved the federal government providing two-thirds, and the states one-third, of the additional money needed. The SRS would be used to determine baseline funding; and each private school would receive 20–90 per cent of this amount depending on the 'capacity of parents to pay' based on a modified SES formula.

By the time of the 2013 federal election, all states and territories except Queensland, Western Australia and the Northern Territory had signed agreements. The difference between the various agreements, and the fact that Prime Minister Gillard had promised that under the new arrangements 'no private school would be worse off', meant that already the much-vaunted needs-based model was coming apart at the seams. However, since the federal Coalition had promised a 'unity ticket' on Gonski—albeit with a funding commitment that spanned four years rather than six—it was presumed that no matter which party was elected, the broad principles enunciated by Gonski would survive.

It was not to be. After a number of changes of position, the newly elected Abbott Liberal/National Party Coalition government made it clear that Gonski was effectively dead. When the Coalition government's first budget was released in May 2014, the funding for school education was loosely based on the first four years of the agreements with the states and territories, with the addition of funding for the non-signatories.

Crucially, however, the agreements for years five and six, which comprised the bulk of the additional funds, were torn up. Instead, the Abbott government insisted that, from 2018, federal funding would increase at the rate of the consumer price index (about 2.5 per cent), rather than on the basis of any educational justification. The loss of the promised funding in the final two years—the bulk of which would have gone to public schools—resulted in a significant reduction in the amounts agreed to by the states.

The about-turn of the Abbott government caused a return to the bitter divide and acrimony of the pre-Gonski decades. It was clear that, under the Abbott government scheme, the increase in Commonwealth funding for private schools within five years would be nearly double that of the public sector. It was also obvious that the federal government had no appetite for ensuring that the states—the main funders of public schools—allocated their money on the basis of need within a consistent framework of understanding and monitoring educational disadvantage.

For a time, even a change of prime minister did not alter anything since, for his first eighteen months as Prime Minister, Malcolm Turnbull seemed to have no interest in returning to the Gonski principles. And then in May 2017, Turnbull called a press conference and, flanked by his Education Minister Senator Simon Birmingham and David Gonski, announced a new plan for school funding. Dubbed Gonski 2.0, the plan injected an additional $19 billion into Commonwealth funding over a decade, and promised to ensure that all schools and states would move to an equal share of the Gonski-recommended SRS. This involved the federal government by 2023 meeting a 20 per cent share of the SRS with federal funds for public schools, and an 80 per cent share for private schools, with state governments expected to provide 80 per cent for public schools.

Despite the government insisting that the deal injected unprecedented sums of money into schools and would mean nearly 400 private schools would be worse off than under the previous formula, the plan was attacked from all quarters. The Labor Party and public education lobby groups pointed out that the total amount of promised federal funding was still well short of the original amount promised in years five and six of the original Gillard plan. Public education advocates were also angered because most states and territories currently provide between just 70–75 per cent of the SRS, leaving the public system to receive a lower percentage of total government funds than private schools. And no sooner had Gonski 2.0 been announced than the Catholic church mounted a national campaign against it.

They were incensed that the plan stripped away the special deals which had favoured them for two decades, and knew that a number of their schools would lose money.

The entitlement discourse was still dominating the schools funding debate, and public schools were still being short-changed. And things were not to get any better after Turnbull was toppled by a party-room coup, and Scott Morrison became the new prime minister. In an attempt to appease the Catholic lobby, in September 2018 Morrison announced an additional $4.6 billion over ten years for private schools. Of this, $3.2 billion was ostensibly to introduce the new income-based formula that was to take the place of the SES locality-based methodology used for assessing 'need' when distributing federal money to private schools, and $1.2 billion was allocated to support 'parent choice'. According to Prime Minister Morrison, the latter was designed to make the system more equitable, despite not offering one extra cent to public schools, which carry the bulk of educationally disadvantaged students.

So, a decade after an exhaustive review designed to address growing inequalities in schools funding, Australian education had returned to the starting point. Just as it appeared there was a resolution to the endless public/private debates, successive federal governments undermined needs-based principles by caving into the entitlement philosophy, and so guaranteed a return to old jealousies and self-interested lobbying. Meanwhile, the inequities that produced the current system continue to diminish public education. In 2019, the Grattan Institute calculated that in the previous decade real resources available to schools were increased by more than $2 billion, but when wage growth was taken into account, private schools received more than 80 per cent of that amount (Goss, 2019). That is, despite the Gonski debates, the funding gap between advantaged and disadvantaged schools and between public and private schools has widened (Ting et al., 2018).

This potted history of the school funding debates has given some insights into the underlying philosophy that informs them.

Since the Whitlam government made its landmark decision to fund private as well as public schools in the early 1970s, the discourse has gradually changed from one in which the funding of private schools was justified on the basis of need, to one in which private schools are entitled to government funds on the same basis as public schools. As the discourse has changed, so too have public schools moved from being seen as a public good for all, to being understood as a safety net for those who can't afford private schools. The next section will explore the consequences of the shift in discourse, in particular the financial impact that has led to the residualisation of public schools.

The financial impact

Accompanying the changes described above has been one common theme: from 1973 to 2019, the share of public money from the Commonwealth government going to private schools has steadily increased, with a commensurate decrease in the share for public schools. In 1976, public schools had a 65 per cent share of Commonwealth funding for schools, with private schools having a 35 per cent share (Connors & McMorrow, 2015, pp. 30). By 2019, that had changed to a 20 per cent share for the public sector and 80 per cent for the private sector.

Of course, during the same period state and territory governments continued to provide the bulk of funds to public schools. But even when the funding sources are combined, the change in Commonwealth funding over a period of forty years slowly reduced the difference in funding between public and private schools. In recent times, the various versions of 'Gonski money' have increased the Commonwealth's contribution to all schools. However, the hope that Gonski funding based on need would reduce resource disparities between schools has been dashed because of various deals cut with the private sector, and the fact that the states and territories, which largely fund public schools, have decreased their expenditure on public schools while increasing it on private schools. As Cobbold points out, the bilateral funding agreements between the Commonwealth and state governments mean that public schools will only be funded at 91 per cent of the SRS, while private schools are guaranteed 100 per cent or more of the SRS by 2023 (Cobbold, 2018; 2019).

Bonnor and Shepherd (2015) argue that the only way to really understand the difference in government funding for public and private schools is not to take an average of the funding across all sectors, but to compare the funding of *similar* schools across the sectors. Using ACARA's Index of Socio-Educational Advantage (ICSEA), they show that the differences in public funding between the sectors shrinks significantly when comparisons are made between schools in specific ranges, such as lower educational advantage or higher educational advantage. Indeed, Goss points out that, '. . . nearly one in three private schools in Australia now get more taxpayer dollars than the typical public school of similar size and student background' (Goss, 2019).

In addition to these figures, it is important not to forget that when school fees and charges are added into the amounts, the total income of private schools within these ranges is even greater. This is a crucial point. It makes little sense to only compare the amount of public money each sector receives, when it is the total income from all sources that makes the difference to the quality of the resources and facilities available to students. Trevor Cobbold updated 2013 Senate Estimates figures to estimate the average total income of schools in 2016. He found that the independent school figure was nearly 50 per cent higher than for public schools, with Catholic schools receiving slightly more than public schools (Cobbold, 2017a).

The decision in the 1970s to provide recurrent funding to private schools didn't just rescue the private schooling sector at a time when many schools were going under—it gave it such a boost that the face of Australian education altered dramatically.

The disparities this has created between schools and systems are shocking enough. But when they are considered alongside the fact that it is public schools that take the vast majority of educationally disadvantaged students, and that are very under-resourced compared to most private schools, it becomes a national disgrace. If nothing changes, the consequences are chilling.

The consequences: Residualising public education

It was not long after the flow of government funds to private schools started in the mid-1970s that private schools began to steadily increase their share of student enrolments. From 1972 to 2017, the public system's share of enrolments fell by thirteen percentage points from 78 per cent to 65 per cent, with the enrolment loss being picked up by the private schooling sector, the share of which jumped from 22 per cent to 35 per cent (Connors & McMorrow, 2015). When secondary schooling is taken in isolation, 41 per cent of students now attend private schools (Rowe, 2017). In the 1970s, some private school advocates argued that state aid would enable private schools to hold and then reduce their fees, thus opening up school choice to a greater number of families. In general terms, this is not what happened. After a brief fall in private sector fees (Williams, 1985), since the mid-1980s (apart from a short respite during the recession of the early 1990s) fees in the Catholic sector have risen by 5 per cent per annum in real terms; and over 2 per cent per annum in real terms in the independent sector (Watson & Ryan, 2010). Indeed, a *Financial Review* report estimates that private schools' fees are now exceeding the rate of inflation, sometimes doubling it (Bolton, 2018). In other words, the growth in fee levels has not affected demand for private schools. As fees have risen, so have enrolments increased.

People have many reasons for choosing to send their children to private schools—such as family tradition, religion and networking (see Campbell et al., 2009)—but of course these reasons existed before federal funds were directed to private schools. So what caused the spike in private school enrolments from the late 1970s?

A significant consequence of state aid is that it enabled private schools to improve their position in the education market by making them attractive relative to public schools. As competitive pressures accumulate in the schooling system, so aspirational parents begin to look for market advantage. Greater pressure for places in high-status university courses, for example, has flowed down the schooling system with parents searching for ways to provide their children with a head-start in the academic competition.

Private schools responded by creating an image of being well-resourced, academically rigorous, well-disciplined and promoting the right values. For example, since the 1980s, independent schools have been able to use their money to steadily improve (and publicise) their student:teacher ratios, relative to student:teacher ratios in public schools. Factors like this have convinced many with the means to do so that they should move to the private sector despite increases in fees (Watson & Ryan, 2010). At the same time, the fee structures of private schools present natural barriers to entry for the students who are most educationally disadvantaged and therefore require the most resources, while private schools are able to 'cream-off' the most able children from the same background through scholarships.

But the shift of enrolments from the public to the private sector did more than simply change overall enrolment share—it also had a dramatic impact on the social mix of Australian schools. In the 1970s and 1980s, taking the public and private sectors as a whole, the proportions of low-SES and high-SES students were much the same across both sectors—albeit there were differences within sectors based on fees (private sector) or academic selectivity or location (public sector) (Preston, 2013). Twenty-five years later, all that had changed.

The drift from public to private schools has come largely from the higher-SES families. Teese (2011) has undertaken a revealing analysis of the drift from 1986 to 2006. In terms of primary school students, the public sector share of the highest quartile SES students declined from 74 per cent in 1986 to 63 per cent in 2006; and in the next highest SES quartile its share dropped from 81 per cent in 1986 to 72 per cent in 2006. Over the same time period, the public primary school share of the lowest SES quartile remained almost the same. That is, none of the share of the lowest socioeconomic group was transferred into the private sector in the twenty-year period from 1986 to 2006. As Teese observes,

> while both public and private investment in non-government schooling rose substantially over the period, this supported a transfer of students largely from the upper end of the socio-economic spectrum, leaving the public sector to manage with over four-fifths of all children from the poorest backgrounds. (Teese, 2011, p. 32)

Barbara Preston points out that in 1986 the government and private sectors had similar proportions of secondary students from low- and high-income families. Twenty-five years later, the public sector had almost twice the proportion of secondary students from low-income families, relative to the proportion from high-income families, with the private sector having the reverse (Preston, 2013, pp 6-7).

The term that has been coined for this process is 'residualisation', a concept that focuses on the relationships between sectors (Marginson, 1993; Preston, 2013). The drift described above has involved a gradual loss of support for public schools, particularly from the affluent section of the community. As the overall share of enrolments in the public sector has declined, so has there been a social consolidation, with lower-SES groups being concentrated in public schools in certain areas and higher-SES students in private schools. Sometimes these homogeneous groupings exist in the same local communities. In essence, successive policies have 'funded parents from socially advantaged backgrounds to withdraw their children from public schools' (Teese, 2011, p. 12).

Using the ICSEA, the Gonski Review (2011) showed that, in 2010, 47 per cent of all students in independent schools were drawn from the highest quartile of socio-educational advantage, while public schools drew just 22 per cent of that quartile. Conversely, only 13 per cent of all students in independent schools came from the lowest quartile of socio-educational advantage, while public schools had 36 per cent of that quartile enrolled. Catholic schools fell between these two extremes.[6]

The figures are stark. The drift to private schools means that public schools now overwhelmingly shoulder the challenges associated with having 82 per cent of low-SES students. More than this, public schools carry the vast majority of other groups of students who bring with them various forms of educational disadvantage and challenge, including 84 per cent of Indigenous students, 87 per cent of students in very remote areas, and 76 per cent of students with disability (Cobbold, 2016). It is public schools that are doing the heavy lifting in Australian education.

In addition, public schools are becoming increasingly fragmented. There are, of course, still a number of socially mixed and comparatively well-resourced public schools, usually in the more affluent suburbs—although their numbers are diminishing. And some jurisdictions have tried to stem the drift to private schools by establishing special purpose schools and selective schools. This has tended to divide the public system into a three-tiered system, with a minority of affluent well-resourced

---

6   Another way to look at this is to use the average ICSEA of schools. Bonnor & Shepherd (2015) estimate that in 2014, the average ICSEA for schools in the public system was 983; for schools in the Catholic system it was 1040; and for schools independent schools it was 1071.

schools at one end with the capacity to raise significant funds through parent fees and contributions (Thompson, Hogan & Shield, 2019; Rowe & Perry, 2019), a growing number of poorly resourced and residualised schools at the other end, and groups of schools at or just below the ICSEA average trying to retain students and maintain an acceptable standard of resource provision. This degree of fragmentation erodes the cohesion and the sense of collaboration and collectivity that is so important to a healthy system of public education.

There are a range of consequences accompanying a residualised public education system that are essential to understand if strategies are to be fashioned to turn it around. The consequences include the following.

- As argued in Chapter 2, the increasing social segregation of schooling has a deleterious impact on educational outcomes (OECD, 2018b & 2019). In particular it most effects those schools with the largest percentage of low-SES students, who lose the educational ballast and energy that comes from a genuine social mix. Meanwhile, those who are already educationally privileged continue to prosper. It should come as no surprise that students from low-SES backgrounds are recording educational outcomes up to four years behind their peers from wealthy backgrounds (Perry, 2018; Bonnor, 2019).
- The increasing social and cultural segregation of schools has serious negative effects on other crucial aspects of learning, not least the central role of education in promoting the understandings, skills and dispositions of our future citizens to live harmoniously in a multicultural society. This requires an understanding of and respect for difference. Schools are surely the key arenas in our society within which children and young people can rub shoulders with others from vastly different cultural, religious

and social backgrounds. They can never fully develop these capabilities when they are marooned in cocoons of cultural sameness.
- The families lost to public schools are those who have economic as well as social and cultural capital. This has a devastating effect on the capacity of those schools to raise additional funds for school resources. Of course, many of these schools—the very schools with the greatest challenges and thus the need for most additional resource assistance—are already saddled with inadequate facilities and large classes. Meanwhile they watch affluent schools supplement their school incomes with bequests and parent fund-raising bonanzas. High-SES schools have substantially better facilities than low-SES schools, and these disparities are exacerbated by current funding policy.

These examples are sufficient to demonstrate the negative effects of a funding policy that is producing a residualised public education system in Australia. And, of course, as the advantages garnered by private schools are converted into tangible assets, which in turn attract more anxious parents from the public sector, so the gap between wealthy and poor schools continues to widen.

Privatising public education

The schools funding debate in Australian education has been shaped by neoliberal ideology. In turn it has been one of the factors that has helped to produce all the conditions needed to create a privatising dynamic in public education. The ingredients are an education market and a discourse of choice; education data that appears to show that one part of the market (private schools) is producing better educational outcomes than another part (public schools); aspirational parents looking to position their children advantageously in the market; a media that assumes that education standards in Australia are in decline; and governments searching for a way to improve Australia's standing in the international league tables.

The heady mix of these ingredients has suggested an obvious answer to the policy-makers: if standards are to lift, and if private schools are the market leaders, then it is important that public schools become more like private schools (Mannix, 2013). Stephen Ball and Deborah Youdell (2008) draw a useful distinction between two different ways in which public schools can be subjected to privatisation tendencies—one overt, the other more subtle:

- *exogenous privatisation* (privatisation *of* public education), which involves opening up public schools to be run by private individuals, corporate companies and for-profit or not-for-profit organisations
- *endogenous privatisation* (privatisation *in* public education), which involves importing ideas, techniques and practices from the private sector in order to make the public sector more business-like and 'independent' of systems.

While developments in Australia have mainly been consistent with endogenous privatisation, some conservative commentators have been enthusiastic supporters of an exogenous approach (see Donnelly, 2014b; Jha & Buckingham, 2015). That notwithstanding, it is the more covert forms of privatisation in public education that currently pose the biggest threat. Over the past twenty years, public school systems have been awash with the language and concepts of the corporate sector—key performance indicators, vision and mission statements, branding and so on. Accompanying this language have been private sector management and organisational models, such as the self-managing school, which seek to create public schools as independent units operating competitively in an education market. In addition, as was described in Chapter 2, this tendency to privatise public education has been compounded by the commercialisation of education, as governments begin to usher large private corporations into the education policy space (see Hogan, Sellar & Lingard, 2015). In short, the logic of neoliberalism in education involves a tendency to privatise a public good.

Conclusion

In summary, the 20th-century hope that public education would decouple educational success from social background is clearly under threat. It is not that public schools can't do the job. Indeed, when educational outcomes are compared across public and private schools within the same SES group, public schools do at least as well, and often better, than private schools (Ryan, 2013; Nghiem et al., 2015; Zygnier, 2019). But when public schools are expected to carry the vast bulk of educationally disadvantaged students and are not given the extra resources required to undertake the job, then Australia is on the path to a segregated schooling system that simply reinforces existing inequalities and social divisions.

It is not too late. But, as with climate change, as a society we will have to act quickly. The short history of funding in this chapter has demonstrated how the key philosophical concepts of educational neoliberalism—education markets, choice and the individual consumer—shaped the entitlement discourse that has so dominated the funding debates for the past forty years. Every time a new strategy attempted to shift the discourse back to one based on equity, it was beaten back by the strength of the neoliberal narrative. A new educational narrative must therefore deal with the funding issue in new ways.

It is clear that additional public money must be directed to the most disadvantaged schools, most of which are in the public system. The immediate policy challenge is for commonwealth, state and territory governments to work together to ensure that public schools receive 100 per cent of the agreed schooling resource standard. However, as this chapter has demonstrated, coming up with a fairer funding model is a necessary but not a sufficient condition for creating a more equitable system of Australian education. Unless the tenor of the public–private debate also changes to incorporate the values and principles that privilege the common good rather than individual self-interest, then any new approach is destined to be subsumed by the ideology of neoliberalism.

A new narrative is needed to underscore the importance of public education to Australia's future. Such a narrative will show that the secret to addressing the segregation of the Australian schooling system lies, not in the current trend of making public schools more private, but rather in (re)emphasising their publicness.

Chapter 4

Standardised testing and its problems: A case study of the Programme for International Student Assessment (PISA)

Lying at the heart of the neoliberal policy regime is an obsession with quantitative data, often manifested and justified under the banner of choice, accountability and evidence-based policy. This chapter will suggest that the current obsession with data—what Muller (2018) calls a metric fixation—is nothing more than a wish for certainty, a desire to precisely calibrate and measure educational outcomes in ways that narrow and standardise education. Its ill effects have been well documented, and yet governments continue the obsession. In so doing, they are impoverishing education.

It is important to make the point at the outset that a critique of the neoliberal accountability regime is not an argument against accountability. Gathering evidence—both quantitative and qualitative—is crucial in order to inform all those who have a stake in the quality of our education systems about how things are going. It assures taxpayers that government funds are being spent wisely and appropriately; advises parents about the quality of their child's education; tells educators about areas that need work; and assists policy-makers in making decisions about such matters as resource allocation. But it is the form that accountability takes that is at stake here. It is argued that when approaches to accountability are narrow and pinched—as are those associated with the standardising agenda—they can only serve to severely constrain what is needed for a futures-focused education. That is, it is pointless devising an educational program for the future, only to allow it to be sabotaged by accountability strategies that are incompatible with it.

The problem is that standardising approaches are so entrenched that it won't be easy to shift them. The first step in removing them is to understand how they work and with what effect. Since the Programme for International Student Assessment (PISA) is one of the most influential components of the neoliberal global education reform movement, this chapter will focus on PISA as an example of the blockages that can confront futures-focused curriculum change.

PISA as an example of how a standardising educational agenda is created and maintained

PISA is an OECD-administered test of the performance of students aged fifteen years in mathematical literacy, scientific literacy and reading literacy. It has been conducted every three years since 2000. At the time of writing, the latest published tests were taken in 2015 and the results published in December 2016. The next testing round was undertaken in 2018 and the results will be published in December 2019. A different agency in each country has a contract to implement and interpret the tests on behalf of the OECD. In Australia, this agency is the Australian Council for Eductional Research (ACER).

PISA purports to test 'real-life' skills and knowledge. In 2015,

72 countries participated in the tests, which are two hours in length. In 2015, students for the first time took a computer-based test (before that it had been hand-written). It involves a stratified sample of students in each country—in Australia in 2015 about 750 schools and 14,500 students were involved in the PISA tests. All students undertook the scientific literacy test (the major domain in 2015), as well as items from one or more of the other domains (reading literacy, mathematical literacy). Students and principals also completed questionnaires about aspects of school life. In 2015, Australia was grouped in each subject area with countries that returned similar scores, effectively making it equal tenth in scientific literacy; equal twelfth in reading literacy, and equal twentieth in mathematical literacy. Australia was above the OECD average in all three areas.

In 2013, the Gillard government's Australian Education Bill enshrined the aspiration for Australia to be in the top five schooling countries by 2025. Since PISA is the only means by which such a judgement can be made, it sets the benchmark for Australian education. This chapter will make the argument that the focus on PISA is contributing to a narrow and misguided view of the purposes of education, the standards of Australian education, and the policy approaches needed to maintain and enhance quality. As a result, the obsession with PISA scores is preventing Australian education from grappling with the challenges of the future. The effects of PISA will be examined from four different perspectives.

Perspective 1: PISA narrows our educational discourse

In Australia, for the past decade the self-evident starting point for debates about education has been the claim that standards in Australian education are declining relative to other countries. When there is a challenge to produce evidence for the claim, invariably it is Australia's performance on the PISA tests that is proffered. PISA, it seems, has become the arbiter of education quality. Since its inception in 2000, press commentators and politicians in each country go into meltdown when PISA results are published. The 'winners' are eulogised while those countries that have slipped a few rungs on the league table are excoriated.

The usual script was adhered to after the release of the 2015 test results in early December 2016. When it was revealed that Australia had dropped in scores and its position on the league tables, all hell broke loose. The banner headlines variously described Australia's results as 'a catastrophe' (*Financial Review*, 6 December 2016), a 'crisis' (*The Australian*, 8 December 2016), and 'a disgrace' (*The West Australian*, 19 December 2016). Leaving aside the obvious point about whether being in the top third of countries warrants these descriptions, the key point is that not one question was raised about whether or not PISA is an objective measure of education quality. It was simply accepted that it is, fuelling the belief that education standards in Australia are declining.

This has a number of consequences, not the least of which is that the process has created a sense of educational crisis, with schools and teachers bearing the brunt of criticism, creating a flow-on negative impact on morale. But, more than this, the PISA results are starting to have an adverse effect on the public's confidence in Australian education, and on education policy. Following the release of the results in late 2016, many commentators took the opportunity to push their favourite policy positions to improve Australia's standing in PISA tests—most of them from the neoliberal policy armoury. They included performance pay for teachers, giving school boards the power to hire and fire teachers, introducing intrusive accountability regimes, narrowing the curriculum, stressing rote learning and memorisation, and mandating explicit teaching and direct instruction pedagogies. Apart from the fact that these policies have failed elsewhere (Ravitch, 2016) and rarely have a relationship with the problem they are designed to address, they are incompatible with a futures-focused educational agenda.

Another influence on policy is the pseudo-scientific studies of why the top five countries are more successful than Australia. For many years, the focus was on Finland, but as it slipped in the rankings, commentators turned to some of the East Asian countries like Singapore and South Korea, and cities like Hong Kong. The so-called research consists of visiting countries at the top of the league table, describing some of their structures, practices and processes, guessing which variables have contributed to their success, aggregating them, and then urging that these practices are adopted in Australia. A classic of this genre is the 2012 Grattan Institute Report (Jensen et al., 2012), which, despite containing many methodological problems (see Chapter 5), was used by politicians to inform policy and public pronouncements.

The PISA scores have become so synonymous with education quality, that the data are used unquestioningly in inquiries and reviews (e.g., Gonski et al., 2018, pp. 3–14), or by researchers, as a reference point for determining educational achievement, and by politicians trying to justify standardising policy designed to lift PISA results. In all of these reviews and policies, there is rarely evidence provided to support a relationship between the PISA data and the solutions offered. They simply jump from the apparent problem of declining PISA scores, to a solution—ignoring important intermediate steps, such as assessing the evidence, clarifying the problem, gathering extra evidence, and making a connection between the solution and the problem. PISA has become the lazy way to justify any policy proposal.

It is curious that so much store is placed on the results of a test conducted every three years, in just three subjects, by different companies/groups/agencies in over 70 countries, testing sample groups of students. The narrow base of the test belies its influence in shaping almost every aspect of education policy. Instead of public and professional discussion about the challenges of the future, PISA causes educational discourse to be pinched and backward-looking. Surely in the future we need approaches to accountability that expand and enrich the education debate, rather than impoverish it.

Perspective 2: PISA narrows and standardises curriculum and pedagogy

As a consequence of the restricted focus of the tests, PISA narrows and standardises curriculum and pedagogy. Although reading, maths and science are important, they tell us nothing about outcomes in such crucial areas as the arts, history, geography, health and physical education, English literature, and civics and citizenship, to name just a few areas of the formal curriculum. Inevitably, the favoured three curriculum areas become the core subjects, attracting most of the allocated curriculum time and resources, with other areas being relegated to the margins. And yet, as will be argued in Part 3, in a globalising world, people need skills that are as much right-brain directed—such as design and art—as left-brain cognitive skills of the sort tested by PISA. PISA tells us nothing about how education systems are faring in relation to these fundamental capacities. Results at one stage of schooling every three years in only three areas of the curriculum are too narrow a base upon which to make claims about the quality of Australian education.

More than this, the PISA scores mask some important aspects of student learning. The league table of countries, based on raw scores, obscures from public view contextual information that provides a fuller picture of student learning—and suggests that a high league table ranking may not be all that it seems. For example, the raw scores reveal nothing about student engagement. The summary of attitudes to science buried deep in the PISA report indicates that students from the top countries tend to have some of the lowest rates of wanting to pursue a science-related career (Australia is in the top grouping), or of enjoying their science learning. In the 2006 science results, Finland came out on top in cognitive outcomes, but finished nearly bottom in the level of student interest in science; and in 2015 Finland finished well below Australia in terms of student wellbeing. One wonders if the top results have been gained at the expense of turning students off the study of science, and, if so, whether this is something we would want to emulate in Australia.

Then there is the fact that in some countries or regions (e.g., Singapore, South Korea), which are in the top five of PISA league tables, many children are sent to after-hours cram schools to advance their chances of success in a highly competitive and exam-oriented schooling culture. Concerns are now being raised that such approaches stifle creativity, narrow the curriculum and harm student wellbeing (Koo, 2014; Larmer, 2015). Why copy that approach? Uncritically importing policies and practices from other countries on the basis of their PISA success is surely fraught with danger.

In constructing the tests, there are many cultural factors that make comparing the educational outcomes of 72 countries highly problematic. These include the difficulties associated with making an international test culturally neutral when it is converted to many different languages. Although the OECD tries to weed out culturally specific items, it cannot do this precisely and, in any case, one wonders what is left of value to test once culture is washed out of language.

There is another way in which culture is homogenised through PISA. As countries seek to maintain or improve their PISA league table standings by borrowing policy, so the official curricula of many countries start to converge. For example, England is implementing the Singaporean maths curriculum, including mandating textbooks and pedagogical approaches; there have been calls for Australia to follow suit. American educator Yong Zhao (2014) describes this as a process of 'global homogenisation' as the supposedly less successful countries begin to copy or borrow from the more successful countries. There are at least two reasons why chasing success in PISA by copying other countries is dangerous.

First, PISA assumes that young people in every country should know the same things and develop the same skill set. However, while there may be many similarities, such an assumption fails to appreciate the different contexts and challenges faced by people across cultures and, thus, the different kinds of skills needed. In any event, there is a strong case to be made that in a globalising economy countries should be looking to differentiate their skill sets, rather than to standardise them. Since the nature of the curriculum is a key determinant of the kind of educational outcomes achieved, then 'global curriculum homogenisation' is surely counterproductive to a country's interests (Zhao, 2014).

Second, transplanting curriculum and pedagogy from a successful PISA country to a less successful country is dangerous since it ignores the cultural factors contributing to educational outcomes. John Jerrim (2015) looked at the performance of students who were second-generation East Asian students in Australia, and who had been educated only in Australian schools. He found that, in the 2012 PISA tests, the scores of these students outperformed the scores of students in nearly every other participating school system, including those at the very top of the PISA tables such as South Korea, Hong Kong and Singapore. Research like this demonstrates the powerful influence of background and culture, suggesting that it is very dangerous to correlate PISA scores with a certain kind of curriculum or pedagogy, or make sweeping generalisations about the quality of a schooling system in a specific country.

Perspective 3: PISA gives an inaccurate reading of educational outcomes

A third perspective on the PISA story relates to whether or not it provides quality information upon which to make decisions.

Given the ways in which the PISA tests are used to inform education policy, clearly a lot of trust is being placed in the test itself. But what would happen if it could be shown that the results of PISA tests, or the ways in which they have been interpreted, need to be taken with a grain of salt, or are faulty? Where would that leave the research based on PISA results or all the policy strategies designed to address the PISA effect? There are a number of methodological problems associated with the PISA tests that cast a dark shadow over their accuracy.

In 2013, the *Times Educational Supplement* published some articles pointing to some of the 'profound conceptual errors' upon which PISA is based. One article claimed that these flaws render the league tables 'useless' (Stewart, 2013). To understand this argument, it is important to realise that when students sit the test, they do not answer all the questions in the three domains. Every three years the tests have a main focus subject; in 2015, it was scientific literacy. All students answered all the science questions, while some students answered some of the reading items and others answered some of the maths items. Many students were not tested at all in one domain. Despite this, the OECD produced full rankings for all subjects.

The OECD justifies this approach by saying that since its interest is system-level assessment, it does not generate scores by individuals but instead uses Rasch modelling to calculate 'plausible values for each student'. That is, it produces system-wide aggregates based on working out what the scores would have been if all students in all countries answered the same questions. This is very complex territory. But there is now a raging debate between some mathematicians about the efficacy of the OECD approach. Leading mathematician Professor Svend Kreiner, a former student of Georg Rasch (the Danish mathematician and statistician who created the Rasch model), argues that the model cannot be used unless all questions have an equal degree of difficulty in all countries. Since this cannot be guaranteed in PISA, the 'plausible values' are unreliable, which means that the league table rankings are meaningless (Kreiner & Christensen, 2014). Other statisticians and educational researchers agree that the validity and reliability of the test is, at best, dubious (Carnoy, 2015; Fernandez-Carno, 2016).

There are also problems with using the PISA data to make comparisons between countries and previous test results. First, as mentioned earlier, there are many difficulties associated with making an international test culturally neutral when it is converted to many different languages. A second problem is that some of the top place getters in PISA (e.g., Hong Kong, Macao, Taipei and Beijing–Shanghai–Jiangsu–Guangdong) are cities/regions, not countries. This makes comparisons problematic. If it is valid to compare the results of cities with countries, why not make the ACT, with its comparatively affluent demographic, our representative in the PISA tests. Australia would then rise to fifth on the science ladder!

The third problem is associated with how the tests are conducted. What happens in one country is never identical to what happens in another, and these differences—even when very small—affect the capacity to compare the results across countries. One example relates to the sampling processes. Some participating countries exclude more schools from the tests than others; or have a smaller percentage of their fifteen-year-old population at school. This makes comparisons between participating systems very problematic.

For example, when Shanghai–China finished top in each of the three domains in the 2012 PISA tests, Tom Loveless from the Brookings Institute in Washington argued that Shanghai's sampled students were not a representative sample of the students in that city. He pointed out that Shanghai's sample of fifteen-year-old students did not include the thousands of students from poor rural areas whose parents have moved to the city in search of work. These people hold a *hukou*, the Chinese equivalent of an internal passport, which identifies them as belonging to their former region, not Shanghai, and are thus ineligible for public services in Shanghai, including the mainstream public schooling system. The *hukou* system means that rural children, many of whom have low levels of literacy, are either left behind in their villages or driven back there to attend high school; or are placed in inferior and very poorly resourced separate schools for migrants in Shanghai. Their absence clearly skews the PISA results by removing from the population of fifteen-year-olds in the city many of the students who would drag its PISA scores down (Loveless, 2013). The OECD failed to respond adequately to the Loveless critique, until its Education Director, Andreas Schleicher, admitted to a House of Commons Education Select Committee that in fact only 73 per cent of students were represented in the Shanghai province's sample of students in the 2012 test (Stewart, 2014).

Finally, there is the issue of comparing PISA results from one testing period to the next. Prior to 2015, PISA tests were paper-based. This changed in 2015, when tests shifted to being computer-based. When the 2015 results were released, there was a puzzling reduction of up to 10 per cent in the percentage of students achieving high test scores from a number of the top-five countries, including East Asian countries and cities such as Taiwan, South Korea and Hong Kong. There is now strong speculation that the drop was a result of the changed delivery mechanism for the tests. The person in charge of PISA, Andreas Schleicher, has admitted that the OECD cannot explain the reasons for the drop, and that the decline may be to do with the fact that computers were used for the first time. This renders claims about the decline in scores as highly suspect, and once again calls into doubt the reliability of the PISA test itself (Ward, 2017).

These and other technical issues suggest that the doubts overshadowing the technical aspects of PISA are now of such gravity that they demand a product warning when results are released. Instead, journalists and ministers for education fall over themselves in the rush to make comment and devise policy in the belief that PISA scores offer a precise reading of the health of an education system. If the PISA tests are too narrow and contain serious technical flaws, then the use of PISA data to pass judgement about the educational quality of a country is problematic at best, and potentially dangerous at worst. It is not the basis upon which education policy should be made.

Perspective 4: PISA does not provide a sufficient evidential basis for policy-making

The data from the PISA tests has a significant impact on policy-makers in many countries. Every three years when the results are published, the league tables become the focus of attention in all the countries involved. Any shifts in a country's position on the league tables of mathematics, science and reading is taken as evidence that policy is working or that drastic action is needed. The scores have become the de facto measure of educational quality and achievement. This is damaging enough on its own, but it is what follows that does the real damage.

The OECD, which is the lead testing agency (setting and implementing the test), is also the body that interprets the data and the results. This conflict of interest is ignored when the OECD publishes papers on policy implications drawn from the combination of the PISA data and the aggregated responses to survey questions by students and principals. Questions about the methodological issues are forgotten, and when the papers are published, policy-makers and commentators at the national level take notice. The 'findings' become the latest educational truths and provide the justification for the next round of policy changes in individual countries. There are some significant problems with this approach to policy-making.

Even ignoring the methodological issues with PISA described in Perspective 3 above, it makes no sense to use the data for policy-making because the tests and the survey questionnaires are cross-sectional, meaning the same group of students is not followed longitudinally. Every three years, the new PISA test is completed by a new group of sample students, which means it is hazardous to make causal links between gains in student achievement and inputs at the school level. Similarly, since PISA does not examine teacher practices directly or associate individual teachers with students, making causal connections on the basis of anecdotal evidence is highly problematic.

And yet, despite these problems, the OECD arrives at conclusions about why test results in some countries are higher than in others, and disseminates its findings. For example, in 2016 it published five volumes of its key findings, one of which had the title *Policies and Practices for Successful Schools* (OECD, 2016b); included under the heading 'What 2015 PISA results imply for policy' were findings related to such aspects as learning environments, class size, school autonomy, teaching approaches and equity. The usual logic is that since best practice resides with the highest scoring countries, improvement in rankings for those countries further down the tables means adopting the policies of those in the top five. In the years between PISA tests, the OECD mines the data for educational lessons and promulgates its policy 'findings' through reports, papers and conferences.

The Head of PISA at the OECD, Andreas Schleicher, has become something of an international educational guru, travelling the world and giving advice to the countries he visits. His information base relies entirely on PISA data, and the many correlations he makes between the PISA scores and a range of variables. Thus, in 2017 he was in Australia 'reading the riot act' (Dodd, 2017) to educators and policy-makers, and unfavourably comparing us to the mainly East Asian countries that sit above Australia on the league tables. Schleicher has now written a book providing advice on how to build a 21st century school system (Schleicher, 2018), the main messages of which are once again almost entirely based on PISA data and the dubious correlations made with a number of variables. The unfortunate thing is that, rather than simply adding to the policy mix, such information takes on the aura of uncontestable truth and is lapped up by policy-makers looking for answers. Carnoy and Rothstein (2013) observe from a US perspective that such an approach is

> oversimplified, exaggerated, and misleading. It ignores the complexity of the content of test results and may well be leading policy-makers to pursue inappropriate and even harmful reforms that change aspects of the U.S. education system that may be working well and neglect aspects that may be working poorly. (Carnoy & Rothstein, 2013, p. 7)

Combining the perspectives on PISA: How a flawed test produces flawed research and flawed policy

The four perspectives above argue that the PISA 'research' is deeply flawed, and yet it is accepted in the public arena as scientifically accurate, and enables generalised claims about the decline in quality of Australian education to be made. This section will take an example from research into the impact of classroom disciplinary climate on student learning, which uses data from the 2015 PISA tests, to demonstrate the dubiousness of the whole process.

PISA and its 'research' on disciplinary climate

During the PISA testing process, other data are gathered to flesh out a full picture of some of the contextual and resource factors influencing student learning. Thus, in 2015 principals were asked to respond to questions about school management, school climate and school resources, and student perspectives were gleaned from a range of questions and responses relating to science, which was the major domain for that year. These questions focused on such matters as classroom environment, truancy, classroom disciplinary climate, motivation and interest in science.

These data are used to produce key findings in relation to school learning environment, equity and student attitudes to science. Such findings emerge after multiple cross-correlations between PISA scores, student and school socioeconomic status, and the data drawn from responses to questionnaires. They are written up in volumes of OECD reports, replete with charts, scatter plots and tables (e.g., OECD, 2016b).

In the 2015 PISA tests, one of the topics about which students were asked to respond related to classroom discipline. They were asked: How often do these things happen in your science classes?

- Students don't listen to what the teacher says.
- There is noise and disorder.
- The teacher has to wait a long time for the students to quieten down.
- Students cannot work well.
- Students don't start working for a long time after the lesson begins.

Then, for each of the five statements, students had to tick one of the boxes on a four-point scale from (a) never or hardly ever (b) in some lessons (c) in most lessons (d) in all lessons.

Even before looking at what is done with the results of the questions posed in PISA about classroom discipline, alarm bells are ringing. For a start, the five statements listed are based on some unexplained pedagogical assumptions. They imply that a disciplined classroom environment is one that is quiet and teacher-directed; but there is no rationale provided for why such a view has been adopted. Nor is it explained why the five features of such an environment have been selected above other possible features. They are simply named as the arbiters of disciplinary climate in schools.

However, let's accept for the purposes of this analysis that the five statements represent a contemporary view of classroom disciplinary climate. The next problem is one of interpretation. Is it not possible that students from across 72 countries might understand some of these statements differently? Might it not be that the diversity of languages and cultures of so many countries produces some varying interpretations of what is meant by the statements? For example, what constitutes 'noise and disorder' in one context/culture might differ from another; or, for different students, a teacher 'waiting a long time' for quiet might vary from ten seconds to ten minutes; or, 'students cannot work well' might be interpreted by some as 'I cannot work well' and by others as 'they cannot work well', and so on.

These possible difficulties appear not to trouble the designers, because, from this point on, certainty enters the equation. The aggregated responses to the five questionnaire items are inverted and standardised with a mean of 0 and a standard deviation of 1, to define the index of disciplinary climate in science classes. Students' views on how conducive classrooms are to learning are then combined to develop a composite index—a measurement of the disciplinary climate in their schools. Positive values on this index indicate more positive levels of disciplinary climate in science classes.

Once combined, the next step is to construct a table purporting to show the disciplinary climate in the science classes of fifteen-year-olds in each country. The table comprises an alphabetical list of countries, with the mean index score listed alongside each country, so allowing for easy comparison. This is followed by a series of tables containing overall disciplinary climate scores broken down by each of the disciplinary 'problems', correlated with such factors as performance in the PISA science test, the socioeconomic profile of schools and students, type of school (e.g., public or private), location (urban or rural) and so on. It is possible to see here how the report—despite the many methodological flaws upon which it is based—has now taken on the aura of scientific precision and accuracy.

An ACER report summarises these research findings from an Australian perspective. First, it compares Australia's 'mean disciplinary climate index score' to selected comparison cities/countries such as Hong Kong, Singapore, Japan and Finland. It reports that:

> Students in Japan had the highest levels of positive disciplinary climate in science classes with a mean index score of 0.83, followed by students in Hong Kong (China) (mean index score: 0.35). Students in Australia and New Zealand reported the lowest levels of positive disciplinary climate in their science classes with mean index scores of –0.19 and –0.15 respectively, which were significantly lower than the OECD average of 0.00. (Thomson, Bortoli & Underwood, 2017, p. 277)

Then the ACER report compares scores within Australia by state and territory; by disciplinary problem; and by socioeconomic background. The report concludes that:

> Even in the more advantaged schools, almost one third of students reported that in most or every lesson, students don't listen to what the teacher says. One third of students in more advantaged schools and one half of the students in lower socio-economic schools also reported that there is noise and disorder in the classroom. (Thomson et al., 2017, p. 280)

It should be noted that there would need to be a number of caveats placed on the research outcomes. First, the data relate to a quite specific student cohort and are based only on science classes. That is, the research findings cannot be used to generalise about other subjects in the same year level, let alone about primary and/or secondary schooling. Second, there are some questions about the classroom disciplinary data that call into question the certainty with which the numbers are calculated and compared. These relate to student motivation in answering the questions, and to the differing interpretations by people from many different cultures about the meaning of the same words and phrases. Third, there are well-documented problems related to the data with which the questionnaire responses are cross-correlated, such as the validity of the PISA test scores as described in the previous section.

In short, it could be that discipline is a problem in Australian schools, but this research cannot provide us with that information. Surely the most one can say is that the results might point to the need for more extended research. But, far from a measured response, the media fed the findings into the continuing narrative about falling standards in Australian education. When ACER released its report, the headlines and associated commentary once again damned Australian schools. *The Australian*'s headline described 'Chaos in the Classroom' (15/3/2017), while Adelaide's *The Advertiser* carried the headline 'Disorder the order of the day for Aussie schools', reporting that

> Australian school students are significantly rowdier and less disciplined than those overseas, research has found. An ACER report, released today, says half the students in disadvantaged schools nationally, and a third of students in advantaged schools, reported 'noise and disorder' in most or all of their classes . . . In December, the Advertiser reported the [PISA] test results showed the academic abilities of Australian students were in 'absolute decline'. Now the school discipline results show Australian schools performed considerably worse than the average across OECD nations . . . Federal Education Minister Simon Birmingham said the testing showed that there was 'essentially no

relationship between spending per student and outcomes. This research demonstrates that more money spent within a school doesn't automatically buy you better discipline, engagement or ambition,' he said. (Williams, *The Advertiser*, 14 March 2017)

Mainstream newspapers all over the country repeated the same messages, and media commentators and politicians had fodder for a fresh round of teacher-bashing. It is instructive to list what has happened to this PISA-based research.

- The mainstream press has broadened the research findings to encompass not just fifteen-year-old students in science classrooms, but ALL students (primary and secondary) across ALL subject areas.
- The research report findings have been picked up without any mention of some of the difficulties associated with conducting such research across so many cultures and countries. The numbers are treated with reverence, and the findings as an immutable truth.
- The mainstream press has cherry-picked negative results to get a headline, ignoring findings in the same ACER report that, for example, Australia is well above the OECD average in terms of the interest that students have in their learning in science, and the level of teacher support they receive.
- Key politicians began to use the research findings as a justification for not having to spend more money on education, and to blame schools and students for the 'classroom chaos'.

These errors and omissions reinforce the narrative promulgated in the mainstream media and by politicians and current policy-makers that standards in Australian education are in serious decline. If such judgements are being made on the basis of flawed data reported in a flawed way by the media, they contribute to a misdiagnosis of the causes of identified problems, and to the wrong policy directions being set.

The information garnered from the PISA process every three years may have the potential to contribute to policy-making. But if PISA is to be used as a key arbiter of educational quality, then we need to ensure that its methodology is subjected to critical scrutiny. And politicians and policy-makers alike need to look beyond the simplistic, and often downright wrong, media reporting of PISA results.

Some reflections on PISA

At the system-wide level, the current standardising approach to education is at odds with the purposes and the form of what is needed for a contemporary official curriculum and pedagogy. In this chapter, PISA was used as a case study of how a specific strategy can serve to narrow the curriculum and provoke a sense of crisis about declining standards in Australia without a rigorous evidential base. It simplifies educational issues by washing out complexity. Making judgements about an education system on the basis of a single number—the validity and reliability of which is open to question anyway—leads to a misdiagnosis of the causes of educational issues and problems, and to the wrong policy directions being set.

It is important to stress again that a critique of PISA is not a defensive educator's response to adverse data. We should always be striving to improve the quality of Australian education, and our schools and policy-makers must be accountable for their performance; and there is a strong case to be made for an international educational dialogue with countries sharing educational ideas, research and practice. However, superficial and knee-jerk readings of international test data are more likely to impede than to advance the quality of education in Australia. In an attempt to arrest the supposed decline of Australian education as presaged by PISA, governments are proposing educational agendas that bear little relationship to the challenges of the future. If the use of PISA as the major benchmark for our national educational aspirations is fraught, what are the alternatives? Given what is now known about assessment and evaluation in education, surely it is possible to develop more open and educative approaches to assessing educational outcomes—both in Australia and internationally—than a test held every year in the case of NAPLAN, or every three years in the case of PISA.

Rethinking approaches to accountability will involve coming to a national agreement about the purposes of accountability, including supporting schools to enhance education quality, and providing the community with sound information about educational progress. It is only when purposes are clear that appropriate approaches to accountability can be decided. Inevitably this will involve broadening our evidence options. New approaches might include some light sampling of a range of subjects and domains across a three- to five-year period; working with other countries to find ways beyond standardised testing to assess the development of such important attributes as critical thinking, creativity and intercultural understanding; using a range of mediums for students to demonstrate their learning; and ensuring that methods to assess outcomes reflect agreed goals, and are based on more than just one form of assessment.

One of the dangers is that the OECD will attempt to address the critiques of PISA by expanding the test, without a consideration of the alternatives. Already it is seeking to address mounting criticism about the narrowness of PISA's scope by developing standardised tests for 'collaborative problem-solving', 'creative thinking skills' and 'global competence' to be added to the current PISA testing regime (Schleicher, 2019). However, unless the sorts of problems identified in this chapter are addressed, the new tests will carry all of the same flaws and indeed may compound them.

As is argued in more detail in Chapter 10, there is still a great deal of uncertainty about how to teach for and assess 'soft skills'. Given this uncertainty, how can we be sure that a standardised test written for over 70 countries is the best way to assess general capabilities?

It is only when broad agreement has been reached about the scope of Australia's accountability approach that consideration can be given to the role that an international test like PISA might play in such an approach. In other words, PISA should serve the purposes of Australian education, not the other way around.

Once the role of PISA in an accountability approach is agreed, the next task is to consider the flaws in the current PISA testing regime, and ways to overcome these. One of these is the ways in which PISA data is used. At the very least we must ensure that policy, media commentary and research premised on PISA test results acknowledge the difficulties and limitations of the tests, and are more tentative about using PISA as the sole arbiter of what constitutes quality in education. More than this, if PISA is going to contribute to a robust evidential base about Australian education, then policy-makers need to assure themselves not only that the test results are valid, but also that they are being interpreted correctly. Sellar et al. suggest that

> valid use of test scores could be improved by adopting an *argumentative approach*, where each intended use of the test scores must be argued for and subsequently evaluated. (Sellar, Thomson & Rutkowski, 2017, pp. 73–74, emphasis in original)

Such an approach would overcome the simplistic ways in which commentators and policy-makers are inferring causal correlations; where, for example, decline in performance is attributed to a single cause that then becomes the focus of a new policy imposition. Such simplistic correlations ignore the broader social and structural issues that contribute to educational outcomes.

If PISA is going to contribute to 'evidence-based' policy, then its use in each instance needs to be justified.

In this chapter, PISA has been used as a case study of one of the key planks of the neoliberal educational agenda. It is argued that, as it is currently constructed, interpreted and used, PISA is counterproductive to quality education. Unless its stranglehold is loosened, any reform agenda is doomed to fail.

Chapter 5

Evidence-based policy: The use and abuse of research

In Chapter 2 it was argued that one of the damaging effects of neoliberalism in education has been to contribute to the construction of a knowledge base and discourse that is commodified, simplified and technicised. This is a very general claim and begs the question of how such a discourse is built and sustained. There are a number of techniques and practices that contribute to shaping the ways in which education in Australia is perceived and talked about, and the kind of policy that is developed and implemented. One of these relates to educational research, and this chapter will use two case studies to explore this aspect of the contemporary policy environment. The first looks at what passes as educational research; the second explores how research is used in the service of a neoliberal agenda.

Case study 1: A think tank report

One of the features of the neoliberal policy environment has been the influence of non-government organisations on the processes of policy development and enactment. Thus, think tanks, 'edubusinesses' and consultants are combining to form new policy networks that alter the traditional ways in which we have understood the process of policy-making in education (Ball & Junemann, 2012). The larger question of how these new networks operate and influence policy is an emerging focus of study (e.g., Thompson, Savage & Lingard, 2015). In this section I want to take one aspect of that issue, by looking at the question of what passes for research and how it is used by policy-makers.

The Grattan Institute is a non-partisan think tank which investigates problems and solutions in a range of policy fields. In the area of school education, the Grattan Institute has become a significant player in both shaping and reinforcing government policy. Since January 2010, it has produced many research reports on school education, that are invariably picked up by mainstream media and increasingly by politicians.

Like many think tanks, the Grattan Institute's reports are often constructed as research projects. That is, rather than simply piecing together an argument based on research conducted by other individuals or groups, Grattan often claims to conduct the research itself. This adds credence to its findings, which then become justifications for policy directions and help to create or normalise current political assumptions. For this reason, the quality of its 'research' is an important issue, and its various reports warrant scrutiny. This section will look at one of those reports.[7] The report has been selected not only because when it first appeared it was influential in policy-making circles, but also because in many ways it is representative of the genre of reports that came before and after it, such as those produced by

---

7 It must be stressed that the critique of the selected report which follows, only relates to that report. It does not of course apply to the Institute's many other reports, each of which—like any piece of research—would need to be analysed on its own terms, and many of which have made important contributions to the education debate.

the international firm McKinsey and Company (e.g., Mourshed, Chijoke & Barber, 2010; Mourshed, Krawitz & Dorn, 2017). These reports, which purport to provide evidence about how whole education systems can improve, have been widely promoted in the press and embraced by education bureaucracies.

On 17 February, 2012, the Grattan Institute launched its *Catching Up: Learning from the best school systems in Asia* report—a co-authored report with the lead author being Dr Ben Jensen, the then-Program Director for School Education at the Grattan Institute. The report had an immediate impact. On the day of the launch, the national paper *The Australian* led with a front-page story titled 'Lessons from Asia show way forward for schools' and an editorial headed 'A salutary lesson from the world's top school systems', which repeated the report's 'findings' that Australian students are well behind their Asian counterparts in terms of educational outcomes. The editorial enthusiastically endorsed the policies and practices of the East Asian countries described in the report, bringing together some of its key messages:

> The findings are disturbing: OECD figures show that Australian students are well behind their Asian counterparts in reading, maths and science. On some measures they have gone backwards. The reading level of an average 15-year-old in Canberra in 2009 was six months behind the average 15-year-old in 2000, even though spending had increased by 48%. (*The Australian* Editorial Board, 'A salutary lesson', 2012)

The following day, *The Weekend Australian* ran a full page on aspects of the report describing it as a 'blueprint for reforming Australian schools', accompanied by an article by Ben Jensen titled 'Shanghai success a lesson in delivery' (Jensen, 2012a). The stories fed into and reinforced taken-for-granted assumptions, such as that standards are declining in Australian education; that class size does not matter; that merit-based pay is the best way to motivate teachers; and that giving schools greater autonomy in an education market will enhance quality.

Six days after the release of the Report, the then-federal Minister for Education, Peter Garrett, waxed lyrical about the report at a school leadership conference, describing it as 'more than interesting, you might say it is amazing' (Garrett, 2012). With such accolades, it was not long before journalists and politicians were using the report to justify a reduction in expenditure on education. On the day of the report's release, the *Sydney Morning Herald* commented that 'Jensen says the decline in performance in many Australian schools—despite increased funding—proves money is not the answer' (Harrison, 2012).

Not surprisingly, this refrain was picked up by the then-opposition spokesperson on education, Christopher Pyne. Speaking at the Sydney Institute on 16 July 2012, Pyne repeated the assertion that Australia's reading performance is in decline, and then cited the Grattan Institute report to claim that this decline has occurred 'despite education spending over the same period increasing in real terms by 44%. We're paying more and achieving less' (Pyne, 2012).

Indeed, the Grattan research quickly became Pyne's prime authority for attacking the first Gonski Report on the grounds that schools didn't need more money, just better teachers; for the claim that reducing class size is incredibly expensive and does not meaningfully improve student performance; for criticising the quality of teacher education in Australia; and for arguing for greater principal autonomy to hire and fire teachers.

The report's research findings also became the 'go-to' authority for many journalists and commentators. For example, Judith Sloan, in an article in the *The Australian*, used the Grattan Institute report as her major piece of 'evidence' to argue that, given our declining standards and the fact that the research shows that class size does not significantly influence student performance, there is actually a case for **reducing** real per-student spending on Australian schools or maintaining it at present levels by allowing class sizes to increase. (Sloan, 2012; my emphasis)

In short, the report achieved widespread publicity in the media and was embraced by policy-makers. For many journalists, its 'findings' became the facts from which the education debate started. Judged from this perspective, it was a success for the Grattan Institute. Months after its release Ben Jensen was so certain of its accuracy and insights that he berated educators who refused to learn from the successful countries in Asia, accusing them of ignoring evidence, recycling stereotypes and prejudices, and being isolationist (Jensen, 2012b).

A report that is so influential in the public arena deserves scrutiny. After all, what would happen to the claims based on it if its methodology is found to lack the rigour expected of educational research?

Background to the report Catching Up: Learning from the best school systems in Asia

The process for writing the 124-page report began in September 2011 with a high-powered roundtable including the then-Labor Prime Minister Julia Gillard; federal Minister for Education, Peter Garrett; CEOs of education systems from around Australia; and senior education policy-makers from what are described as four of the world's top five school systems, Hong Kong, Shanghai, South Korea and Singapore (Jensen et al., 2012, p. 6). This assemblage of key policy-makers says something about the new kinds of policy networks that have been formed (Ball & Junemann, 2012).

After the roundtable, researchers from the Grattan Institute visited the four East Asian countries where, the report tells us, they met educators, government officials, school principals, teachers and researchers. This 'field' research was supplemented by the collection of (unspecified) documentation from central, district and school levels. The research report was written on the basis of this information.

The report is largely descriptive. Using PISA scores as its major evidence, the report first establishes that schools in the four East Asian education systems are more successful than Australian schools and then identifies what it claims are the factors that explain why these systems are moving ahead of others. This is followed by a short exposition on what constitutes effective teaching and learning, while the rest of the report provides descriptive examples of the 'reforms' that promote it. Thus, it uses the Hong Kong education system as a case study of 'best practice' reform and then draws from the four East Asian education systems to describe approaches to initial teacher education and various practices, such as school principal education, induction and mentoring, classroom observation and teacher career structures. The sometimes stated, sometimes implied, judgement throughout the report—and certainly the public utterances by its main author after its release—is that Australian education systems do not measure up to the quality of East Asian education; and that the adoption of some or all of the strategies and policies of these four countries would improve Australian education immeasurably.

Since the report garners much of its gravitas and subsequent support on the basis that it is 'research', it is important to assess it on that basis. It will be argued that its claims do not stand up to scrutiny, for at least four reasons.

Concern 1: *The inadequacy of its methodology*

The report does not outline or justify its approach or methodology. Importantly, it does not explore the strengths and difficulties associated with comparative educational research of this type and certainly it does not cite any literature that might provide a justification for the approach used. Instead, it assumes that it is possible to simply describe a range of policies and practices in different countries and to correlate these with PISA results.

There are numerous problems with the research methods used in the report. It does not explain the reason for the selection of the practices that are examined and described or why other factors are deemed unimportant; there is no description of the policy documentation that is reviewed; no list of the teachers and policy-makers interviewed, or how and why they were selected and in what numbers; and very few quotes from interviewees, with no sense of the most dominant views in terms of numbers. These are significant omissions, since their absence gives the reader no way to judge the rigour of the research process.

Concern 2: *The report's acceptance and reinforcement of dominant assumptions.*

The report's foundation assumption is that it is possible to make judgements about the quality of education systems on the basis of PISA outcomes. Using this assumption, the authors are able to justify the focus on Asia, which has four of the five highest performing systems—Hong Kong, South Korea, Shanghai and Singapore—as determined by the 2009 PISA results. There are a number of problems associated with this unexamined assumption.

The use of PISA as the measure of education quality is not accompanied by any of the qualifications about the PISA tests documented in the literature and described in Chapter 4. These include concerns about:

- the propensity of some systems to prepare students for the test (such as the extensive use of after-hours tutors in some countries)
- the difficulties associated with making an international test culturally neutral

- the variation in sampling across various jurisdictions
- the validity of the test
- the unexamined values and beliefs embodied in the test about what constitutes valued knowledge and about curriculum
- the narrowness of what the test measures.

And yet, far from being tentative, the Grattan report goes on to use the OECD formula, which converts PISA scores into education months, to make claims about the disparities in learning levels between countries:

> In Shanghai, the average 15 year-old mathematics student is performing at a level two to three years, on average, above his or her counterpart in Australia, the US, the UK and EU21 countries. Korean students are at least a year ahead, on average, of USA and EU students and seven months ahead of Australian students in reading. (Jensen et al., 2012, p. 10)

These measures appear to have a precise scientific objectivity. When they enter the public domain, the fact that they are associated with a narrow band of learning is forgotten and it is not long before generalisations are made about the differences in quality between education systems. Once this pivotal assumption is accepted, a number of other things follow. For example, the Grattan Institute researchers are able to make assertions about the impact of educational reforms without having to actually evaluate the reforms. Since they coincide with an increase in PISA scores, the success of the reforms is apparently self-evident. Thus:

> In just five years (in reading literacy), Hong Kong moved from 17th in 2001 to 2nd in 2006, only one point behind the mean of 1st placed Russia . . . Hong Kong's reforms have driven this rapid improvement in student's reading. (Jensen et al., 2012, p. 46)

The only other evidence that is used to corroborate the success of the (mainly) top-down reforms are comments made by the designers of each reform itself and those in charge of its implementation. It won't surprise that the people who designed and/or supervised the implementation of the reforms thought the reforms were of a very high quality! For example, in the chapter on 'best practice reform', which describes the changes in education in Hong Kong since 1999, quotes from key decision-makers are highlighted with no attempt made to balance these accounts, or at least explain alternative views. Thus, the report notes, citing the Hong Kong Education Bureau, that:

> Hard working teachers are a strength of Hong Kong's system. Hong Kong recognised that as the frontline workers responsible for implementing reforms in schools or classrooms, teachers needed additional support to develop the capacity to implement change. Many elements of the reform supported teachers. (Jensen et al., 2012, p. 30)

These views are not triangulated with research in classrooms; nor is there reference to the research published in peer-reviewed journals that documents the fierce opposition by many teachers to the managerialist and market-based nature of the reforms, and to the associated appraisal system that emphasises 'performativity' and 'accountability' (Choi, 2005).

Concern 3: The report simplifies the complexity of education

The research confuses correlation with causation. Even accepting the test results, there is no explanation offered as to why the authors have selected, from all the possible practices and policies in schools and education systems, those that are described in the report (e.g., teacher induction and mentoring, and classroom observation). They are simply cherry-picked from different countries and then lumped together with the assumption that they have contributed to the improvement in PISA scores. There is no examination of the connection of these variables with one another or with wider social and cultural settings.

By removing complexity in this way, the report washes out consideration of the effects of socioeconomic background on educational outcomes. The report deems the four East Asian countries to be highly equitable, since the gap between the top- and the bottom-performing students in PISA tests is less than it is in Australia. The explanation offered for this is the range of curriculum and professional development 'reforms' that are described in the report. Nowhere is there any consideration of differences between schools, or the range of complex social, economic and cultural variables that contribute to educational inequality.

There is a total disregard for the vast literature that shows how education tends to reflect wider social inequalities and what this means for policy and practice. In addition, complexity reduction enables the authors to claim that improving student learning outcomes is simply a matter of focusing on teaching and learning, as though matters such as the extent and quality of resources, class size and school funding are not important factors depending on context and circumstance.

Another example of complexity reduction is the assertion that a key characteristic of high quality education systems is 'High Efficiency', which is understood as spending less:

> The world's best school systems are rarely the world's biggest spenders. Korea spends much less per student than other education systems, yet achieves far better student performance. Many systems continue to increase expenditure with little impact. Australian school expenditure has increased dramatically. Between 2000 and 2009, real expenditure on education

increased by 44%. The average cost of non-government school fees rose by 25%. Despite these increases, Australia was only one of four countries that recorded a statistically significant decrease in PISA reading scores from 2000–2009. (Jensen et al., 2012, pp. 10–11)

The report leaves the implications of this statistic unstated, but it is clear what is meant. After all, the authors could just as easily have correlated the increase in expenditure with the maintenance of its success in science and said: *Because of these increases, Australia was able to maintain the average of its PISA science scores from 2006–2009.* This is no less fatuous than correlating PISA outcomes with expenditure without any analysis of how money was spent and with what effects, let alone exploring the connections between variables. Not surprisingly, this section of the report was pounced upon by politicians and the media who made the simple correlation—spend less and improve quality.

Concern 4: Confusion of messages

Many of the messages in the report are contradictory. For example, a whole section is devoted to teachers as researchers, with much made of professional learning communities and research groups in Shanghai with teachers working together 'in exploring new ways of working based on theory, strengthening the link between theory and practice' (Jensen et al., 2012, p. 91) and being expected to publish in academic journals. And yet, in another section of the report, the approach to teacher education in Singapore is described and lauded because the sole teacher education provider, the National Institute of Education (NIE), decided to

> cut subjects such as history and philosophy of education, and curriculum and assessment design, from their undergraduate teacher education syllabus . . . (because) feedback from teachers,

school principals, and the Ministry of Education showed that these subjects were not leading to sufficient increases in students' learning. Instead NIE focused more on subjects emphasising practical classroom teaching. (Jensen et al., 2012, p. 18)

It is hard to reconcile a claim that understanding philosophy is of no assistance in linking theory and practice, or that curriculum and assessment design might not contribute to pre-service student learning. On the face of it, such a narrow and impoverished view of what constitutes undergraduate student learning in education renders teachers technicians rather than researchers, and can only diminish rather than enhance the professional status of teachers and the quality of student learning. And yet the report does not discuss the apparent contradiction between holding the concept of 'teacher as researcher', as it does, and dismissing the study of philosophy and history of education as unnecessary for undergraduate education.

Conclusion

The four concerns described above are surely enough to raise significant questions about the research itself and the implications of its findings for policy and practice in Australian education. They demonstrate that 'evidence-based policy' should mean more than treating all research as equal, and then selecting that which confirms a predetermined policy position. New ideas and new evidence are important ingredients in any dynamic education environment, but they must be accompanied by a healthy scepticism about the quality of the information.

It is important to stress again that the critique of this specific report does not extend to other Grattan Institute reports. Each report must be treated on its merits. The point of this case study has been to illustrate what happens when the findings of a research project are accepted without demurral by policy-makers and commentators, and then used to shape assumptions and perceptions and contribute to policy. If this critique has any substance, then the uncritical embrace of the report's findings is troubling. It demonstrates that the first port of call—for policy-makers, educators and commentators—should have been an investigation of the rigour of the research, before it was used to substantiate education policy or the views that contribute to it. Without that test, the notion of 'evidence-based policy' is simply an empty signifier.

Case study 2: Using research to support a key plank of the neoliberal agenda

If the first case study looked critically at reports that purport to be 'research', the second investigates how research is both used and abused to support a key concept in the neoliberal policy armoury. It will focus on the issue of 'school autonomy' that is a key part of the suite of neoliberal ideas that include school choice, devolution, education vouchers and education markets. In particular, this section will look closely at the claims made by one influential conservative commentator about 'school autonomy'. This will provide not only a sense of the shaky ground upon which much of the 'school autonomy' discourse is based, but also a sense of how research can be used and abused in the service of a specific ideology.

School autonomy and neoliberalism

One of the shibboleths of the neoliberal narrative is that public schools should be autonomous because autonomy improves educational outcomes (Pyne, 2014; Caldwell, 2015). The problem with this claim is that the meaning of 'autonomy' is opaque, hiding a range of possibilities. On the one hand, it could denote freedom from the sort of heavy-handed policy impositions on schools that were described in Part 1 of this book. This concept of autonomy invokes the idea of teachers and principals having the freedom to work together to fashion educational programs that suit their local context, and to collaborate with other public schools, sharing ideas and resources to strengthen each school and the public system as a whole. It is an interpretation of 'autonomy' that should be part of any new educational narrative, as will be argued throughout the book.

On the other hand, autonomy can be interpreted as promoting stand-alone, independent public schools, competing against other schools for a share of the market. In this version, quality is improved not through collaboration but through competition, where fear of failure becomes the driving force. Successful schools will thrive while unsuccessful schools will go to the wall unless they change. The focus on competition, consumer choice and education markets means that it is this version of autonomy that is pushed by a neoliberal policy agenda.

In Australia, the concept of school autonomy has been in play for many years. However, to date it has been a type of autonomy that straddles variations of both versions described above. Thus in the ACT, Victoria and South Australia, efforts have been made to provide schools with greater flexibility in making decisions about resource allocation and staffing than can be achieved in a more structured bureaucratic system—although, ironically, the imposition of NAPLAN, professional standards, national curriculum and intrusive accountability regimes has meant that curriculum freedom has been severely curtailed. Nonetheless, this form of autonomy is a work in progress, and there needs to be ongoing research into the ways by which schools can be given the freedom to make school-based decisions which suit the context of the school, while being supported by education systems. The tension between school autonomy (meaning greater flexibility) and being part of a public system that seeks to ensure that all schools are properly resourced and can collaborate to maximise quality across the system, is ever present. For example, how does the system encourage schools to have greater flexibility with staffing, while ensuring that there is an equality of staffing across a jurisdiction? These are ongoing issues that are worthy of continued debate and analysis in order to find the best balance. But that form of 'school autonomy' is not the focus of this section.

There is another version of school autonomy in Australia that goes beyond the idea of flexibility and embraces notions of independence and corporate governance. Some jurisdictions, such as Queensland, Western Australia and the Northern Territory, have adopted the idea of independent public schools (IPS), an idea that has also been strongly advocated by successive national governments. In these schools, principals, in conjunction with independent school boards, have more freedom to make decisions about matters such as student support, staff recruitment, financial management, governance and accountability. The idea is to make public schools operate more like private schools while still being part of a public system (Mannix, 2013; Cavill, 2014). Of course, it does not play out as simply as that, and many IPS principals still argue that it is important to collaborate rather than compete with other public schools even while they are pushed to be more entrepreneurial (eg., Gobby, 2019).

In other words, the idea of 'school autonomy' is being realised in different ways in different parts of Australia. However, it is the language around school autonomy that reveals a lot about how neoliberal policy discourse is sustained. In particular, this language signals an intention to maintain and extend the privatising dynamic in public education. It is here that the views of conservative educational think tanks and commentators are important to analyse since they are strong advocates for 'school autonomy' of the privatising ilk. Often they argue that the IPS model does not go far enough by calling for the introduction of US-style charter schools and the introduction of 'for-profit' schools in Australia (eg., Donnelly, 2014a; Jha & Buckingham, 2015).

So, what evidence is used to build the case for the neoliberal version of school autonomy? Scott Eacott points out that empirical evidence that 'school autonomy' improves student learning outcomes is very thin on the ground (Eacott, 2015). The case is largely based on questions about the success of overseas experiences with school autonomy. The 'evidence' is usually introduced into the public domain through the mainstream media, and it has created an environment in which policy-makers are looking to consolidate and extend neoliberal versions of 'school autonomy'.

This section will review and assess the kinds of arguments that are made for 'school autonomy' using a case study of the work of one commentator, Dr Kevin Donnelly, who has been at the forefront of the argument for extending the privatising version of 'school autonomy' in Australian public education. Dr Donnelly has a fierce commitment to neo-conservative values and approaches, mixed with a belief in a number of key tenets of neoliberal philosophy such as choice and competition. Over the past two decades, he has been critical of Australian public schools, particularly using the pages of the national paper *The Australian* to attack what he describes as the 'provider capture' of public education by the 'cultural left educational establishment' comprising teacher unions, education academics, education bureaucrats and faddish teachers. This alliance of 'left-wing cultural warriors', he claims, has lowered standards in public education (e.g., Donnelly 2012, 2018d, 2019).

Donnelly has been a long-time advocate of what he calls 'a more market-driven approach to education represented by school autonomy' (Donnelly, 2015). In his many newspaper articles on this topic, he argues that neoliberal versions of autonomy produce better educational outcomes. A key feature of this work is his claim that a number of overseas countries have raised educational standards through market based school reform. This case study will draw from articles Donnelly has written on this topic over the past decade, to outline and explore some weaknesses with the 'research evidence' he uses to make his case.

Conflating the key concept of school autonomy

The first problem is that Donnelly conflates different forms of school autonomy. In his many articles extolling the virtues of school autonomy, Donnelly invariably refers to the success of overseas approaches, frequently citing research studies from various countries to support his case, and concluding that the consensus is

> that not only is empowering schools and their communities—whether charter schools in the US, free schools in England or partnership schools in New Zealand—inherently worthwhile, it also represents an effective and cost-efficient way to lift standards and outcomes. (Donnelly, 2014a)

Far from teasing out the various forms that school autonomy can take, Donnelly simply treats all examples as though they have the same characteristics. Thus, he draws from across the autonomy continuum, randomly using examples from community schools of the 1970s, private schools overseas, non-government schools in Australia, privately managed schools in the United States, India and New Zealand, and free schools in England (see Donnelly, 2014a & b, 2015). This extraordinary confusion of structures, approaches and styles is lumped together and treated as though they all represent a common version of school autonomy. It appears that Donnelly believes that the form autonomy takes, whether fully or only quasi-privatised, is immaterial. It is well recognised that there are significant problems with aggregating research studies in this way; and with taking research findings from one setting and transferring them to another setting in a totally different context, as though the findings are universally applicable (Steiner-Khamsi, 2004, 2016).

How have 'autonomous schools' fared overseas?

The second problem is that the evidence offered to demonstrate the success of the potpourri of overseas 'autonomous' schools to which Donnelly refers does not stack up, even when each country is looked at separately. Let's examine what has happened in four of the countries that Donnelly uses to make his case, all of which are drawn from the extreme 'privatising public education' end of the school autonomy curriculum.

Africa

To support the argument for school autonomy Donnelly draws from some totally private examples such as the low-fee private schools in Africa, India and England championed by education free-marketeer Professor James Tooley (Tooley, 2009, 2018):

> Research carried out by James Tooley comparing the performance of low cost private schools in the slums of many Indian and African cities against state managed schools also demonstrates that autonomy and school choice are beneficial. (Donnelly, 2014b)

In *The Beautiful Tree*, Tooley—a long-time champion of the education free market—describes the growth of low-fee private schools run by private entrepreneurs and operating in some of the poorest areas of the world such as India and Africa (Tooley, 2009). He claims that, wherever they have sprung up, these schools outperform public schools.

Donnelly does not point out the possible conflict of interest that Tooley has in arriving at such a conclusion, given that James Tooley has set up a company to build a chain of private schools in Ghana in partnership with Pearson—the world's biggest educational publisher and owner of the *Financial Times*; and has recently established a chain of schools in the United Kingdom (Tooley, 2018). Nor does he say that Tooley is so ideologically committed to a free market in education that he is even opposed to charter schools and free schools because they are still public. That is, Tooley believes that government has no place in education at all: the state should move aside from education (Wilby, 2013).

Instead, Donnelly accepts Tooley's claim that these low-fee, for-profit private schools in some of the poorest areas in the world outperform their state school neighbours, and so assumes that this is evidence that supports the push for school autonomy in public systems in developed countries. There are at least two problems with his proposition. First, as a study by Claire Mcloughlin from the University of Birmingham points out, the evidence about the educational outcomes from these low-fee private schools is, at best, inconclusive (Mcloughlin, 2013; Srivastava, 2015, 2016). Second, and more importantly, Donnelly is generalising from totally different contexts and about totally different phenomena. How is it possible to translate findings about tiny, privately operated (and for-profit) schools in very poor countries to a public system with large schools in a wealthy country? Donnelly tries to use research to sustain the pretence that it is possible.

> The Australian Education Union is also opposed to school autonomy programs like the Independent Public School initiatives . . . Ignored is the research by German academic Ludger Woessmann that concludes 'Across countries, students tend to perform better in schools that have autonomy in personnel and day to day decisions'. (Donnelly, 2015)

Unfortunately for Donnelly, the academics he cites to support his case have serious reservations about taking research from one context and applying it to another.

> Our results indicate that the impact of school autonomy on student achievement is highly heterogeneous, varying by the level of development of a country . . . **It suggests that lessons from educational policies in developed countries may not translate directly into advice for developing countries, and vice versa.** (Hanushek et al., 2012, my emphasis)

It is revealing that the researchers Donnelly uses to substantiate his case for school autonomy have expressed serious warnings about using their research in a way that ignores context.

New Zealand

In 2014, Donnelly touted the benefits of the Partnership schools in New Zealand which were New Zealand's equivalent (Donnelly, 2014a) of charter schools—public schools run by private organisations—and were established in 2012. Five years later, the New Zealand Government made the decision to abandon the Partnerships model on the grounds that they had not worked as planned, and refused to allow any more to be established (Bracewell-Worrall, 2018). Instead, the existing Partnership schools have become state-integrated schools. This was not the first time that New Zealand had flirted with the 'autonomous schools' model, and been forced to abandon it.

Before Partnership schools a version of school autonomy—called *Tomorrow's Schools*—had operated for 25 years in New Zealand. The Chief Researcher at the New Zealand Council for Educational Research (NZCER), Dr Cathy Wylie, argues that since its inception in 1989 and despite the claims about what these schools would achieve, *Tomorrow's Schools* did not result in any significant gains in student achievement, new approaches to learning or greater equality of opportunity. Instead it had a number of predictable deleterious effects, such as promoting competition between public schools and widening the gap in student achievement between rich and poor without any overall gain in achievement, fragmenting the public system and making principals operate like entrepreneurs rather than educational leaders (Wylie, 2012). Wylie maintains that New Zealand needs to totally rethink the school autonomy model to encourage stronger connections and collaboration across the system, suggesting a return to more central and regional support for schools—the antithesis of Donnelly's case for autonomous public schools.

Sweden
Another system that Donnelly quotes in support of school autonomy is that of Sweden.

> The benefits of school autonomy are especially evident in the recent experience of school reform in Sweden and the Netherlands (where in) . . . the early 1990s, the state-controlled Swedish education system was deregulated and since that time there has been a dramatic increase in the number of non-government schools. (Donnelly, 2009)

In fact, the Swedish experiment has been a disaster. Sweden converted to the idea of outsourcing education to private equity firms in the 1990s, and introduced a school voucher system to enable parental choice. It was not long before several big firms entered the market, the largest being JB Education (owned by Danish private equity firm Axcel), which immediately took over many schools and collectively enrolled over 11,000 students. In a lax regulatory environment, and with companies with an eye on profits, it was not long before things began to go wrong. Soon the 'free schools' (which now comprise about a quarter of Sweden's secondary schools) were being criticised for poor educational practices, deteriorating results, widening inequality and exacerbating social segregation (Wiborg, 2014; West, 2014). Of course, it may not be the case that these effects were directly a result of the introduction of free schools—but certainly it shows Sweden cannot be used as an example of the success of choice and autonomy.

In 2014, JB Education went bankrupt and immediately closed its schools, sacking staff, leaving 11,000 students in the lurch, and owing millions (Orange, 2013). Many other free schools are in financial trouble for a range of reasons. Advertising and marketing have diverted attention from education; the local community has felt alienated; and public confidence in education has fallen (Weale, 2015). The approach has been an abject failure.

The point is that there are too many studies showing that the unfettered school autonomy experiment in Sweden is fraught with problems to enable claims to be made that this form of school autonomy raises educational standards.

Charter schools in the United States

Donnelly also supports his argument for 'autonomous' schools by citing charter schools in the United States:

> Charter schools, where schools are freed from government control and where decisions are made at the local level, give schools the autonomy to best reflect the needs and aspirations of their communities. (Donnelly, 2016)

Charter schools, whch began in the 1990s, receive public funding and are bound by an individual school charter and not by the government regulations that apply to state schools. They are run by education management organisations and not-for-profit groups, and some for-profit groups. In other words, they are public schools which have been privatised.

There are approximately 7000 charter schools in the United States with over two million students and they have all adopted very different approaches. Some have sought to reduce costs by hiring inexperienced teachers, paying teachers and staff less, increasing class sizes and standardising curriculum. Others have adopted progressive pedagogies and pay teachers more than their state school counterparts (e.g., Ravitch, 2013). Since the charter school sector comprises thousands of different entities, it is methodologically dangerous to generalise about them. And yet that is what Donnelly does when he makes claims about the impact of charter schools.

Researching the educational outcomes of charter schools
There are many research studies that explore the educational outcomes and effects of charter schools, most of which use standardised test results as the benchmark for education quality. Of course, as argued in other chapters, the narrowness of this measure produces a thin version of educational quality. Using statistical measures like standardised test results as the sole measure of education quality (e.g., Hanushek, Link & Woessmann, 2013; Fuchs & Woessmann, 2007) reveals nothing about broader aspects of education quality, owing to the lack of qualitative information gained from observation, interviews, questionnaires and so on. That is, education—the most human of activities—is totally stripped of the presence of human beings with thoughts and feelings, resulting in an absence of information about the nature of relationships, school environment or community engagement. More than this, the research rarely explains the causal link between improved test scores and degrees of school autonomy. It is simply assumed.

However, even if this narrow measure of quality is accepted, taking all of these studies together, the best that can be said about charter schools in the US is that the results are mixed in terms of student learning outcomes. Thus, in 2019 the Centre for Research on Educational Outcomes (CREDO) did a study of charter schools in Ohio and concluded that some charters perform worse than traditional public schools, some perform better and roughly half do not differ (CREDO, 2019). This finding is consistent with research that has been conducted across the US over the past decade.

Most studies have concluded that, on average, the scores on standardised tests are no different if charter schools and public schools enrol the same kinds of children. For example, the US Centre for Reinventing Public Education undertook a meta-analysis in 2011 of 25 studies of charter school performance and found

> compelling evidence that charters under-perform traditional public schools in some locations, grades and subjects, and out-perform traditional public schools in other locations, grades and subjects. (Betts and Tang, 2011, p. 1)

In 2009, the performance of charter schools in sixteen states and the District of Columbia was assessed by researchers at CREDO. They found that

> a decent fraction of charter schools, 17%, provide superior education opportunities for their students. Nearly half of the charter schools nationwide have results that are no different from the local public school options, and over a third, 37%, deliver learning results that are significantly worse than their students would have realised had they remained in traditional public schools. (CREDO, 2009, p. 1)

Another analysis by CREDO (2017) found that, even after controlling for differences in student populations, the effectiveness of charter school organisations varies across states, with the strongest positive effects among traditionally underserved populations, such as black and Hispanic students. They also found that charter schools run for profit were far less successful than non-profit charters.

For these reasons it is pointless to cherry-pick research to make the case one way or the other. For every piece of research cited by Donnelly to demonstrate the success of charter schools, it is possible to produce research that shows the opposite. Overclaiming through the selective use of research does not advance educational debate in the public sphere.

Charter schools and equity
Of course, educational outcomes, as measured by standardised tests, are not the only important things to measure when looking at impact on the quality of education. Donnelly also ignores a number of the problems for public education that have been produced by privatised models of public education like charter schools, especially related to equity. Indeed he goes so far as to claim:

> As proven by the success of charter schools in the USA, especially in disadvantaged communities ... school autonomy also helps to **strengthen** equity in education.' (Donelly, 2014b, my emphasis)

How does this claim stack up against the evidence? There is a lot of empirical research that shows that, in order to turn a profit, many charter schools engage in practices that would not be tolerated in a public education system serving the common good. For example, as Dianne Ravitch (2013) has argued, in order to attract custom and improve results, many for-profit charter schools exclude the weakest students and enrol lower proportions of disability students and English language learners than traditional public schools; many hire unqualified teachers and spend more on administration and less on instruction than traditional public schools; and some have been mixed up in shady real estate deals and been closed down because of corruption, embezzlement or bankruptcy.

More than this, a number of research studies demonstrate that charter schools diminish three of the most powerful characteristics of public education: diversity of student population, community and collaboration. First, for a range of reasons, charter schools are more segregated than local public schools. For example, Frankenberg, Siegel-Hawley and Wang (2011) found that charter schools are more racially segregated than traditional public schools in virtually every state and large metropolitan area in the US. In some areas white students are overrepresented in charter schools, while in other charter schools black and Hispanic students are overrepresented. An Associated Press study of school enrolments in charter schools show that more than 1000 have minority student enrolments of at least 99 per cent and the numbers are rising steadily (Moreno, 2017). These students tend to be in schools that receive low performance ratings, while white students are overwhelmingly in schools that are highly rated (Perry, 2017).

However, the pattern of segregation is uneven across the US. In Nevada, charter schools serve significantly lower percentages of the most challenging students than do traditional public schools. This includes students with disabilities, English language learners and children who get free or reduced-price lunches (Pak-Harvey, 2019). It should be noted here that charter schools are not the cause of increased segregation in the US schooling system—segregation in schools has been a feature there for many years—but at best they are not helping the situation and at worst they are contributing to it. It is difficult to teach students to respect and work and live harmoniously with difference—an important outcome in increasingly diverse societies—in schools that are racially, culturally and socially homogeneous. Surely that problem with charter schools should be noted.

Second, charter schools tend to destroy local community involvement in public schools as children travel across cities to get to their school of choice. Third, they have severed any sense of a supportive public system. In an era of high-stakes testing, charter schools competed, not collaborated with, their public school peers. As Ravitch observes:

Some children have gained; most have not. And the public schools, an essential element in our democracy for many generations, have suffered damage that may be irreparable. (Ravitch, 2013, p. 179)

None of this evidence speaks to the idea that charter schools *strengthen* equity in the US, as claimed by Donnelly. By 2019 it is becoming clear that the charter school movement is fast losing public support. Mayors, Governors, education boards and politicians are voicing deep concerns, some arguing for a moratorium on new charters being established (Schneider, 2019). The early promises that charter schools would become 'incubators of innovation', provide a quality alternative choice for families stuck in 'failing' schools and lead to system-wide improvement, have not only come to nothing but have in some ways been reversed. Thus, innovation is stifled by the dead hand of competition where schools focus on strategies to improve standardised test scores rather than trial pedagogies that might truly engage a diverse student population. And far from increasing quality, in some areas there has been a diminution of educational outcomes.

The only lesson to be gleaned from a study of charter schools in the United States is that Australia must stay well clear of privatised models of public schooling.

Conclusion

At the start of this section it was argued that the concept of 'autonomous schools' can be understood in at least two ways. The first interpretation involves providing greater flexibility for public schools, allowing them to collaborate and share as they shape educational programs to suit local contexts whilst retaining the strength of belonging to a public system. The second interpretation involves stand-alone public schools competing against each other in an education market by operating more like private schools. It is this version of 'school autonomy' that is dominant in the neoliberal education policy agenda.

This section has used the work of one proponent of the neoliberal version of 'school autonomy' to explore some of the arguments that are employed in the public arena to support it. The case study demonstrates the importance of closely analysing the claims that are made for 'school autonomy', especially when they are based on the experience of other countries. It served another purpose by highlighting questions that might be asked to interrogate various models of 'school autonomy'. They include questions such as does the model:

- Promote or hinder a public school's connections with its local community?
- Enable public schools to collaborate and share to raise the standards of the whole system, or create a system of winners and losers?
- Increase or lessen the possibility of segregation by cultural or social grouping?
- Provide safeguards to ensure that schools serving large populations of educationally disadvantaged students do not fall further behind in resource provision, or exacerbate resource inequality?

If the answers to questions such as these suggest that parents and students are seen as consumers making educational choices in a free market; if principals and school boards are to be charged with the task of maintaining and increasing market share; and if schools are to be expected to compete for 'custom'—then it is clear that this is 'school autonomy' interpreted through the prism of neoliberalism. It is not a version of autonomy that will address the current inequitable outcomes in Australian education. Reinterpreting the meaning of such core values as freedom and autonomy is an essential feature of a new educational narrative.

Chapter 6

Outside influences on education policy

Another characteristic of educational policy-making in neoliberal times is the powerful influence of a network of economic, political and social actors, including entrepreneurs, think tanks, advocacy groups, media corporations, politicians and very wealthy philanthropists and foundations. In the United States and the United Kingdom these new actors have exerted a significant corporate influence on 'school reform' consistent with the strategies of the global education reform movement (GERM), influencing almost every aspect of education (Ball & Junemann, 2012; Au & Ferrare, 2015; Sen, 2016). In so doing, they have injected a strong neoliberal ideology into education,

> blurring the once fairly clear lines between public and private, as private corporations assume ever more control over publicly funded endeavors. (Roberts-Mahoney, Means & Garrison, 2016, pp. 2–3, quoted in Sen, 2016, p. 136)

Over the past few years, traces of this corporate influence has emerged in Australian education, albeit in a more diluted form than it has taken in the United States. However, it is important to understand the various manifestations here in order to fully grasp its powerful impact. This chapter will investigate two ways that corporate networks have put their stamp on Australian education policy over the past decade. The first involves borrowing policies from other countries by transporting them directly to the Australian context; the second describes the increasing influence of non-educators from the corporate sector in educational debates and decision-making. Each will be dealt with in turn, with examples of how they interact.

Borrowing education policy

It is now well established that the transfer of policies from one country to another is highly problematic (Steiner-Khamsi, 2004, 2016). Differences in context and culture demand that, at the very least, ideas from one setting are treated with some caution and trialled before they are imposed in another setting. And yet successive governments in Australia have continued to adopt policies developed and implemented elsewhere. To examine how policy borrowing has worked in practice, this section will use an example of policy borrowing from a decade ago, the consequences of which still echo in the educational landscape today.

The story starts in New York in 2002 after the election of the Mayor of New York, billionaire businessman Michael Bloomberg. During his campaign, Bloomberg had pledged to reform the public school system that, he claimed, was 'in a state of emergency' (Ravitch, 2016) and needed to be fixed with an injection of practices from the corporate sector. Within a few weeks of becoming Mayor, Bloomberg announced the appointment of Joel Klein as Chancellor of the New York City Department of Education, the largest public school system in the United States. Klein, a New York lawyer and businessman who had minimal experience in education, started his tenure by denigrating the standard of public education in New York. He claimed a particular concern for students from the most disadvantaged backgrounds with the lowest educational outcomes, and vowed to close the 'achievement gap'. Klein brought in international management consulting firm McKinsey and Company, and a number of leaders from the corporate world, to devise a reform strategy that applied business principles to public education.

There are two stages in the story after that. The first stage (2003–2007) involved establishing a centralised, top-down and hierarchical model of decision-making that enabled the City Department of Education (DOE) to mandate uniform reading and mathematics programs in every school. These programs prescribed the content to be covered and the approach to teaching it, with every teacher being tightly supervised to ensure they were carrying out what was required. Standardised tests in reading and mathematics were used to inform the DOE about progress being made, with little attention being paid to other subjects like the arts, civics, science, history or literature.

In 2007, Klein declared that the first phase of top-down control and centralisation had been a success, and that the system was ready for a more decentralised model. Instead of close supervision of schools by superintendents, now compliance would be achieved through self-regulation. Thus the second stage (2007–2010) involved neoliberal market reforms such as choice, school autonomy, competition and incentives—all under the broad umbrella of accountability, and relying on the invisible hand of the market. This seemingly benign approach did not of course mean that central control had been relinquished. Now it was exercised at a distance through target setting, achievement benchmarks, incentives for successful schools, and threat of closure for failing schools. The strategies included such elements as:

- Using annual standardised test results as the indicator of educational quality that allowed 'like' schools to be

publicly compared. Once again the focus was solely on mathematics and reading;
- Awarding to every school a grade with associated consequences, and making these public. Schools receiving an A or B grade would receive financial rewards; schools with D or F grades would be given targets to meet the following year or be treated as failing schools and risk closure or the removal of the principal and some or all staff; and schools receiving three Cs in a row or less would be treated as failing schools;
- Giving bonuses to principals and teachers on the basis of improvements in standardised test results;
- Establishing charter schools—autonomous schools, funded from the public purse, but which run as private entities and compete for custom in an education market—and creating 'small schools' out of the large schools that failed and were closed;
- Pushing the cause of the private company *Teach for America*, which organises programs involving the recruitment of the 'top' graduates from a range of areas (e.g., law, finance, science etc.), giving them six weeks teacher training, and then placing them in the most disadvantaged schools to work with the most disadvantaged students. This 'infantry' of 'quality' teachers would be used in the fight to reduce the equity gap.

Within two years of introducing this program, Joel Klein was widely spruiking the unparalleled success of his accountability approach. Using the standardised test results he showed not only that standards were improving rapidly, but that the 'achievement gap' was closing fast. 'Failing' schools were closed, and new charter schools or smaller schools funded by Bill Gates were established in their place—in the face of vociferous teacher, parent and student protests about the unfairness of the strategy and the destruction of established public school communities.

Klein was unphased by the protests and, emboldened by his success—which he trumpeted far and wide at home and abroad—claimed that his policies were lifting educational performance and closing the 'achievement gap'. Test scores continued to go up every year, and indeed the 2007 results caused the Broad Foundation to award New York City its annual prize as the nation's most improved urban school district. Things got even better in 2009 when 84 per cent of elementary and middle schools received an 'A' grade report compared to 23 per cent in 2007 (Ravitch, 2016). Klein was riding high and Mayor Bloomberg used the results to bolster his re-election.

During this triumphalist period, Julia Gillard, then the Australian federal Minister for Education and herself a lawyer, was drawn into the Klein orbit. It was not long before Gillard was a convert, and in 2008 she issued an invitation to Klein to visit Australia and talk about the educational transformation of New York. As Gillard eulogised:

> No one who has witnessed Joel's marshalling of evidence about the systemic improvements he's made in New York schools could be in any doubt about the effectiveness of his approach. His message is morally compelling and intellectually convincing. (Gillard, 2008a)

Not surprisingly, the 'transparent accountability' agenda announced under the banner of Australia's 'Education Revolution' bore a striking resemblance to the intent and substance of the Klein agenda, including having an ambition to 'close the achievement gap'(Gillard, 2008b). The agenda comprised:

- My School—the website that allows people to compare the performance of like schools, with the sole information about educational outcomes being NAPLAN results;
- additional funding to schools that lift their NAPLAN results;

- performance bonuses for teachers and principals;
- autonomous (self-managed) schools, described as 'empowering local schools';
- financial and moral support for Teach for Australia (the Australian version of its American counterpart).

The alignment with the Klein agenda puzzled many educators at the time, given the considerable research evidence that existed showing that similar accountability strategies in other countries narrow the curriculum; cause schools to throw up smoke screens such as excluding certain students from tests in order to improve results; and damage the sense of school community as parents begin to eye off 'better performing schools'. Where it had been implemented, the performance bonus culture had not resulted in improved educational outcomes (other than teaching for the test) and instead had diminished teacher collegiality and collaboration. In short, the policy that was being borrowed from New York did not have a good track record (e.g. Nichols, Glass & Berliner, 2006; Apple, 2006; Ball, 2008).

But, even if the government had paid no attention to the research evidence, it would have been expected that it would undertake some due diligence in respect to the claims made by Joel Klein before transplanting his policies. It failed to do this. Indeed, just as Minister Gillard was announcing her new suite of policies, back in New York things were starting to fall apart for Joel Klein. Many people were raising publicly their concerns about the standard of the tests that lay at the heart of his suite of policies. It was suggested that the annual New York tests were getting easier; that they were too narrow, too short and too predictable; and that since questions varied little from year to year, teachers were able to prepare students for the test. More than this, it was claimed that the cut-off scores for achieving a proficiency level were being lowered each year. In short, people were claiming that the tests results were being manufactured to make the Klein strategy look like a raging success.

Eventually the evidence of grade inflation was too compelling to ignore and forced the city to commission an independent review to be conducted by Professor Daniel Koretz of Harvard University. The review found that the New York tests did not stand up to scrutiny, and when benchmarked against US national tests, educational standards in New York had not risen. As a result, the 2010 tests in New York were adjusted to better equate with national standards. Under the revised test regime, the grades plummeted and passing rates dropped by more than 25 per cent. In some schools the percentage of students passing dropped by more than 50 percentage points, and in other places it was much worse. For example, the percentage of third grade students proficient in maths at Public School 179 in the Bronx had been 91 per cent in 2009 and fell to 21 per cent in 2010. The *New York Times* reported that

> . . . overall more than half of public school students in New York City failed their English exams and only 54% passed in Maths . . . (T)he drop-offs were most drastic for black and Latino students, as well as those with disabilities and those still learning English, primarily because many of the students had been just above the minimum proficiency rates under the old standards. (Medina, 2010, p. A1)

Once the central piece of the Klein agenda was revealed as a sham, the rest began to fall like a house of cards. The teacher performance bonus was scrapped; charges were levelled that the claims about the educational outcomes of charter schools were overblown; and evidence showed that public non-charter schools were becoming residualised. New York parents began protesting at public meetings, particularly angered by the fact that student performance had been exaggerated, thus denying some students remedial or diagnostic assistance; and providing a false picture of student progress. It was, according to the famous US educator Diane Ravitch, 'institutionalised fraud' (Ravitch 2016). Just as the anger was boiling over, Joel Klein revealed that after eight years in education his time as Chancellor was up and he had accepted an offer from Rupert Murdoch at News Corp, leaving New York schools to pick up the pieces.

And so it came to pass that the agenda that then-federal Education Minister Gillard had been so quick to borrow for the Australian education system had unravelled, with school progress since 2002 remaining flat when tests results were corrected against national standards, and the equity gap just as wide as it had been in 2002. All of this of course had been predicted by those who pointed to the dangers of such an agenda as revealed by educational research in a number of countries.

Many of the policies Klein espoused in the United States were picked up too easily by Australian policy-makers and transferred without consideration of their weaknesses and problems, and their suitability for the Australian context. It is an all too familiar story in the neoliberal standardising agenda, and it is crucial that the uncritical borrowing of policies from other countries are not a part of a new educational narrative.

The influence of non-educators

In Chapter 2 it was argued that one of the adverse consequences of neoliberal education policy is the deprofessionalisation of educators. Far from being trusted, educators are often blamed, and rarely consulted, except about the detail of policies that have already been determined. It is a further irony of neoliberal policy that as trust in educators has declined, so has there been an increasing use by policy-makers of the views of people who have no expertise in education, such as businesspeople, economists, journalists and lawyers.

In the United States, for example, the heavy hitters in the corporate world—e.g., Gates, Walton, Murdoch, Broad (collectively forming what Diane Ravitch calls the 'billionaire boys club')—have entered the field, not just as donors of private funds, but as designers of education policy. They are pouring buckets of money into neoliberal schemes based on education markets and 'transparent accountability', and dismantling public education (Ravitch, 2016). Their 'solutions' have been picked up by successive governments and turned into policies.

The starting point for the involvement of these businesspeople is a low regard for educators and public education, and a conviction that their business knowledge can be applied to education. Thus, consistently over the last decade, very wealthy businesspeople have been pronouncing on the problems in education, coming up with solutions and then funding programs that are promised to deliver results. They rarely do. Sometimes the programs are for-profit business activities, sometimes they are philanthropic. This section will look at examples of each.

Transforming learning through a $500 billion business opportunity

In 2008, Rupert Murdoch, presented the Australian Broadcasting Commission's prestigious Boyer lectures which he titled *Golden Age of Freedom*. The fourth of his seven lectures was dedicated to education. Murdoch started his lecture by claiming:

> The unvarnished truth is that in countries such as Australia, Britain and particularly the United States, **our public education systems are a disgrace**. Despite spending more and more money, our children seem to be learning less and less—especially for those who are most vulnerable in our society. (Murdoch, 2008, my emphasis in bold)

His evidence for saying this is not revealed, but having said it—that is, having dismissed the public education systems in three countries—he goes on to apportion blame and then propose three strategies for turning things around. First, higher standards need to be set. The implication here is that educators are setting low or inadequate standards—again an unresearched accusation. But given that the question of standards is a vexed one in the education literature, it is interesting to note Murdoch's contribution to the debate. For him, standards in education mean that:

> . . . we ought to demand as much quality and performance from those who run our schools as we do from those who provide us with our morning cup of coffee. (Murdoch, 2008)

It is difficult to discern what that actually means—but it is an important benchmark because his second strategy involves holding schools to account and closing them when they fail to reach these standards. This sets up his third strategy, which is that corporations (remember that he is talking at the time of the Global Financial Crisis) should get heavily involved in schools, especially at the lower levels, because:

> . . . corporate leaders know better than government officials the skills that people need to get ahead in the 21st century. And businessmen and businesswomen need to take this knowledge and help build school systems that will ensure that all children get at least a basic education. (Murdoch, 2008)

There are a number of techniques at work here—constructing educators as the enemy; describing a problem without any evidence and then proposing solutions; transferring business models to education, and so on. One wonders what Murdoch would say if educators told him how to run his media empire! For the next few years Murdoch refined a three-part educational narrative. The first part is his conviction that schools have not moved with the times, and have failed children. For example, in a speech at a G8 summit in Paris in 2011, he claimed that 'today's classroom looks almost exactly the same as it did in the Victorian age' and that education is 'the last holdout from the digital revolution' (quoted in Bradshaw, 2011). The second part involves his answer: that educational transformation can be achieved through technology. The third part is about profit, with Murdoch revealing that he saw K–12 education in the US as a '$500 billion sector in the US alone that is waiting desperately to be transformed' (quoted in Mencimer, 2011).

The three parts came together in 2012 when Murdoch outlined plans to make News Corporation a leading provider of educational materials within five years. He acquired a majority interest in Wireless Generation—a company that produced software for assessment, curriculum instruction and compilation of student data for school districts and state governments—and used this as the basis for a subsidiary company called Amplify. Murdoch's vision was that Amplify would transform the ways that children in public schools are taught, by integrating technology into the classroom. In so doing, the profit from education would comprise 10 per cent of News Corps total revenue.

Murdoch appointed Joel Klein, the former lawyer who was coming fresh from his period as Education Chancellor of the New York City school, to head Amplify. Both Klein and Murdoch—the lawyer and the businessman—wanted a technology-based solution to the problems that they had diagnosed in American education. Their answer was to develop and lease to schools custom-made digital tablets containing new online curriculum and assessment materials—with many video games—based on the Common Core Standards that a majority of American states had adopted. The dream was that every American child would own a tablet and be able to progress their learning at their own pace, and interact with the teacher.

Amplify struggled to get off the ground right from the start. Educators were cynical about what looked like private profit-making at the expense of public schools, suspicious that the technology was being supported by education authorities to enable larger classes and fewer teachers, and frustrated when the technology regularly failed to perform (Kadaras, 2017). In addition, teachers were annoyed by the continual unsubstantiated assertions that they were providing low quality education in ways that hadn't changed for over a hundred years.

For its part, Amplify made some basic errors in its approach. Instead of trying to understand current teaching contexts and meeting identified needs, the company believed that they could arrive at a universal solution that would be readily adopted by teachers. As Greg Whitby (2013) has argued, the promise of the new technologies lies in how they can support educators to rethink pedagogy and traditional structures and processes. They are not an end in themselves, containing all the answers! Amplify made little attempt to work with teachers as professionals to understand the theory and practice of current teaching approaches, and how these might be supported and extended by the Murdoch tablet technology. As a result, the resources were seen as just another 'add-on' to a busy teacher's load (Horn, 2015). More than this, they failed to take into account the research emerging about some of the negative effects on children of a constant exposure to digital technology (Kadaras, 2017).

Within five years, despite ploughing nearly one billion dollars into the product, and employing 1,200 people, Amplify was bleeding money and Murdoch was forced to sell it. In stark contrast with his earlier claim that the skills of corporate leaders are needed to build school systems, Murdoch's strategy to fix education was a sorry failure. Another scheme concocted by people with no expertise in education, addressing problems they didn't understand, and looking to generate profits, had failed (Colby, 2015).

The Murdoch story from the US can be seen as part of a developing trend in a number of countries where edubusinesses try to shape educational agendas while making profits (Hogan, 2015). Often they are more financially successful than Murdoch at 'transforming' education and consolidating a neoliberal policy agenda, and indeed some are involved at almost every stage of the policy cycle. For example, in the US the multinational company Pearson—previously a print publishing company based in the UK, now a global company that integrates education services in over 90 countries—is not only producing education texts, but is also developing, implementing and marking standardised tests in a number of states, conducting teacher certification, and promulgating 'evidence-based' research on what constitutes good teaching practice. Through such avenues, businesses are becoming far more powerful than educators, parents and students who are inevitably marginalised or excluded (Thompson, Hogan & Shield, 2017).

The edubusiness trend is becoming apparent in Australia. For example, Pearson now has a toehold in Australia, having been engaged by ACARA to undertake the logistical work for the NAPLAN tests in a few states. Pearson has placed a lot of emphasis on its social responsibility, and certainly its influence does not yet have the same reach as in the United States. However, policy-makers and educators in Australia need to be clear about the extent to which private companies should be engaged in the policy production cycle, and ensure that what has happened in the United States does not happen here.

There are many dangers inherent in a private company, set up to serve its shareholders and make profits, having significant influence over aspects of public education. Not the least of these is the trend to privatise a public good as more control over key education tasks is handed over to private interests. Taken too far, the commercialisation of education consolidates it as a commodity in an education market, rather than a public good serving public purposes.

Philanthrocapitalism and education

Over the past two decades, another privatising shadow has been cast over educational policy-making through the emergence of philanthrocapitalism. This involves extremely wealthy business-people contributing vast sums of money to a specific cause, to be used in the same way that business operates in the for-profit capitalist world (Bishop and Green, 2008). It comes straight from the neoliberal play book. Before describing the dangers of philanthrocapitalism, it is important to draw a sharp distinction between it and traditional philanthropy.

Traditional philanthropy involves businesses or wealthy individuals donating money to a 'good cause', and allowing those with expertise in the field to determine how it is spent. In school education in Australia, this form of philanthropy has operated for decades, mainly in relation to donations to private schools for infrastructure projects. More recently in Australia the question of philanthropy in public education was raised by the Gonski funding review (Gonski, 2011). It recognised that the additional resources obtained through philanthropy is one of the reasons that private schools, usually in high socioeconomic communities, boast superior facilities that in turn exacerbate resource inequality in Australian schooling. The Gonski Review argued that public schools, especially those serving low socioeconomic areas, should also be able to benefit from philanthropy. However, since these public schools often do not have the necessary networks or the time and resources to approach donors, Gonski recommended that the Australian Government establish a fund to support schools, especially educationally disadvantaged schools, 'to develop philanthropic partnerships' (Gonski, 2011, p. 206).

There are many issues associated with applying the traditional philanthropic model to public schools in Australian education which need serious consideration. The most obvious objection is that the existence of private funding may enable governments to escape their obligation to properly fund schools from the public purse. This argument is based on the belief that since education is a public good, it should be funded by the public through taxation, rather than through individual largesse which can be withdrawn at any time. This public process emphasises that since education makes a significant contribution to the whole society, it must be properly funded by that society. However, if safeguards are put in place to ensure that philanthropy is an addition to, not a replacement for, public funding then this objection can be overcome.

Another issue is that philanthropy can exacerbate inequalities if its beneficiaries are randomly selected by individual donors. The Gonski recommendation addressed this concern by suggesting a national fund to coordinate the distribution of philanthropic money on the basis of need. Since that time a philanthropic organisation called Schools Plus has been formed through the collaborative effort of a number of not-for-profit organisations to help disadvantaged schools access funds for school-determined projects through donors. The Australian government has supported this organisation through seed funding, and by granting it deductible gift recipient status. Since its formation in 2013, Schools Plus has supported curriculum and resource projects in over 100 schools, and made a difference to the lives of many students. Traditional philanthropy organised through a planned and coordinated approach can be a force for good.

Philanthrocapitalism stands in stark contrast to the traditional philanthropic model. Rather than philanthropists donating money to a good cause and allowing those with expertise in the field to determine how it is spent, the philanthrocapitalist is heavily involved in deciding what the money is spent on and how it is spent (Bishop & Green, 2008). Although this has not been the model adopted in Australia, it is important to understand how it works in the United States, where it is strongest, in order to know what Australia should guard against if elements of philanthrocapitalism are imported into Australian education.

Philanthrocapitalists are very wealthy businesspeople—examples are Bill Gates from Microsoft or Mark Zuckerberg from Facebook—who have decided to spend some or most of the profits from their businesses on helping to solve the big social problems of our time by using business methods. Through foundations established for the purpose, they decide what the money will be spent on, determine what outcomes are expected and are often involved with the detail of the strategy to be used. Given the size of the sums they donate, governments are loath to stand in their way, and indeed public policy can begin to be determined by private individuals despite their lack of expertise in the chosen field. This diminishes democratic processes of public involvement in public policy and reduces the sense of public ownership that comes with public accountability. It also marginalises the knowledge and expertise of those working in the field.

In education in the United States there are growing concerns about the damaging effects of philanthrocapitalism that largely stem from such factors as the donor's lack of knowledge about the contexts in which 'reforms' are introduced and about the processes of educational change (Bosworth, 2011; Schneider & Menefee-Libey, 2018). The Bill and Melinda Gates Foundation (BMGF) will be used as an example of how philanthrocapitalism is playing out in education in the United States.

Over the past two decades, BMGF has poured vast sums of money into education projects that have been designed by the foundation to address problems identified by it. Invariably the projects have been consistent with a neoliberal policy agenda. School District policy-makers have been seduced by the large sums of money on offer, and have shaped policy programs to accommodate them. Unfortunately, each project has had significant problems associated with it, and most have failed—in the process causing considerable damage to the school communities they were designed to assist.

The first BMGF project operated between 2002 and 2009 and involved spending over US$2 billion to help break up many 'low-performing' large public schools into smaller schools of 400 students or less on the grounds that smaller schools worked better than larger ones. This included donating large sums of money—along with other philanthrocapitalists such as the Broad Foundation and Walton Foundation—to charter school organisations in order to expand the number of public schools run by private organisations. This was consistent with their stated aim of overhauling public education through choice, competition and standardisation. In the process, many school communities were damaged or destroyed—and to what end? After a few years, Bill Gates was forced to admit that, despite some 'encouraging successes' in small pockets, the scheme had been a failure overall.

> In the first four years of our work with new, small schools, most of the schools had achievement scores below district averages on reading and math assessments. In one set of schools we supported, graduation rates were no better than the statewide average, and reading and math scores were consistently below the average. The percentage of students attending college the year after graduating high school was up only 2.5 percentage points after five years. Simply breaking up existing schools into smaller units often did not generate the gains we were hoping for. (Gates, 2008)

BMGF didn't blame itself, or consider that it may have neglected a number of factors that contribute to educational improvement. The reason for the failure, according to Gates, could be placed at the feet of schools: principals and teachers who didn't change their established culture and practices sufficiently to accommodate the vision that BMGF had for education. This diagnosis presented Gates with the target for his next education project—improving teachers. In the same speech in which he admitted the failure of his small schools' project, Gates laid out the shape of his next:

we're going to sharpen our focus on effective teaching—in particular supporting new standards, curriculum, instructional tools, and data that help teachers—because these changes trigger the biggest gains, they are hardest to scale, and that is what's holding us back. (Gates, 2008)

The BMGF contributed $215 million to a six-year project, partnering with a number of public school districts and charter school management organisations to 'help' teachers become more effective. Their approach was to use standardised test scores, combined with a peer observation scheme, to identify which teachers were most effective in improving student academic performance, and to reward them with bonuses. The BMGF ignored warnings from educators—including the American Statistical Association (ASA, 2014)—that linking teacher evaluation to student test scores that had been designed for another purpose was unfair and statistically invalid, and that teacher bonuses had done a lot of harm elsewhere. Unsurprisingly, the scheme failed. Many teachers—even those who had initially supported the scheme—were resistant, arguing that the approach did not and could not accurately evaluate teacher effectiveness, and that it worked against collaborative teaching. After just a few years some School Districts withdrew, and a major evaluation of the project by the Rand Corporation concluded that the scheme had failed to achieve its goals of improving student achievement. It pointed to a number of problems with the project, including using standardised test information to make judgements about teacher effectiveness, just as educators had warned when the project began (Rand Corp, 2018).

In addition to the teacher effectiveness project, BMGF provided several hundred million dollars to develop and implement the controversial Common Core curriculum standards—a national set of mathematics and language arts standards adopted by the majority of states. Many felt that the standards had been developed without the contribution of educators, and like the earlier projects, the initiatives were developed too quickly and too much change was expected of teachers in too short a time. In May 2016, the BMGF's CEO, Sue Desmond-Hellmann, issued an open letter that was in effect another mea culpa.

> Unfortunately, our foundation underestimated the level of resources and support required for our public education systems to be well-equipped to implement the standards. We missed an early opportunity to sufficiently engage educators—particularly teachers—but also parents and communities, so that the benefits of the standards could take flight from the beginning . . . This has been a challenging lesson for us to absorb, but we take it to heart. The mission of improving education in America is both vast and complicated, and the Gates Foundation doesn't have all the answers. (Desmond-Hellmann, quoted in Camera, 2017)

Still not deterred, in 2017 Gates announced that over the next five years, BMGF is going to spend $1.7 billion on 'providing better curricula (learning resources and lesson plans) and professional development'. Although this latest initiative at least started with the recognition that professional learning is best done collaboratively and contextually—BMGF will support networks of schools working on locally identified problems and solutions—there are still concerns that the materials to be developed will be based on a lock-step and uniform approach that shackles and constrains teachers (Tampio, 2019).

So what does the BMGF experience over the past twenty years tell us about philanthropy and education? The issue is not that people like Bill and Melinda Gates have an interest in education but that they have become more influential in education policy-making than educators themselves. Given the amount of money at its disposal, the BMGF vision for education is exerting a major influence on education policy in the United States. Its programs affect what happens in many school communities, and when the programs fail, it is the schools who are left to repair the damage while the private sponsor walks away. It is surely galling to educators to have a foundation constantly intervene in their work by deciding what the problems are and how they can be resolved without consulting those involved, and then to apologise because the work was more difficult than the foundation had realised. As *The Times* Editorial Board puts it:

> Philanthropists are not generally education experts, and even if they hire scholars and experts, public officials shouldn't be allowing them to set the policy agenda for the nation's public schools. The Gates experience teaches us once again that educational silver bullets are in short supply and that some educational trends live only a little longer than mayflies. (*The Times* Editorial Board, 2016)

It is not being argued that such philanthropy is not offered with the best of intentions but, rather, that philanthrocapitalism usually involves funding projects for 'problems' that have been identified by wealthy businesspeople without the involvement of those who are the focus of the project, or who have educational expertise. Such projects side-step the democratic process of determining policy through public and professional discussion and, since they are privately funded, are not publicly accountable. As Reich observes:

> Big Philanthropy is definitionally a plutocratic voice in our democracy . . . an exercise of power by the wealthy that is unaccounable, non-transparent, donor-directed, perpetual, and tax-subsidized.' (quoted in Madrigal, 2018)

This does not mean that we reject philanthropy in Australian education, rather that we need to work out the criteria for making judgments about when and how it can add value, and insist that these are applied when philanthropists wish to contribute money to support educational practice. Earlier it was suggested that philanthropy should not relieve governments of their obligations to properly fund education; and should aim to reduce rather than exacerbate existing educational inequalities. The American case study suggests another important criterion that will help to guard against the siren call of a wealthy billionaire wanting to change education on the basis of her/his personal diagnosis and prescription.

Australian education must ensure that philanthropic money is directed at assisting educators, particularly in educationally disadvantaged schools, to design strategies that address issues or problems that are identified by educators in their local contexts. It is a model that has been adopted by Schools Plus in Australia. And it appears that the latest BMGF initiative involving collaborative and contextual professional learning may also be heading down that path, albeit belatedly. In such ways, philanthropy could be designed so that it enriches education without undermining the professional expertise of educators, exacerbating inequality, or sidelining democratic processes of policy determination.

Conclusion

The argument in this chapter is that it is difficult to develop sophisticated policy approaches to address complex educational issues when those designing the solutions do not have educational expertise or are also trying to turn a profit. A new educational narrative would insist that if education is a public good, then education policy-making should be an important part of our democratic processes, not the purview of a small group of wealthy businesspeople. This would not only ensure that the community has a sense of ownership of its schools, but that policy-makers are publicly accountable for their decisions. Allowing the educational agenda to be set by people who are privately wealthy can only smooth the path to a commercialised and privatised system of public education.

Part 3

Changing the educational narrative

Overview

Parts 1 and 2 have argued that educational policy has been taking us down the wrong track for the past three decades, with devastating consequences for Australian education. Despite its failures, the ideology of neoliberalism, upon which the policy direction is based, has been resilient and proven difficult to dislodge. School-based educators have battled hard to shift the educational discourse towards a more futures-focused agenda, but have lacked a coherent narrative capable of challenging the dominance of neoliberalism. As a consequence, if Australian education policy is to change direction, there is a need for a powerful alternative educational narrative that looks to the future and trusts the expertise of educators.

Part 3 begins the task of developing a new narrative for Australian education.

Chapter 7 explores the various emphases represented in the educational literature, and concludes that there is a common missing element—a consideration of the *purposes* of education. This is the starting point for a new educational narrative.

Chapter 8 discusses the question of educational purposes, and then proposes four broad purposes and their implications. From this discussion emerge two further elements of a new educational narrative: the *principles and values* that inform policy and a *process* to enable ongoing curriculum renewal to replace the traditional stop–start process of curriculum change. The chapter ends by proposing a six-step process.

Chapter 9 trials the process outlined in Chapter 8 using a case study of a broad societal trend—the fourth industrial revolution. This trend is explored through the lens of the four purposes of education. The process helps to identify the kind of capacities that people will need now and into the future to not only cope with, but help to shape, the significant technological disruptions that comprise the fourth industrial revolution.

Chapter 7

The perils of ignoring the purposes of education

The elements of a new educational narrative

In Part 1, the argument was made that the current educational policy regime, which has been in place for over 30 years, has damaged Australian education and is ill-suited to meeting the challenges of the future. However, so embedded is neoliberal ideology in the psyche of policy-makers that it will not be easy to alter the course of education policy.

Part 2 explored various aspects of the neoliberal agenda as it has played out in Australia, looking particularly at how and why it has been sustained. Each chapter showed in its own way how the key tenets of neoliberalism in education—choice, competition and the education market, privatisation, commercialisation, and standardised data to facilitate customer choice—are expressed and reinforced through different mediums. These mediums include funding policies, accountability strategies, what is accepted as educational knowledge and research, and the transfer of ideas from other countries. In other words, neoliberal policy in education is more than just a range of strategies. It is an ideology that saturates the educational landscape, shaping every educational practice in its image.

It follows that changing the neoliberal educational narrative requires more than just picking off the low-hanging fruit like NAPLAN. Unless the core of the neoliberal educational narrative is changed, the removal of one neoliberal tool will only result in its replacement with a new look but the same intent. In other words, critique of a specific neoliberal policy is a necessary but insufficient strategy for change. What is needed to unsettle the dominance of neoliberalism in education is a new, more progressive, and futures-focused narrative for education with a strong philosophical core. That task is the focus of the rest of the book. So where to start?

There are many people who have developed ideas and strategies about the direction education should be taking now and into the future. Thus, a starting point in the search for a new narrative is a review of the ways in which the educational literature analyses what education should look like in the future. Such a review may provide some clues about the key elements of a sturdy educational narrative.

How are others thinking about educational futures?

Although considerations about the future are often present more by implication than by design in the educational literature, some of the major emphases can be organised into four categories. The title of each category seeks to encapsulate a different philosophy about, and approach to, education in the future: *revert, reboot, reframe* and *replace*—the four Rs, if you like. Each approach has a unique core that distinguishes it from the other categories and that connects the disparate ideas contained within it. The four categories are a heuristic to help clarify the major contesting ideas, and so this section describes rather than analyses these ideas.

However, the four Rs will be referenced throughout the book in a more critical way in order to assess their suitability for meeting the challenges of the future.

Revert

At its core, this approach sees desired educational futures as involving a reversion to the key features of the past. It is exemplified by those who argue that the tried and true practices of the past have been undermined by trendy fads engineered by the cultural left, which have lowered standards and reduced rigour (e.g., Donnelly, 2012, 2018a, b & c). From the revert perspective, the future lies with a return to the established educational traditions, which include teacher-directed teaching, strict discipline, an emphasis on the canons of literature and the Judeo-Christian heritage and tradition, rote learning, competition and choice. These beliefs are summarised in an Australian book titled *Reclaiming Education* (Runcie & Brooks, 2018), which, according to former prime minister Tony Abbott, contests the 'postmodern brainwashing' endemic to contemporary Australian education and argues for a return to teaching the story of western civilisation and its values (Abbott, 2019).

A similar stance is taken by the English educator Daisy Christodoulou (2014), whose book *Seven Myths About Education* has had a significant influence on the debate in England. She argues that too many students in England leave school without basic literacy and numeracy skills, and suggests the fault lies with a number of myths that dominate contemporary education. In her book, Christodoulou describes and critiques seven of these myths, and concludes by arguing their reverse. This leaves her with an educational agenda for the future based on traditional educational approaches. These include reifying teacher-led instruction and moving away from such ideas as 'learning by doing' and student engagement in projects and activities.

Another perspective within the revert approach is represented in the work of Michael Young (2008, 2014). His concerns are that current curricula are marginalising powerful disciplinary knowledge. Young points to attempts to cater for the interests and motivation of non-academic students who, from the 1970s onwards, were staying at school for longer periods in increasing numbers, as the start of a trend to diminish the knowledge base of the curriculum. This resulted in the introduction of programs oriented to everyday contexts, such as work-related and community-oriented activities, which, he says, make it difficult for students to use disciplinary-based knowledge independently of its context. Young claims that the current focus on competencies and integrated teaching have confirmed these trends, which are short-changing young people.

Young stresses the important role of schools as institutions involved in the transmission of knowledge from one generation to the next. He maintains that this role has been weakened, as the focus has shifted to learning and educators have stopped talking about what students should know. Rejecting the idea that the official curriculum represents the 'knowledge of the powerful', Young proposes instead the notion of 'powerful knowledge' that should be available to all. Powerful knowledge draws on the work of communities of specialists and is organised through disciplines. Educators use their knowledge of how students learn to recontextualise disciplinary knowledge as school subjects.

Although there are real differences in the ideas described here, the common element in the revert category is the argument that, far from rejecting what has been valued in the past, the pathway to the future in education should involve returning to key practices of the past, in particular the discipline-based curriculum. The existence of schools as institutions—as well as their structures, processes and organisation—are either not questioned or are reaffirmed. The major focus is on curriculum and pedagogy, with an emphasis on the acquisition of knowledge to which many children and young people would not have access at home or in their communities if schools did not exist.

Reboot

In essence, this approach assumes that the ways things are organised now in education—the curriculum, pedagogy and school structures—are adequate to meet the needs of the future, but that the future consists of improving the quality of education by focusing on what works best. It is exemplified by Professor John Hattie, whose work is based on synthesising over 800 meta-analyses of the factors that have the most impact on student learning. In his well-known book *Visible Learning*, Hattie (2009) calculates the effect size of 138 influences on educational outcomes and places them in rank order. He argues that teachers and education systems should focus on those variables with an effect size of $d = 0.4$ or greater. Thus, variables located at or above this designated hinge-point exert the greatest influence, while those variables below it are a distraction.

Visible Learning has become an international bestseller in education, and was hailed by the *Times Educational Supplement* as teaching's Holy Grail. Professor Hattie has become something of an international educational guru (Eacott, 2017) and, although his work has attracted some sustained critique for its methodological flaws (e.g., Beregron & Rivard, 2017; Snook et al., 2009), many education systems around the world have used it as the basis for professional development programs, and for policy directions.

Hattie argues that it is time for a reboot of Australian education (Hattie, 2017). Using NAPLAN results, he claims that too many schools are 'cruising'. For the purposes of this section, it is his prescription for the reboot that is important. Working from his effect size evidence, Hattie argues that success is produced by such factors as teachers working together to evaluate their impact ($d = 0.93$), giving students explicit success criteria at the start of a series of lessons (d = 0.77), developing high trust in classrooms so that errors are seen as learning opportunities (d = 0.72), and ensuring a balance of surface and deep learning (d = 0.71). There are, of course, many other factors on the list, but these are enough to demonstrate that, for Hattie, teacher expertise, as defined by the effect size evidence, is much greater than structural influences such as class size, whether a school is public or private, or how students are grouped.

You will note here that Hattie is not arguing for a return to the past, nor for a focus on what students should learn (e.g., disciplinary knowledge) but, rather, on the process of learning and on teacher expertise. It is an argument that has attracted a great deal of support from media commentators and politicians who maintain that teacher union demands for extra funding to educationally disadvantaged schools, particularly public schools, are ill-conceived. Ignoring external factors such as socioeconomic status, or internal factors such as the quality of available human and material resources, they focus instead on teacher quality, where, they argue, the emphasis should be on improving what currently happens rather than rethinking it (e.g., *The Australian*, editorial, 18 June 2017).

Hattie has been used as an exemplar of this approach but there are, of course, many other educators and scholars who broadly accept the current organisation and operation of schools, while suggesting that certain aspects need rebooting. This might involve, for example, such disparate topics as new strategies for classroom management, adding student self-assessment to existing assessment approaches, or supplementing direct instruction with inquiry pedagogy—with each author proposing and defending their formula for improving the quality of teachers and teaching. In addition, some advocate weaker versions of strategies described in the next section on reframing, such as personalised learning, or flipping the traditional model of teacher input in the classroom followed by application in homework activities.

The key point is that from a rebooting perspective, these strategies aim to refine or improve a particular aspect of pedagogy or curriculum, rather than make wholesale changes to practice on the basis of a very different philosophy. This focus on the processes of teaching and learning leaves largely untouched questions about what is taught and why, and the ways in which schools are organised and structured.

Reframe

The reframing approach starts with the changing world into which young people are moving, especially related to globalisation, technological change and new economies, and examines the implications for schooling. Although there are many different strands and approaches proposed, it is possible to identify a theme common to all of them: that traditional approaches to schooling are no longer adequate to meet the demands of the contemporary world. Thus, the ways in which schools are preparing young people for that world—through curriculum, assessment, pedagogy, learning environments and so on—need to be reframed.

One dominant element is the claim that a curriculum based solely on disciplinary knowledge is insufficient for the challenges of new times. Thus, many education systems around the world are stressing the skills and dispositions needed for coping with the rapidly changing nature of work wrought by globalisation and new technologies. These are being identified and added to the official curriculum with labels such as competencies, capabilities and skills for the 21st century. They include skills and dispositions such as critical and creative thinking, information literacy, communication, personal and social capacities, collaboration, intercultural understandings, resilience, agility and adaptability, and ethical understandings (e.g., Bellenca & Brandt, R, 2010; Fadel, Bialik & Trilling, 2015; Trilling & Fadel, 2009).

The phrase *learning to learn* captures the aims of the approach to 21st century skills, and is often used as its overall descriptor.

There are also a number of well-known approaches that start from dissatisfaction with the disciplinary silos of the current official curriculum. These strategies try to reframe curriculum and pedagogy into a coherent and integrated whole. For example, some use a multidisciplinary approach that explores the disciplines through common themes (e.g., Christian 2004 & 2018; Christian, Stokes-Brown & Benjamin, 2014); some organise the curriculum through an interdisciplinary approach that focuses on common learnings or big ideas drawn from the disciplines (e.g., Spady, 2014); and some, like the Big Picture schools, employ a transdisciplinary approach to structure the curriculum around negotiated student questions, concerns or interests to be explored through problem-based or project-based learning, often in real-life settings (e.g., Washor & Mojkowski, 2013). A common key element in the latter approach is using and building on the funds of knowledge students bring to the learning situation (Moll et al., 1992; Zipin, 2017).

Associated with a demand for curriculum change is the case for pedagogical change. Proponents of the need to reframe schooling maintain that, if students are to become independent learners, there needs to be a shift from a teacher-led to a student-centred pedagogy. There are many proposals that fall under the banner of being student-centred. Some, such as project-based, inquiry-based and problem-based learning, emphasise collaborative learning involving students working together to investigate questions or problems they have identified as being important to answer.

Other strategies take a more individual approach, such as personalised learning, which focuses on the learning of each child in order to enhance educational progress and achievement (Pane et al., 2017; Prain et al., 2015; West-Burnham & Coates, 2005). Tailoring education for every learner starts with an understanding of each learner's needs, upon which basis individual programs are designed to challenge and support their learning and to monitor progress. In other words, learning starts with the learner, not the teacher. Personalised learning is appearing in various guises around the world, sometimes in individual subjects supported by commercially developed materials, sometimes across the curriculum as a whole-school approach. Increasingly, its proponents are exploring the use of big data, learning analytics and cognitive technologies to help identify insights about individual students and possible learning pathways.

Inextricably linked with all of these different stances on integrated learning is the impact of digital technologies. Of course, the use of new technologies is common to each of the four approaches, and is shaped by the philosophy of each. Thus, digital delivery can be used to transmit content (revert), or make current pedagogies more efficient (reboot). From a reframing perspective, the new technologies are a way to transform how education operates.

An example of this thinking can be found in the work of Greg Whitby (2013), who argues that the structures and processes of schooling are based on an industrial model that hasn't changed for the past 150 years. Thus, students are organised by year levels into standard groups and learn in a classroom with a teacher out the front. This model was designed, he says, for a different time and purpose, and must change since it does not meet the needs of the future.

Coming from a personalised learning perspective, Whitby maintains that technology should be used to help develop an alternative model of schooling, and not be seen as an end in itself. That is, it is not sufficient for students and teachers simply to use technology; rather, technology must help a rethink of pedagogy, school structures and learning spaces. Thus, teachers should use digital technologies to provide opportunities for learners, individually and collaboratively, to follow and extend their interests and passions through project-based activities and problem-based learning, in flexible groupings and learning spaces. In short, technology, says Whitby, provides the opportunity to break free from the shackles of how schooling has always been done, to create a genuinely student-centred education that caters for the needs of all students.

This section has only described a small handful of examples from the huge range of reform literature to illustrate the essence of the reframe category. But they are enough to show that, while the strategies vary, they are all based on the common belief that schooling, as it is currently organised and operated, is in need of some radical changes if it is to meet the challenges of the 21st century. It is important to note, however, that no matter how radical or reforming, this approach stills affirms the importance of schools as institutions. Such is not the case with the next, and final, of the four Rs, which rejects the schooling model altogether.

Replace

In essence, this approach argues that schools are artefacts of the industrial age and should be phased out. The basis of this view is the fact that the world's knowledge is online and available at the click of a mouse, along with associated developments such as the digital revolution, AI, algorithms, machine learning and robots. Its proponents argue that the rapidity and impact of these technological changes have irrevocably changed the purposes and processes of education. Schools are no longer relevant in this new world and must be replaced by new approaches to learning. In this sense, the replace approach is a 21st century version of Ivan Illich's 1971 classic *Deschooling Society*.

The genesis of the approach can perhaps be traced back to Professor Sugata Mitra and his famous hole-in-the-wall project. In 1999, Mitra placed a computer in an empty ATM hole in a slum area in New Delhi, and left it. He came back after eight hours and found children of many ages, most of whom had never used computers, browsing the internet and then using it to answer questions. He repeated the experiment in other parts of India, including small, rural and remote villages. For example, he set one group of children a question about DNA replication and came back two months later to discover that they had made some progress. Before he left again, he asked a young woman to be a surrogate 'granny' to the children by giving them encouragement and praise. Mitra claims that after another two months their progress was significant, and he began to publish about the approach, describing it as minimally invasive education (Mitra & Rana, 2001). In England he set up what he called the *granny cloud*, where volunteer grannies were available to provide help, advice and encouragement via Skype to groups of children who were investigating key questions at various places around the world. He described these groups as self-organised learning environments, or SOLE (Mitra, 2005).

In 2013, Mitra won a million dollars for presenting the best TEDx talk of 2013 about his 'school in a cloud'. During that talk he described what had happened and summarised his conclusions and his developing educational philosophy. His starting point was the pronouncement that, given that the information stored on the internet is available in the cloud at the click of a mouse, 'schools as we know them are obsolete . . . they are wonderfully constructed . . . it's just that we don't need them any more' (Mitra, 2013). With the right conditions, he said, learning just happens—we don't have to make it happen, as schools do. Mitra's formula for the right conditions are broadband, plus collaboration, plus encouragement. In this model, not only traditional educational approaches, but also teachers, get in the way of real learning. Thus, a 'school' can be in the cloud with a curriculum organised around the 'big questions', with one teacher/facilitator to provide learning support.

Mitra became an overnight sensation and, ironically—given that the implication of what he was saying is that teachers are redundant—he began to be a regular on the education conference circuit. By this time he had formed a company, HiWEL (Hole in the Wall Education Ltd), and his experiments with the school in the cloud expanded to a number of other countries, including Cambodia, Nigeria and Botswana. In England, the approach was picked up and used in a few schools, leading some to argue that Mitra's learning formula and approach is applicable in school settings provided that significant curriculum and pedagogical changes are made (e.g., Quay, 2013).

Mitra's work attracted real interest from educational technology businesses around the world, especially in Silicon Valley. It wasn't long before it was being used to argue that technology in education settings has the potential to set children free. A number of American billionaires began to pour money into educational programs based on software packages and devices such as tablets and desktop computers (Peretti, 2017). Many of these programs are more individualised, or personalised, than the collaboration inherent in SOLE, but common to all of them is the fact that large groups of students can work on their own or in groups, with a single teacher whose role it is to be consulted only if the students have a problem.

At first glance, it might appear that the use of new technologies in this way is similar to strategies proposed by Whitby (2013) in the reframe approach described in the last section. But there is a significant difference. The reframers are not arguing that schools and teachers are obsolescent but, rather, that the new technologies offer the opportunity for schools to be organised more flexibly, with teachers playing a range of roles from instructors to facilitators of student learning. By contrast, from the perspective of the replace approach described in this section, technology is seen to offer new ways to learn that make schools and teachers redundant. Although this may not happen immediately, they claim that the advent of the digital revolution and AI (e.g., will robots substitute for teachers?) will make it inevitable.

What is missing from the four Rs?

The four categories—the four Rs—are simply a device for organising the mountain of literature that has been published about the direction education should take. While they are not discrete categories, and a number of similar strategies appear in two or more of them—albeit with emphases that vary according to the ontology of the category in which they appear—they are sufficiently different to be able to discern the motivation lying at the heart of each. These are summarised in Table 1 below.

Although the four categories represent significantly different stances, each, to a greater or lesser extent, has a common key weakness. That is, each downplays, assumes or omits the purposes of education. It is not tenable to consider questions about future directions for schooling without a clear understanding and articulation of the purposes a broad approach to education is designed to achieve. Without an understanding of purpose it is impossible to assess the applicability, relevance and

Table 1: Categorising ways of thinking about futures in Australian education

Category	Central focus
Revert	strategies that reinstate the key features of the past
Reboot	strategies that focus on the quality of teachers and teaching
Reframe	strategies that depart radically from the past by making significant changes to curriculum, pedagogy, assessment, and school organisation and culture
Replace	the promise of new technologies means that schools are becoming obsolescent and teachers either redundant or peripheral

appropriateness of the strategies proposed for the future. That is, it is the question of the purposes of education that form the first element of a new educational narrative. Chapter 8 will take up the question of purposes and use them to identify other elements.

Chapter 8

Towards a process for thinking about futures for Australian education

The importance of establishing educational purposes

In Chapter 7, after categorising four broad perspectives in the literature relating to the direction that education policy and practice should take in the future—revert, reboot, reframe and replace—it was pointed out that what was common to all of them was a lack of explicit attention to the purposes of education. Purposes are present, either by implication or omission, but are rarely consciously articulated and pursued. This is a significant lacuna that must be addressed in a new educational narrative, since purposes provide the rationale for any endeavour and so give meaning to the goals and the strategies that are set in any educational system.

In the absence of a well-articulated set of purposes and an understanding of the implications of these for student learning, the setting of goals and strategies becomes a hit-and-miss affair. For a start, there are no criteria against which to judge whether a goal is fit for purpose, or if the strategies are expansive or adequate enough. Gert Biesta (2012, 2016) argues that the absence of a consideration of purposes has resulted in the 'learnification' of education, whereby there is talk of 'learning' and 'learning spaces' and a neglect of 'what' is learned. He goes on to claim:

> The question of purpose is in my view the most central and most fundamental educational question since it is only when we have a sense of what it is we want to achieve through our educational efforts—and 'achieve' needs to be understood in a broad sense, not in terms of total control—that it becomes possible to make meaningful decisions about the 'what' and the 'how' of our educational efforts, that is, decisions about content and processes. (Biesta, 2012, p. 38)

In the absence of clearly articulated purposes, education can be shaped to serve—by design or default—particular interests or ideologies that are at odds with broadly accepted notions, such as that access to quality education is the right of all children and young people. In contrast, explicit purposes offer a benchmark against which to assess the quality of educational policy and practice. It is for these reasons that the search for a new educational narrative will start in this chapter with an exploration of the kinds of purposes school education should seek to fufil in the 21st century.

The expression 'explicit' purposes has been used to highlight the importance of educational purposes being public and transparent, rather than existing by default. This raises the question of who decides on the purposes at any historical juncture, and how the decisions are made. In the history of Australian schooling, purposes have tended to be determined by the prevailing social and economic order. For example, when public education systems were established in the various colonies in the late 19th century, it was clear that one of the primary purposes of school education was to conserve the established social order. The state decided that the economy needed workers with basic literacy and numeracy skills, and civil society required law-abiding citizens who would not threaten the status quo. Public schools were established and organised to achieve this purpose. Thus, compulsory public education was initially confined to basic or elementary schooling, with a narrow subject-based curriculum emphasising rote learning and testing. A more expansive secondary education was available, mainly to the wealthy who paid fees at private colleges (Campbell & Proctor, 2014).

Over time the economy slowly industrialised, and a number of social and political changes led to wider participation by citizens in democratic life. These developments meant that a different form of education was required, and so there were increasing expectations of governments to expand their educational provision. Gradually, the purposes of Australian government schooling became less limited, resulting in changes to the nature and scope of schooling. Thus, during the 20th century, the compulsory school leaving age slowly rose, the curriculum broadened and increasing numbers of students began to attend secondary schools. School education came to be seen as central to the project of nation-building. Not only did it enhance the life chances of individuals, but it also had a number of public purposes, such as developing skills for the economy and fostering the skills and understandings for active citizenship (Campbell & Proctor, 2014).

Nonetheless, there was an emerging recognition that education was serving particular groups in society, giving some young people the edge over others on the basis of socioeconomic and cultural backgrounds. Equity in education came to be a focus of educational research and policy-making but, although some strides have been made, at the current stage, after two decades of the 21st century, we are still a long way from understanding in full the kinds of structures and practices that will promote educational equity.

At the same time, social, cultural and economic developments in late 20th century and early 21st century post-industrial societies have disrupted the 20th-century settlement around the purposes of school education. Trends such as the growth of artificial intelligence and machine learning, the merging of biotechnology and information technology, the increasing cultural diversity of Australia's population, the flood of data posing questions about privacy and individual freedoms, the globalisation of economies and cultures, and pressures on the environment, are all challenging individuals and the very nature of work and citizenship.

These massive social, cultural, environmental and economic challenges pose significant questions about the purposes of school education, and yet such questions are rarely the focus of educational discussion or debate in the public and professional arenas. At best, it is assumed that schools are there to serve the interests of the economy and the labour market; other purposes, if they are mentioned at all, are treated in a perfunctory way that suggests the fulfilment of a duty before getting on with the real work of establishing goals and strategies. The result is that often the stated purposes have little obvious connection to the education strategies proposed. Two significant documents in the contemporary education landscape will be used to illustrate this point.

The first example is the document that currently guides the future directions for Australian education—*The Melbourne Declaration on Educational Goals for Young Australians*.[8] Every ten years since 1989, the body comprising the state/territory ministers for education and the Commonwealth Minister for Education—the name has changed over the past thirty years, but it is currently called the Education Council—has produced a statement about the goals and aspirations of Australian education. If there was ever to be a statement of educational purposes, it would be contained in this document. And yet the

---

8   At the time of writing, the Melbourne Declaration was under review.

nineteen-page *Melbourne Declaration* starts with just one short paragraph alluding to its purposes:

> In the 21st century Australia's capacity to provide a high quality of life for all will depend on the ability to compete in the global economy on knowledge and innovation. Education equips young people with the knowledge, understanding, skills and values to take advantage of opportunity and to face the challenges of this era with confidence. Schools play a vital role in promoting the intellectual, physical, social, emotional, moral, spiritual and aesthetic development and wellbeing of young Australians, and in ensuring the nation's ongoing economic prosperity and social cohesion. (MCEETYA, 2008)

That paragraph is followed by a very brief description of five major changes/trends in the world in the decade since the previous declaration (the Adelaide Declaration of 1999)—global integration and social mobility; the rise of Asian nations; globalisation and technological change; complex environmental, economic and social pressures; and continuing advances in communication and information technologies.

There is no detailed examination of the nature of these changes, nor what they might mean for the sorts of capacities that schools need to help young people to develop. Rather, on the basis of a short and very vague two-page preamble, the Melbourne Declaration posits two goals and nine strategies (Commitments to Action) that make up the remainder of the document. It seems that there is a lack of understanding that purposes are much broader and deeper than goals. Goals tell us what we want to achieve, while purposes tell us why. In other words, goals serve purposes. By foregrounding goals and not purposes, the Melbourne Declaration lacks a rationale. As a result the strategies appear to be free-floating, and so the document is honoured more in the breach than the observance.

The second example is the report of the review panel established by the Turnbull Government in late 2017. Led by David Gonski—the person who also chaired the well-known report into education funding six years earlier—the panel was charged with designing a blueprint for Australia's educational future. If ever there was a need for a clear articulation of educational purposes to lay the basis for the review and its recommendations, it was this report. And yet, when the report—*Through Growth to Achievement: The report of the review to achieve educational excellence in Australian schools* (Gonski et al., 2018)—was released, there was no reference to the purposes of education in the 21st century. Beyond vague references to a 'rapidly changing' world and to preparing students for the labour market, the report failed to make a case for education's role in meeting the challenges facing Australia.

Despite its claimed concern to bring education into the 21st century, the report was also surprisingly free of any reference to key current and future challenges—including environmental challenges, threats to democracy, the implications for work of such developments as AI, robotics, machine learning and so on. Without a consideration of purposes and the implications for education of key societal issues or trends, the Gonski recommendations comprised sheer guesswork. There was no obvious link between what they proposed and the nature of the challenges.

So, what can be done to bring educational purposes to centre stage of education policy-making? How can we prevent educational purposes being determined by default by the weight of dominant social and political interests, rather than by conscious and deliberate decision-making following widespread community and professional discussion?

The once-a-decade statement on the future directions for Australian education is an ideal vehicle for the country to establish the purposes of its systems of school education and then to use these to develop goals. At the time of writing, a review of the

Melbourne Declaration had just commenced. It is to be hoped that the state/territory and Commonwealth ministers for education ensure that there is a widespread process of discussion and consultation with the education profession and the wider community, one that starts with a deep consideration of the purposes of Australian schooling and uses these to guide the development of the document. In this way, there will be a sense of ownership of and commitment to our schools and their purposes among the Australian community. Importantly, such a process will inform a new narrative about Australian education that will help to break the stranglehold of the standardising approach to education policy.

Given the current absence of educational purposes, the next section will propose some purposes and explore their implications for developing a new educational narrative.

Purposes: The first element of a new educational narrative

Building on the work of scholars from the UK and US (Goodlad, 2008; Inglis, 2004; Labaree, 1997), and an Australian Research Council project in which I was involved with some colleagues in Australia (Reid et al., 2010), I propose four key purposes of school education.

- The first is a *democratic purpose*. Schools are the main means society has to systematically develop young people as citizens who are able to play an active and constructive role in democratic life.
- The second is an *economic purpose*. Schools make an important contribution to the Australian economy by preparing people for work in the many occupations that comprise the contemporary and future labour markets.
- The third is an *individual purpose*. Schools provide opportunities for all children and young people to 'acquire

knowledge that takes them beyond their experience' (Young & Lambert, 2014, p. 10) and which enables them to lead rich, fulfilling and productive lives. This purpose emphasises that there does not have to be a utilitarian purpose for education—it is significant in its own right.
- The fourth is a *social and cultural purpose*. Schools are an important means by which children and young people develop the understandings, skills and dispositions necessary to play an active role with their fellow citizens in a diverse and multicultural civil society.

There are at least six salient aspects to these purposes that should be noted and that have significant implications for schools. First, it is the mix of these purposes that make up the educational settlement at any historical juncture. In recent times there has been an emphasis by policy-makers on the economic purpose of education, at the expense of the other three purposes. This book is based on the belief that although they may be expressed in different ways, each of the four purposes is important, and therefore it is a crucial and ongoing task to ensure that they are all represented in educational policy and practice.

Second, the purposes have been described in a neutral way that masks the fact that, when they are realised in practice, they are based on values and assumptions that shape them in specific ways. Each purpose can only mean something when these values are declared and the detail is fleshed out. For example, the democratic purpose will result in very different practices depending on the understanding of democracy that informs it. This might range from democracy being largely a matter of voting for representatives every three or four years, to it being a process that encourages active and engaged participation in all aspects of democratic life. The point is that the role and nature of education will vary depending on the view of democracy adopted. It will become clear that an underlying value informing the view of each purpose in this book is a belief that education should be instrumental in shaping a fairer and more socially just society.

Third, the purposes have public as well as private benefits in mind. That is, the outcomes of school education go beyond individual interest. A democratic society depends on its citizens being in possession of a range of what Connell (1995) calls 'capacities for social practice'—that is, capacities[9] that enable them to contribute to the economy, the polity and the civil society, to lead productive and fulfilling lives, and to contribute to social change. These need to be developed, practised, sustained and renewed. Thus a key, yet much neglected, aspect of the public purposes of education is to improve the conditions for deliberation and debate in the public sphere by providing the young with the skills, dispositions and understandings required to engage with others about the common good.[10] If education places a greater emphasis on the individual purposes of education than it does on its public purposes, then the public sphere can only be diminished as people lose the capacity for communicative relations and for thinking beyond individual interests. These are high stakes.

Fourth, it doesn't advantage society to have people who lack these skills and understandings, who are alienated and disenchanted, or who act purely from self-interest. This makes equity a central concern for school education. It must ensure that *all* citizens have the same opportunities to develop the capacities

---

9   In this book 'capacities' is used as an overarching term for knowledge, skills, dispositions and values. When curriculum matters are discussed in Part 4, the terminology of the Australian Curriculum is followed, where knowledge is represented in the learning areas, and generic skills, dispositions and values are described as general capabilities.

10 Where the term 'common good' is used in this book, it is based on the meaning ascribed to it by Robert Reich: 'The common good consists of our shared values about what we owe one another as citizens who are bound together in the same society—the norms we voluntarily abide, and the ideals we seek to achieve . . . A concern for the common good—keeping the common good **in mind**—is a moral attitude. It recognises that we're all in it together. If there is no common good, there is no society' (Reich, 2018, p. 18; emphasis in original).

implied by the purposes—a challenge that has consequences for curriculum, school structures and resourcing. In a democratic society, something as basic and important as school education should not be provided unequally on the basis of wealth or birth.

Fifth, the purposes reaffirm the importance of schools as institutions. Thus, the achievement of successful outcomes related to each purpose demands a systematic approach led by people with expertise. Since schools comprise teachers trained to work with children and young people, they are better equipped than any other organisation in our community to undertake the educational task. In addition, the four purposes have an important social as well as individual emphasis, and so demand an educational approach that encourages group and collaborative work rather than solo learning. As social institutions that place young people in an environment with many of their peers on a daily basis, schools are unlike most other organisations in our society. In short, the purposes described above suggest that Mitra's claim that schools are obsolescent (see Chapter 7) fails to take into account the important social function of schools.

Sixth, each of the purposes implies that there are a number of understandings, skills and dispositions that schools should aim to develop in students. This demands looking at each of the sites served by schools—the polity, civil society, the economy and the individual—and asking about the capacities for social practice that are needed to operate productively in each. It doesn't automatically follow that it should be the job of schools to nurture all of these capacities—presumably some may be best developed through other sites, such as the family or workplace—but most will require skilled educators for optimum development.

It follows from the sixth point that educators, as well as politicians and the community where possible, need to systematically and regularly analyse and discuss the main developments and trends in society as a prelude to developing policy and practice in education. That is, previous attempts to arrive at a futures-focused educational agenda have concentrated on *what* should be taught by peering into the future and making some shrewd guesses about the world into which students will be moving. It is being suggested here that it is the *process* of educators, community members and policy-makers discussing key societal trends that is a key element of the futures-focused discourse, and the lack of such a process the reason a futures narrative has failed to gain any traction in education policy-making.

The analysis of the implications of educational purposes has revealed the two other elements of a new educational narrative: the importance of *values and principles* and the need for an agreed *process* to enable ongoing decision-making in the face of rapid change in the contemporary world. Each will be discussed in turn.

Values and principles: The second element of a new educational narrative

If purposes are the bedrock of the educational narrative, then values and principles are its soil. That is, educational policies are both nurtured by, and must be consistent with, an articulated set of values and principles. Once again, these can only be developed through wide-ranging professional and community discussion and must always be open to review. For the purposes of this book, a number of values and principles will be suggested as examples of the kind of narrative that would contest a neo-liberal discourse.

Throughout the book it is argued that the challenges of living in the contemporary world can only be dealt with adequately when there is a collective sensibility—that is, when, as a community, we look out for others, think about the effects of individual and social actions on the wider community and are not obsessed with how we can advance our individual interests. Bringing this back to education, it is argued that we need schools and education systems to be based on a commitment to the common good. As Robert Reich says:

> If the common good is to be restored, education must be reconnected to (our) public moral roots. We must stop thinking about it as a private investment that may lead to a good-paying job, and revive the . . . understanding of it as a public good that helps to train young people in responsible citizenship. (Reich, 2018, p. 176)

Of course, any education system would need to come to a general agreement about the sorts of values that best serve the common good, but it would include such values as social justice, care, compassion, empathy, collaboration, equity, community, generosity, integrity, respect and so on. Immediately, when they are written down like that, the stark contrast with the values of neoliberalism—individualism, competition, materialism, consumerism and self-advancement—becomes obvious.

Listing common good values in this way serves no purpose unless they are translated into action and lived out. Deciding on the values that should lie at the heart of every school and education system is just the first step. The next is to achieve a common agreement about what each value means and what it might look like in practice. It is then possible to make decisions about how to teach for the agreed values; ensure that they are modelled in the environment of every educational institution and system; and use them as a benchmark against which to assess policy and practice. When these steps are built into the fabric of education—the ongoing practices, policies and relationships of every school and education system—the values will really come to life.

If values describe the sorts of qualities an education system should display, principles are rules or beliefs that are consistent with the values and that should inform policy and practice. This book implies or suggests a number of principles consistent with the kind of values described above, covering such key aspects of education as educational structures and environments, relationships, and curriculum and pedagogy. As with purposes and values, there is no recipe for principles. They need to be worked on by the participants in the education system, and this is an ongoing task. The following are examples of the kind of principles that might form the basis of an alternative narrative for Australian education—one powerful enough to overcome the claims of neoliberalism.

Examples of principles that might form the basis of a new narrative for Australian education

Australian education must:

- ensure that public schools are well-resourced, inclusive, non-segregated and open to all, and are seen as the major educational providers in Australia
- guard against privatising education by ensuring that all schools receiving public money serve public purposes
- be concerned about inequitable educational outcomes and work hard to understand the causes of inequality and how they can be diminished and overcome
- value a broad and comprehensive curriculum
- use approaches to accountability that cover the breadth of activities which make up a rich educational experience, and do not attempt to punish and blame but, rather, contribute to a joint endeavour to achieve a high quality of education
- enable pedagogies that are flexible and are chosen to suit the purposes of learning, the context of learners, and what is to be learned
- actively encourage the involvement of parents, students and community members, as well as educators, in the

life of each school and in consideration about the broad purposes, values and goals of education
- recognise, value and trust the voice of teachers in the development of education policy, and the professional knowledge and skill they bring to educational decision-making and practice
- ensure that schools have the flexibility to shape programs that suit each school context, while being part of an agreed common curriculum program
- support teachers through the provision of professional development programs and resources that address mutually agreed issues and goals
- cultivate a culture of research and inquiry in schools and education systems and so on.

Although these principles are provided as suggestions only, they reflect the kind of new educational narrative for which this book will argue. It should be noted that each of the values and principles suggested above is at odds with the ways in which the neoliberal policy regime has structured education in Australia over the past three decades. For example:

- policies or practices that tend to privatise public schools are inconsistent with the values of the common good
- relying on standardised test results as the sole measure of education quality is incompatible with a principle that asserts the importance of a rich curriculum and broad approaches to accountability
- naming and shaming schools is not congruent with a value that prizes trust and collaboration
- ignoring the fact that the current funding policy has led to the segregation and stratification of our schooling systems is not accordant with a principle that enunciates a commitment to equity in education.

To tolerate inconsistences like these is to create change in name only. Chapter 2 described seven damaging consequences of the neoliberal policy regime in education. If implemented, the values and principles outlined in this section would go a long way towards addressing each of those consequences.

An agreed process for decision-making: The third element of a new educational narrative

The traditional approach to decision-making at the system level has been for those in the 'centre' to come up with ideas for policies and strategies, engage in some 'consultation' with the field, decide on a new strategy or 'reform' and implement it. Under the neoliberal policy regime, often there is not even a pretence of 'consultation'. Problems are identified, solutions arrived at and policies announced with little input from those whose work is at the heart of these decisions. What is common to both approaches to decision-making is that once a 'reform' (e.g., a new official curriculum) is introduced, it usually remains in place for a lengthy period of time (say, 5–10 years) before the next version comes on board. Such an approach suited a time when societal change was slower than it is today, and so did not have the same impact on what is taught and how. But in contemporary times and into the future, change is a constant, and indeed is speeding up. In this environment a new approach to educational decision-making is needed.

If the future is uncertain then it is clear that educational policies and strategies must be flexible and open to change, not fixed and immovable. A process that addresses the problems with the traditional approach to educational change must have at least three features. First, it should ensure that the voices of educators are central to any change or development. Second, it must place a focus on broad societal trends, so enabling schools to identify the capacities that are required to deal with and shape these trends. Third, it should enable educators, in an ongoing way, to decide on the educational implications of the societal trend being analysed and what additions or modification are needed to adjust to them. The reference points for the investigation of the societal issue are the purposes of education, and the values and principles that support them, and so it is assumed that these are agreed and kept under review over time.

The importance of educators engaging in discussions about broad societal trends and their educational implications may seem to be an obvious point, and yet it seems that most professional conversations avoid such discussions. If they occur at all, it is usually in a perfunctory way, naming the trends and then jumping to a description of what are seen as educational approaches that best suit the future, without any deep analysis of what these trends mean for the work of schools.

The six-step model proposed below is based on the three features identified. Since it is crucial to develop a deep understanding of a societal trend or issue before identifying its implications for educational policy and practice, education is not considered until the fourth step of the process. This is an attempt to overcome the weakness of futures-focused education reports that offer a superficial coverage of contemporary and future change before making a giant leap to policy proposals.

The six steps of the proposed model are as follows.

Step 1: If, as has been argued, thinking about education policy and practice from a futures perspective should start with an examination of key societal trends, then Step 1 in the process will involve identifying one or more trends, understanding its parameters and exploring it in depth. By trends is meant such broad themes as:

- *environmental* challenges brought about by climate change and the depletion of natural resources
- massive *economic* changes wrought by innovations in

science and technology (including developments in biotechnology, nanotechnology, AI, and machine learning) and financial interdependence
- *social and cultural* challenges such as the increasing diversity of populations produced by such factors as migration, population growth and urbanisation; the social dysfunction created by job displacement and growing inequalities of wealth within and between countries; and war and terrorism
- challenges to democracy brought about by such disparate factors as social media, metadata, fake news and the rise of populist politics.

All of these key societal trends demand a response from governments, agencies and individuals at regional, national and global levels.

Step 2: Having grappled with the nature and extent of the selected trend, Step 2 involves investigating its impact, using the domains represented by the purposes of education as the reference point for the analysis: work and the economy; democracy; the individual; and social and cultural life.

Step 3: If the response to these trends is to be informed, appropriate and timely, people need to have a range of capacities – as citizens, workers and members of communities—to enable them to analyse the trends and to act. Thus, having identified what are thought to be the impacts of the trend in the various domains, the task in Step 3 is to describe the capacities (knowledge, skills and dispositions) people will need to handle the trend in order to achieve socially and individually desirable outcomes. It should be noted that this step will involve clarifying the values that inform analysis and decision-making.

Step 4: In this step, education is foregrounded for the first time in the process. It involves identifying which of the capacities described in Step 3 should be allocated as the responsibility of schools, and then deciding how these capacities should be represented in, and developed through, the official curriculum (what is intended to be taught). There will be a range of possibilities here, from confirming or making minor modifications to existing policy and practice, to planning and implementing significant changes to curriculum policy and/or practice. The step also involves identifying the blockages to change and developing strategies to deal with these.

Step 5: This step involves identifying approaches to pedagogy and assessment that best suit the capacities described in Step 3. Again there will be a range of possibilities here, from confirming or making minor modifications to existing policy and practice, to planning and implementing significant changes to current approaches. The step also involves identifying the blockages to change and developing strategies to deal with these.

Step 6: If the change is to occur in more than name only, then there must be a set of supporting conditions in schools and education systems. The role of Step 6 is to identify the conditions and practices that will support the change, and those that may block it and should be removed. These range from physical resources, to human resources, to the culture of an organisation, and they need to be tailored to suit the demands of the change in specific contexts such as classrooms, schools and education systems as a whole.

The six-step process is summarised in Table 2 below.

How and where will the process be used and by whom?

In this book, the six-step process will be trialled in a case study (Chapter 9) and then used to develop the contours of a new and alternative narrative for Australian education—one that is sturdy enough to challenge the iron grip of the standardising discourse in education policy. This will enable the efficacy of the process to be tested, and its usefulness for other purposes to be assessed.

Table 2: The steps of a process for thinking about futures in Australian education

Steps	The focus of each step
Step 1	Identify a broad societal trend and explore it through research, reading and discussion.
Step 2	What is the impact of this trend, particularly on those areas covered by the purposes of schooling: work and the economy; democracy; individuals; and social and cultural life?
Step 3	On the basis of the analysis in Step 2, what understandings, skills and dispositions do people, individually and collectively, need to handle the consequences of this trend so that there is a good/socially desirable outcome?
Step 4	What are the educational implications of the responses to Step 3? How can they be built into the official curriculum, and what are the blockages that need to change?
Step 5	What are the educational implications of the responses to Step 3? How can they be built into pedagogy and assessment and what are the blockages that need to change?
Step 6	What conditions and practices will enable the changes identified in Steps 4 and 5?

In particular, it is suggested that, given the process has a wide scope and sweep—taking in the official curriculum, approaches to teaching and assessment, accountability and cultural factors—it can be used at system-wide levels for thinking about educational futures and at the level of individual schools. At both levels, educators need to be intimately involved at each stage. Marginalising educator voices, as the standardising agenda has done for so long, is not an approach suited to the 21st century.

In the long run the process could contribute to a new way for systems to function and plan. Thus, at the school level it could be used as the basis for a discussion about curriculum and pedagogy, with policy and/or practices being modified or changed as a result. It would be an ideal way to engage all stakeholders in a school community—educators, students, parents—in ongoing discussion and debate about educational purposes, curriculum and pedagogy, and the future. However, it would need some planning and resource support—not the least being the need to release schools from some of the counterproductive burdens of the standardising agenda.

At the system-wide level, there could be an aggregation of ideas emerging from schools, with the system responding by providing resources, offering relevant professional development programs, changing policy or altering the official curriculum. In other words, the process suggests a way to establish a more dynamic relationship between schools and systems—one based on partnership, rather than the current model of top-down imposition. In this way, the fulcrum of the standardising model would shift from schools serving the policy-makers to the other way around. Of course, there are obviously many other possible models. Schools and systems could try the approach in this book or a modified version of it, or develop their own.

The rest of the book will use the process to suggest a new narrative for Australian education that can meet the challenges of the future. It follows the structure represented in Diagram 1 below. Thus, Chapter 9 is a case study of the impact of the momentous shift to digitalised technologies. The case study is used to model Steps 1–3 in action. Then, in Part 4, the educational implications of the case study will be explored. Chapter 10 discusses ideas about possible new directions for curriculum; Chapter 11 looks at the implications for pedagogy and assessment; and Chapter 12 looks at the kind of school and system-wide cultures that will help to realise a futures-focused educational

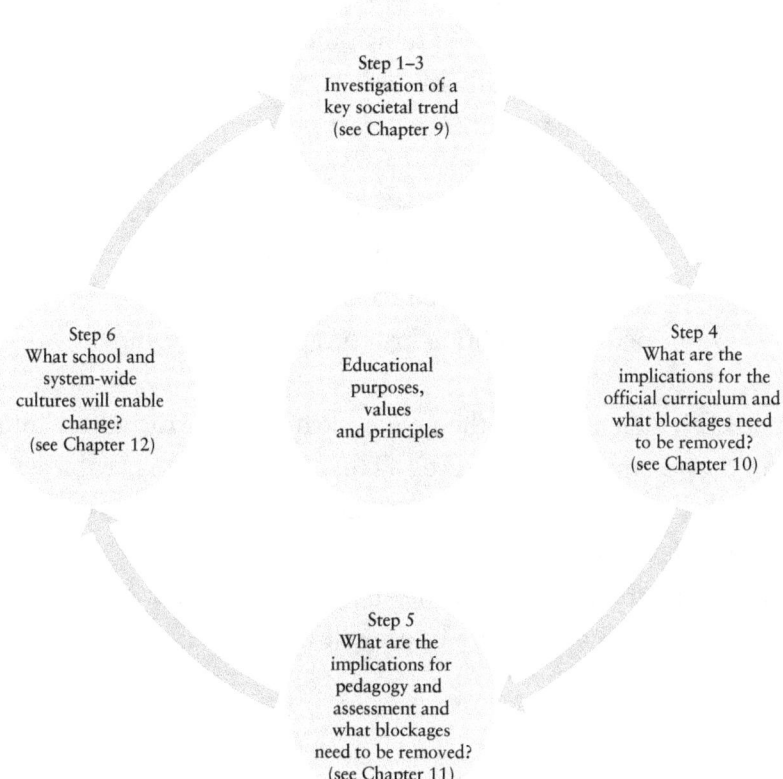

Figure 1: A process for thinking about futures for Australian education

agenda. The Epilogue will discuss some of the ways a new educational narrative can get political and professional traction and challenge the dominance of the standardising discourse.

The elements of a new educational narrative

In summary, the focus on educational purposes has revealed the three key elements of a new educational narrative. They are:

- *Purposes:* that are the bedrock of the narrative, setting out why education is needed in the contemporary world.

- *Values and principles:* that are consistent with the purposes and that challenge the selfish individualism and standardisation of the neoliberal policy narrative.
- *A process:* that enables educators and policy-makers, in an ongoing way, to understand, monitor, evaluate, and assess broad societal trends and the changes they are bringing in the various arenas covered by the purposes of education. This information is used to make decisions about curriculum, pedagogy, school structure, and environments.

All three elements of the new educational narrative are interrelated and must be addressed. Thus, the purposes, values and principles must serve as reference points for deciding on the kinds of strategies that are suggested by the process. Is the process sturdy enough to challenge the neoliberal discourse? It is to a trial of the process that the book will now turn.

Chapter 9

Using the process: A case study of the fourth industrial revolution

Setting up the process

In the previous chapter it was proposed that if educational responses are to meet the challenges of the future, they must be based on a deep understanding of what is entailed in those challenges. This means that educators should engage regularly in systematic investigations of key social, cultural, economic, political or environmental issues, in order to identify the capacities required to live in the present and shape the future. Armed with this knowledge, educators can assess what they are teaching and how—and then, where necessary, adjust approaches to better suit the demands of the future. In other words, if—as has been argued—purposes must precede action, then ongoing examinations of key societal trends provide a way to clothe broad purposes with detail.

For these reasons, Steps 1–3 of the six-step model proposed in Chapter 8 deliberately avoid educational considerations, focusing instead on the kinds of capacities people need to shape and work productively with the broad trends that are changing our societies. Step 1 involves selecting and describing the features of a key contemporary societal trend or issue. There are any number of trends/issues that could be chosen, such as climate change, globalisation and its consequences, inequality within and between nations, threats to democracy and so on. For the purposes of the book, what has been called the fourth industrial revolution has been chosen as the case study.

Imagining the process in an education setting: Learning District

The reader may like to imagine the process in use in a specific setting, such as a school, a school district or a whole system. There are any number of ways the process can be designed over long or short time frames, so what follows is just one example to give a sense of what is possible. If it is of no interest or help, just skip to the next section.

Let's assume that the action takes place in an imaginary district—the Learning District—which comprises fifteen preschools, primary schools and high schools, all in close proximity in the southern area of a city. Learning District is one of a number of districts in the public education system, and the purpose of each is to facilitate collaboration between schools, share resources and promote professional development. After consulting the staff in each of the sites in the Learning District, the decision has been taken to make the fourth industrial revolution the professional development and curriculum planning focus for the next eighteen months, using the six-step model. It is agreed that Steps 1–3 will be covered in Terms 1, 2 and 3 of the first year.

A planning committee is given the task of organising the program. The first step involves understanding the trend itself. The process starts with a professional development (PD) day involving all staff at the beginning of the school year, with a keynote speaker from the neighbouring university, a panel comprising parents and teachers with expertise in the topic, a film and group work. By the end of the PD day, staff have a broad appreciation of the scope of the topic; enough information to decide how they will continue to explore the fourth industrial revolution and its impact for the next three terms; and are able to share suggestions about human and material resources available across the district that might assist the process.

The PD day creates an air of excitement and staff are looking forward to exploring the topic in greater depth. The investigation of the fourth industrial revolution continues at two levels. First, at the district level, a website is established where all staff can find or upload readings and other resources, and share ideas and insights. Second, each site has a small planning committee that develops a site-based program looking at the impact of the fourth industrial revolution. Most sites agree that there should be a regular slot at staff meetings where time is set aside for discussion and debate; in addition, special interest groups are formed to explore specific aspects of the trend. Some schools run separate parent and/or student meetings to discuss the fourth industrial revolution, others decide to invite parents and students to key staff events so that they can widen the range of insights available and contribute to a sense of the whole school as a learning community. As the process unfolds, some teachers build a study of the fourth industrial revolution into the formal curriculum. In effect, there is a common theme across each site, with an emphasis on discovering new things about what is happening.

At each site during the process, articles and books are circulated, visiting speakers are invited, teachers, parents and students with expertise in aspects of the topic share their understandings, films and documentaries are shown, and posters are put up. All staff keep their own record of notes, questions and ideas.

After coming to grips with the main elements of the trend (Step 1), the rest of the time is spent moving backwards and forwards between Steps 2 and 3, exploring the impact of the fourth industrial revolution (Step 2) on each of the arenas covered by the purposes of education—work, democracy, individuals, and social and cultural life—and identifying the capacities needed by people to shape and work productively with the possibilities it produces (Step 3). A list of the capacities that people might need is recorded in a visible place in the staffroom and, at regular intervals during the process when there is consensus, new capacities are added. At this stage, it is sometimes hard not to discuss the educational implications, so it is agreed that when that happens any questions or observations are recorded but not discussed—put aside until the next stage of the process (Steps 4–6).

As the process unfolds, staff find that not only are they discovering new insights for their own professional development, but that they are using some of the material in their own teaching. It has also created a sense of common purpose across the district and within individual sites. By the end of Term 3, there is a lot of raw data, and each site has developed a list of the capacities that people will need into the future. These are taken to a second Learning District PD conference near the end of Term 3.

What follows sets out the kind of information and analysis that might have emerged from Steps 1–3 during the process described above. It will give the reader a sense of the model at work. To emphasise that the process is not a lock-step approach, the description and analysis has been loosely organised to reflect the to-and-fro interaction between Steps 1–3 viz.,

- the key features of the fourth industrial revolution
- the impact of the fourth industrial revolution on work, democracy, individuals, and social and cultural life
- the capacities needed to respond to the fourth industrial revolution and its impacts.

What is the fourth industrial revolution?

The second half of the 20th century saw the invention and introduction of stand-alone computers using digitalised technology that enabled the organisation and storage of large amounts of information. During the 1970s and 1980s computer science developed quickly, resulting in the capacity to link computers through the internet, and it was not long before many other technologies became digitalised. By the turn of the century these developments had begun to change the shape of societies around the world, although of course it was in the developed countries that the biggest uptakes of the technologies occurred.

The use of the new technologies has been given a variety of titles. Each title describes a particular aspect of the technologies such as the 'computer age' (focusing on the machine at the heart of the changes), the 'digital age' (focusing on how computers record and transmit information); the 'new media age' (focusing on the new types of media enabled by digitalisation); the 'information age' (focusing on the general outcome of enabling greater access to information); or the third machine age (focusing on the capacity of machines to learn).

However, such labels do not adequately capture the sheer scope and scale of the changes that have occurred in the past twenty years. As the pace quickens, many scholars have begun to argue that the changes are so widespread that they are of the same order as the changes brought about by the first industrial revolution two centuries ago. One of these is the American economist and social theorist Jeremy Rifkin, who, in 2011, wrote a book titled *The Third Industrial Revolution: How lateral power is transforming energy, the economy, and the world.*

Rifkin uses historical analysis to explain how, over the past 250 years, three industrial revolutions have created wholesale societal transformations in the way we work, live and govern ourselves. Of course, none of these three revolutions are discrete—each develops with elements of the previous revolution continuing to operate for quite some time. Rifkin argues that what is common to each industrial revolution is the emergence, and then convergence, of technologies that take on a new form in each revolution and fundamentally change the way we manage, power and move economic activity. He describes this process as involving

> new **communication** technologies to more efficiently manage economic activity; new sources of **energy** to more efficiently power economic activity; and new modes of **transportation** to more efficiently move economic activity. Each of these defining technologies interacts with each other to enable the system to operate as a whole. (Rifkin, 2016; my emphases)

Thus, in the first industrial revolution, the three technologies were steam-powered printing and the telegraph (communication), coal in plentiful supply (energy) and steam-powered locomotives (transport). Those three technologies changed with the arrival of the second industrial revolution in the 20th century, which brought telephone, radio and television (communication), centralised electricity and cheap oil (energy) and internal combustion engines (transport).

Rifkin proposes that in the late 20th and early 21st centuries, societies are transitioning—at different speeds—to a third industrial revolution, which is building a new system-wide infrastructure based on digitalisation. Even while economies are still closely tied to the second industrial revolution, with its reliance on fossil fuels, elements of the third industrial revolution are beginning to disrupt old ways of doing things, spurred by increases in computer power, growth in the amount of online data sets for machine learning, and the development of powerful algorithms that are used for a multitude of purposes. These developments are used in different ways by and through such disparate technologies as personal computers, mobile phones, robots and so on. They are changing entire systems of work, governance and production in our society.

Rifkin suggests that these digitalised technologies contain the new forms of the three elements in a third industrial revolution that is changing the ways we manage, power and move economic activity. It involves

> a digitalized communication Internet . . . converging with a digitalized renewable Energy Internet, and a digitalized, GPS-guided and soon driverless Transportation and Logistics Internet, to create a super-Internet to manage, power, and move economic activity across society's value chains. These three Internets ride atop a platform called the Internet of Things . . . [where] sensors will be embedded into every device and appliance, allowing them to communicate with each other and Internet users, providing up to the moment data on the managing, powering and moving of economic activity in a smart digital society. (Rifkin, 2016)

Such has been the breathtaking speed and impact of these developments that the chairman of the World Economic Forum, Professor Klaus Schwab (2015, 2016), argues that we are now in a fourth industrial revolution. Schwab recognises that technological breakthroughs in a number of fields, such as artificial intelligence, nanotechnology, quantum computing, biotechnology, robotics, 3D printing, autonomous vehicles, and the Internet of Things, had their foundations in the third industrial revolution; however, he argues that such technologies are now combining in ways that mark a radical break from the key elements of that revolution. In the fourth industrial revolution, the lines between physical, digital and biological spheres are being blurred:

> Already, artificial intelligence is all around us, from self-driving cars and drones to virtual assistants and software that translate or invest. Impressive progress has been made in AI (artificial intelligence) in recent years, driven by exponential increases in computing power and by the availability of vast amounts of data, from software used to discover new drugs to algorithms used to predict our cultural interests. Digital fabrication technologies

meanwhile are interacting with the biological world on a daily basis. Engineers, designers and architects are combining computational design, additive manufacturing, materials engineering, and synthetic biology to pioneer a symbiosis between microorganisms, our bodies, the products we consume, and even the buildings we inhabit. (Schwab, 2015)

Thus, for Schwab, it is the convergence of the new technologies in such fields as neuroscience and artificial intelligence that has taken the scope and impact of these developments into a new realm of possibilities worthy of being named as a fourth revolution. Rather than being characterised primarily by changes in technologies, the hallmark of the fourth industrial revolution is the blurring of the physical, digital and biological spheres that is creating possibilities never before imagined.

Despite their differences over nomenclature, both Rifkin and Schwab analyse the third/fourth industrial revolution primarily from a technological perspective, looking particularly at the ways in which it might transform the economy, business and the environment for the better. For example, Rifkin believes that although there are dangers, the new technologies have the potential to establish new collaborative economic systems and, by reducing the human footprint on the environment, can help to combat environmental degradation and the threats posed by climate change (Rifkin, 2016).

Other writers are concerned about the dangers posed by the fourth industrial revolution now, citing the dark side of internet activity such as cyberbullying, cybercrime and terrorism (the 'darknet'), and maintaining that the ways in which digitalised technologies are currently being used could exacerbate inequality, heighten tensions between groups, diminish democracy and threaten individual privacy and civil rights. They claim that the introduction and use of nearly every new technology raises a raft of significant ethical issues (e.g., Avent, 2016; Harari, 2016; Keen, 2018).

Some scholars take a longer term view by looking at what the fourth industrial revolution might mean for humankind itself. For example, historian and philosopher Yuval Harari (2016) argues that humans are increasingly ceding their decision-making about many aspects of personal and work life to algorithms in machines, not least because the machines make better decisions. This applies to areas as disparate as finance, driving and navigation, medical diagnosis, and book and film selection. It will extend as the Internet of Things becomes established and all our household devices are interconnected; as people spend more time in virtual reality worlds; and as AI becomes smarter and expands its capabilities through such developments as machine learning. Gradually, humans may lose the capacity to make decisions about many aspects of their lives as algorithms take control.

Leading AI researcher Toby Walsh points out that currently computers are able to perform quite specific tasks using a lot of data, but can't synthesise or think holistically as humans can. However, given the speed at which AI is developing, this will not be the case for long. AI researchers are using different approaches to develop machine intelligence, such as those that imitate human intelligence, or are based on deep neural networks like those that function in the human brain. As machines develop the capacity to learn and think, it is not beyond the bounds of possibility that they will also develop human emotions.

Harari (2018) points out that running alongside the rapid developments in artificial intelligence, and now converging with it, is research into our brains, bodies and emotions. In the past, humans could control the external world but had little control over what goes on inside them. Now research is revealing that humans comprise biochemical algorithms that have evolved through natural selection and shape our decision-making, emotions and feelings using calculations. However, as the boundaries in the revolutions in biotechnology and information technology increasingly start to blur, so the new technologies could restructure our bodies and minds. If organisms are biochemical algorithms, they can be hacked. This would give us, or enhanced artificial intelligence, the capacity to take

> control of the world inside us, and . . . enable us to engineer and manufacture life. We will learn how to design brains, extend lives, and kill thoughts at our discretion. Nobody knows what the consequences will be. (Harari, 2018, p. 7)

On the basis of his survey of 300 researchers in the area of artificial intelligence, Walsh (2018) reports that a majority believe there is a 50 per cent probability that by the year 2062 (and a 90 per cent probability that by the early 22nd century) we will have achieved general artificial intelligence, whereby AI will supersede human intelligence and be able to better do all the tasks that humans can currently do—faster, longer and without human foibles such as being forgetful or blinded by emotion (Walsh, 2018). Indeed, Walsh postulates that just as *Homo sapiens* outlasted Neanderthals because the former possessed language and the capacity to co-learn and adapt to different environments, so too will the emergence of AI result in the evolution of a new super species he calls '*Homo digitalis*'. This may occur as our bodies and minds become immersed in the digital world.

What does all this mean? The first point to make is that there are no certain future outcomes. As Abraham Lincoln is reputed to have said: 'The best way to predict the future is to create it'. There are any number of ways in which the fourth industrial revolution might shape the future journey of humanity, from the utopian to the dystopian and many possibilities in between. For example, we could ensure that the digital revolution augments and enriches our lives, even while we hold on to the human qualities and capacities that we value; or we could surrender to machines with superior intelligence, live our lives in virtual realities and lose our human qualities. It will be up to humans to choose. The stakes are high.

The point of this book is to make the argument that it is not a matter of allowing the consequences of contemporary trends like the fourth industrial revolution to wash over us, hoping that it will all turn out to be okay. If we are to respond adequately, trends need to be understood and analysed, and strategies developed, enacted and monitored. This demands citizens who have the capacities to do the job—which puts education at the frontline of the response.

How, then, do we make sense of the fourth industrial revolution in order to make decisions about what role schools can play in meeting the new challenges? If, as has been argued, such considerations need to address the purposes of education, the next step is to examine what the fourth industrial revolution means for each of the educational purposes outlined in Chapter 8. This task is complicated by the speed of change. Many elements of the second and third industrial revolution still exist even as new technologies reshape established practices and institutions and create entirely new economic and social possibilities.

Recognising that children and young people in school today are likely to live deep into the 21st century, this complexity will be embraced by canvassing implications for the short term (to 2025), medium term (to 2035) and long term. At the end of each section some of the capacities that the analysis suggests may be important will be enumerated, understanding that such a list will inevitably need to change as circumstances change.

What are the implications of the fourth industrial revolution for work and the economy?

For the past century in Australia, work has been important not just as the basis for sustaining and building the standard of living of the society as a whole, but for individual financial security, mental and physical wellbeing, and meaning and self-identity. Young people have been able to assume that work will be available, and educational institutions have played an important role in preparing them for the workforce. Generally, this has been successful, and Australia has experienced low levels of unemployment, growth in wages and sustained economic growth. The indications are that the impact of digital technologies on work are already disrupting that economic settlement, and that over the next two decades our understanding of work will begin to change irrevocably.

Work in the short to medium term

Automation—AI, robots, driverless cars and so on—is already taking the place of workers in routine manual jobs, such as labourers and assembly line workers, and routine cognitive jobs, such as office assistants and clerks (Peretti, 2017). At the moment, these jobs are being replaced by non-routine manual jobs, such as in the service and security industries, and non-routine cognitive jobs, such as technical engineers and healthcare workers. Thus, over the past 25 years the percentage of unskilled workers in the Australian workforce has declined by over 10 per cent, while there has been a corresponding increase in the percentage of skilled workers (Foundation for Young Australians, 2015, p. 6). Indeed, the level of unemployment in Australia since the 1990s has declined, and the aggregate hours worked by the Australian population, on a per capita basis, has remained stable since the mid-1960s (Borland, 2017).

The big question, however, is whether this pattern can, or will, continue. There is a range of different interpretations and predictions about the future of work in the literature, and it is impossible to be definitive. Some argue that stability in employment will continue in the foreseeable future, albeit with fewer unskilled jobs and changes in some work tasks brought about by technology (e.g., Gittins, 2017; Creighton, 2018). For these commentators, the cry that 'robots will take our jobs' is much over-hyped. They argue that robots have made little impact outside manufacturing, and that multiple-function robots in many cognitive-based fields are a long way off. In any case, they say, just as happened in the first industrial revolution, as new technology makes some jobs redundant, so new jobs rise in their place, spurred by the new technology. Examples include the start-ups made possible via digital platforms, and the need for human workers to program, monitor, maintain and repair the robots (Autor, 2015; Flynn & Robu, 2017).

Others argue that although the level of employment may remain stable, the nature of work will change significantly. A recent study by AlphaBeta investigated two thousand tasks in over a thousand jobs over the past five years and found that over one-tenth of those tasks had been automated (AlphaBeta, 2017). Automation did not mean that people lost their jobs but, rather, that they spent less time on the tasks that involved routine drudgery and that are now done by robots or AI, and more time on jobs that require the tacit and more nuanced knowledge that human workers possess, including analytical skills, creativity, curiosity, and social and emotional intelligence. The AlphaBeta report found that the consequence of this shift has been a fall in workplace injuries and a significant rise in worker satisfaction.

In other words, currently there are many jobs that robots cannot undertake, since the technology is at a stage where robots can only be programmed to do quite specific tasks—Walsh (2017a) calls this 'weak AI'—rather than more complex ones. In more skilled occupations, robots will be used to augment human labour rather than replace it—collaborative robots (cobots) that work alongside humans—and make work more stimulating.

However, many researchers are not as sanguine about the impact of the new technologies on work in the short to medium term. They make the argument that unlike the first industrial revolution, where machines took the jobs of manual workers but could not do cognitive work, in the fourth industrial revolution machines can undertake some cognitive tasks now, and will only get smarter (e.g., Walsh, 2018). In Australia, it is estimated that 70 per cent of young people currently enter the workforce in jobs that will alter dramatically as a result of automation over the next fifteen years, and that 60 per cent of young people are being trained in jobs that will be radically altered by automation (Foundation for Young Australians, 2015, p. 4). One influential study in the US goes further. It estimates that 47 per cent of jobs are under threat of automation in the next two decades (Fray & Osborne, 2013), and a number of other studies support this contention (e.g., Ford, 2015; West, 2018).

In the first instance, job replacement will involve unskilled and semi-skilled workers, but it will inevitably also start to impact on non-routine cognitive jobs. And even where some jobs are retained, there will be fewer of them. Technology has increased the productivity of some highly skilled workers, and so enabled companies to downsize the workforce and concentrate on economies of scale (Avent, 2016). One study estimates that for every robot introduced, 5.6 workers will be replaced (Acemoglu & Restrepo, 2017).

Further, it is not only the existence of jobs, but also the ways in which they are structured that is changing significantly. The traditional idea of the full-time worker in one job for life is disappearing, to be replaced by the flexible worker who changes jobs many times across the course of her/his working life, and may even have a number of employers at the same time. An OECD (2015) report observes that more than half the jobs growth in OECD countries since 1990 has been in roles that are part-time, temporary or self-employed; and in 2014 research firm Edelman Berland estimated that 30 per cent of the Australian workforce have flexible casual and/or part-time work arrangements, such as being moonlighters, freelancers and independent contractors.

Despite the differences in predictions about the speed of change, the common denominator is that the number of jobs, and their type and nature, is altering significantly. In the short- to medium-term future there will be a mix of old and new jobs leavened by the new technologies, which will alter work as we have known it, but the outcomes of which are not inevitable. The impact of the change will depend largely on the capacity of humans to rethink the nature of work and to develop new strategies.

Obviously there will need to be significant investment in ongoing reskilling programs as the nature of jobs change or are left to robots, and/or as new jobs emerge. The immediate challenge is to find ways to blend the old with the new. For example, Stein (2018) points out that there is still a demand for industrial crafts such as engineering pattern-making and moulding. This demand can be met without locking young people into a narrow field by merging digital fabrication skills with traditional craft knowledge and broadening subsequent job options.

In a report on the changing nature of work, the Foundation for Young Australians proposes that work could be organised into clusters, with each cluster having a broadly similar knowledge base and skills that are portable across the many different occupations that comprise that field of work category.

> Of the 7 clusters of work: The Artisans and The Coordinators are likely to experience lower growth and high exposure to automation; The Generators and The Designers are likely to experience moderate growth and medium exposure to automation; and The Carers, The Informers, and The Technologists are most likely to grow and persist into the future. Over time, the jobs that comprise these clusters of work will change, as will the names and number of clusters of work. More job clusters may arise, based on new occupations and new skills being demanded and valued by employers. (Foundation for Young Australians, 2016, p. 9)

Ideas like this can help to make sense of the changing nature of work, ease work transition by broadening career options, and identify ongoing pre- and in-job training programs. This is important at a time when elements of the second and third industrial revolution coexist with the new technologies of the fourth. It is clear that having a commitment to, and the skills for, lifelong learning is crucial in the 21st century.

At the same time, there are many work-related social and political issues that must be addressed, such as issues related to work conditions. In the shift to more flexible and casualised working arrangements with multiple employers, how are important and hard-won working entitlements such as holiday and leave arrangements (e.g., sick, long service and parental leave) and minimum wage structures retained and exercised? This is particularly the case in the gig economy, where workers are finding that the promise of immediacy and flexibility is offset by the lack of security and worker rights (Kessler, 2018). It will be important that workers in the new workplace can combine to ensure they are not exploited by the changing arrangements, and can devise approaches suiting the new circumstances.

In summary, when thinking about the future of work in the short to medium term, it is important not to be too deterministic or pessimistic about the impact of automation on work. At the same time, automation is already affecting the labour market today and, given the speed of technological change, the impact can only widen and deepen. However, in the first instance it will be variable across and within work sectors. The one common element is that workers will need to have the skills and capacity to influence and adjust to change and keep on learning.

But if the short- and medium-term changes described above require strategic action, the trends for the long-term future are already becoming apparent and cannot be left unattended. They demand serious consideration now.

Work in the long term

Beyond the next two decades, it is impossible to; say whether current work arrangements will continue, or if work as we know it will exist at all. The growth in machine learning means that robots will develop an artificial general intelligence enabling them to engage in far more sophisticated tasks than is possible at the moment.

Some researchers are optimistic. For example, Rifkin (2016) argues that increasingly flexible work arrangements may lead to a new economic paradigm—the sharing economy—where, as machines take over work, people move from producing and selling goods to selling services on a digital platform. People will develop portfolios comprising a mix of paid work with a number of employers at any one time, unpaid community service work, and increased leisure time.

Walsh (2018) maintains that in forty years, when machines will be physically and cognitively better than us at most jobs, we may choose to still have people do some or many of the jobs. For example, machines may be able to paint better art or compose better music, but even if machines develop emotions (which is possible), people will still prefer many pursuits to be done by humans. This is because we will appreciate human emotions and skill and social interaction with humans, rather than the impersonal non-human work done by machines.

> The most important human traits in 2062 will be our social and emotional intelligence, as well as our artistic and artisan skills. It won't be the STEM [science, technology, engineering, maths] skills that are currently seen as important for getting a job. The irony is that our *technological* future will not be about technology, but about our *humanity*. And the jobs of the future are the most human ones. (Walsh, 2018; emphasis in original)

However, many researchers writing about work in the future are not as optimistic. Some talk about the end of work, and discuss the features of a post-work society (e.g., Frayne, 2015; Srnicek & Williams, 2015; Thompson, 2015). They maintain that when machines are able to do everything that humans can do and more cheaply, the logic of capitalism means people will lose their jobs. Harari warns about the dangers of a two-tier society that might be produced in the longer term by the impact of automation, with a small number of well-paid elite workers and a vast majority of people—a 'useless class'—being either unemployed as robots take their jobs, or engaged in low-paid work for which it is cheaper to use humans than machines (e.g., Harari, 2016; 2018). Without work, and beaten down by a ceaseless demand to reskill, the mass of people could become a 'useless class', increasingly disillusioned and resentful. Social dysfunction will result.

Like Walsh, Harari is quick to point out that the future does not have to end up that way—there is an alternative scenario. The increased productivity brought about by cheaper production costs as a result of automation will mean that GDP will grow. That is, we could have a more affluent and more environmentally sustainable society with more time for leisure and community activities. However, if that scenario is to be realised—rather than a scenario involving social dysfunction—there will need to be serious community discussion. It might mean for example that we consider such questions as:

- At this early stage in the digital revolution, and no matter how sophisticated AI becomes, how do we decide which jobs we want machines to take and which not?
- As jobs diminish in number, how can the existing work be distributed and/or working hours shortened?
- Should we develop strategies for a post-work society, such as a universal basic income (Bregman, 2018), so that work is no longer such a central part of our lives?

- In a post-work society, what universal basic services are needed to sustain community life?
- As the traditional notion of 'work' changes and people have more time at their disposal, how can we promote meaningful individual and community pursuits that enrich our lives individually and socially?
- How can the concept of work be widened to include parenting, caring and volunteer work?

In short, a dystopian future is not inevitable if people have the political skills to ensure that our society takes such questions seriously. Rather than thinking of ways to compete with machines, it may be better to consider thinking about ways to better distribute wealth, other than through paying wages for traditional forms of work. But given that it is impossible to tell just how quickly technological change will reshape the jobs of today and the future, it is crucial that the conversation starts now.

In summary, students entering school today are going to live through significant changes to work over the coming decades that will have a number of individual, social, political and economic consequences. If personal and social dysfunction is not to result, it is clear that people will need knowledge, skills, dispositions and values that not only suit the changing circumstances of work, but also enable them to critique and shape the way work is constructed now and in the future. What, then, are the work-related capacities that are suggested by the preceding analysis of work in the fourth industrial revolution?[11]

---

11 For the rest of this chapter, the overarching term 'capacities' will be used to differentiate them from the term 'capabilities', which has a more specific curriculum meaning discussed in Chapter 10.

What work-related capacities are needed to handle the impact of the fourth industrial revolution?

There are at least three aspects to the capacities needed for the new workplace. First, no matter how much work changes, and for as long as work exists, there will be a need for skills and understandings that relate to specific jobs or clusters of jobs. These might be the focus of qualifications or certificates and/or they might be learned on the job.

Second, there are general skills and understandings that will apply to most or all employment settings. These generic capacities are crucial if people are to work productively in a changing workplace, and they are therefore shaped by the nature of work and its possibilities.

Third, it has been argued that while the fourth industrial revolution has the potential to remake the idea of work, as well as the nature of work, its consequences are not inevitable. That is, workers and employers can use the promise of the new technologies to shape socially and individually fulfilling responses, rather than be passive recipients of the consequences. This means that people must have the political skills and dispositions to deal with such challenges—and yet these capacities are rarely enumerated in the many lists of what the new worker needs.

The following list of capacities for the changing workplace that will cater for these three aspects has been drawn from the implications of the discussion in this section.

- *Knowledge and lifelong learning capacities:* Workers of the future will still need the foundational skills of literacy, numeracy and digital literacy, as well as the knowledge, skills and understandings relevant to the field of work in which they are engaged. But if work is to change radically as described above, then workers must have the capacity to upgrade/update their work knowledge on a regular basis and to retrain where necessary. In addition, if the amount of time spent at work is to decline as a result of automation, or if we move towards a post-work society, people will need to have the knowledge and capacities that enable them to pursue creative interests (such as music, the arts and making things); enjoy community involvement; re-engage with families; and participate in volunteering activities. Thus, the capacity and appetite for lifelong learning is an important attribute.

- *Capacities for the new work contexts:* If the meaning and nature of work is going to undergo the kind of significant change described in this section, then the worker of the future will need to have a number of capacities including:
  - *Thinking capacities*—machines may be going to do most of the routine work, but we have not yet been able to automate tasks that demand human qualities that relate to thinking and feeling. This means that in the near future workers need to develop and use such thinking skills as critical thinking, judgement, creativity, curiosity, computational thinking (i.e., understanding the fundamental principles of computation), problem-solving and communication.
  - *Social capacities*—if workers are going to have to spend less time on routine individual tasks and more time working with others, including working for more than one employer in different settings, then they will need to have skills for collaboration, teamwork and interpersonal relations.
  - *Political capacities*—if workers are to protect working conditions, help to shape the extent of automation as applied to jobs, and prevent the digital revolution from widening inequalities, then they will need to possess knowledge about our political system; be able to exercise such political skills as lobbying, advocacy

and networking; and have interpersonal skills and a disposition to work for the common good.
- *Dispositions for the new work environments:* If work is important to the shaping of such personal dispositions as self-identity and feelings of self-worth, then in a changing working environment, people will need to be resilient, open-minded, respectful of difference, empathetic and committed to the common good.

What are the implications of the fourth industrial revolution for democracy?

One of the early promises of the digital revolution was that it would enhance democracy. In contrast with pre-internet times, it was claimed that the internet provided access to a greater range of news outlets and so would diminish the power of a small number of media monopolies; at the same time, it would foster political participation by enabling people to express their views to a much wider audience. Citizens could engage in horizontal communication with their government, which in turn could make new and powerful connections with their electorate. Rifkin (2014) goes further and argues that the internet can be seen as a 'collective commons' in which anyone can post, download and read material for the purposes of sharing for the collective good. Such collaboration can be systematised through common platforms such as Wikipedia, the free online encyclopedia created and edited by volunteers around the world.

Notwithstanding such possibilities, the digital revolution poses a number of dangers to some of the key features of democracy that can only diminish, rather than democratise, the public sphere (Runciman, 2018). These need to be identified and dealt with if the internet's contribution to democracy is to be more than an empty promise.

A major concern is the negative impact that the digital

revolution is having on our representative form of democracy, especially on the process of elections. At the heart of the problem is big data, which works by gathering large amounts of personal data from social media and using a powerful algorithm to analyse it to develop detailed profiles of individual voters. This enables political parties to identify each voter's emotional triggers and so tailor messages to suit each profile. One high-profile example is that of Cambridge Analytica, the data mining and analysis company that, without authorisation, took personal Facebook data gathered from 50 million Americans in order to target them with personalised political advertisements during the 2016 American presidential elections (Cadwalladr & Graham-Harrison, 2018). Such hyper-targeting lacks transparency and accountability. As Hendrix and Carroll point out in the US context:

> Deploying hypertargeted voter media that constructs narrow or outright fabricated versions of the truth to influence small subsets of voters in strategically important geographies is a scenario our founding fathers never imagined. (Hendrix & Carroll, 2017)

Of course, attempts to manipulate the population using propaganda techniques have long been a feature of politics, but the digital revolution has sped up the process. It feeds into and builds individualised and self-interested attitudes to voting, and diminishes any sense of the common good. As Grayling points out,

> in our present day highly sophisticated techniques are employed by partisan interests to target different facets of the uninformed, prejudiced, self-interested, emotionally driven attitudes of different constituencies of the many, to aggregate them into voting for an outcome which is the partisan interest's own preference . . . The aim of the architects of representative democracy was to prevent a single interest from dominating: in the distortions that

representative democracy has suffered, new manipulators have found a way to pervert that aim. (Grayling, 2017, p. 148)

A broader but related concern involves the fragmentation of the spaces for public discussion (Twitter, bloggers, online single-issue communities, multiple pay-TV channels and so on) that are making the task of deliberation in the public sphere more difficult and more complex than it has ever been before, if not serving to residualise the public sphere itself (Sandlin, Burdick & Norris, 2012). Allied to this are concerns about the toxic impact on civil society as a whole, as social media drives people into like-minded groups where their opinions and beliefs are constantly reinforced. In these echo chambers, people only talk to others with similar views—silos of sameness where biases are confirmed and alternative views rarely considered (Hull, 2017). This intellectual isolation is exacerbated by website algorithms used in, say, Facebook or Google searches, that now selectively guess what information a user would like or want to read based on previous searches. In this way, users are rarely exposed to points of view that vary from their own—isolating them in their own ideological 'filter bubble' (Pariser, 2011), closing minds and reducing the possibility of a truly democratic discourse.

The quality of democratic discourse in the public sphere is also reduced by the proliferation of fake news and conspiracy theories, which are fanned by the speed and reach of the internet. False claims are circulated quickly and across many sites and are therefore difficult to rebut. As Susaria argues:

> The societal consequences of fake news—greater political polarization, increased partisanship, and eroded trust in mainstream media and government—are significant. (Susaria, 2018)

And at a time of the 'death of expertise', where Google has replaced the expert and people reject the concept of expertise itself, it becomes difficult to contest false information (Nichols, 2017). There is a widespread assumption that one opinion is as good as another, no matter the content.

The quality of democratic discussion is also adversely affected by the lack of time for reflection on the complexity of issues. A 24-hour news cycle heightens the immediacy of any single issue and action is quickly organised through social media via hashtag democracy such as Twitter campaigns. Disagreement is expressed through fierce attack and anonymous abuse, and those with the shrillest voices are heard. These factors combine to diminish the possibility of a healthy, restrained and respectful conversation in the public sphere, and so weaken democracy itself. Airoidi (2018) points out that such intolerance has always existed, but that in the contemporary world it has been exacerbated by social media, which has become the stage through which political actors push certain hate-filled positions.

A further threat to democracy brought about by the digital revolution is the power governments now have at their disposal to increase their control over populations through pervasive surveillance systems and access to metadata that can be gathered about citizens (Moore, 2018, Chapter 8). The global surveillance systems unmasked by the Snowden affair in 2013—all facilitated by the new technologies—raise serious questions about the relationship between the individual and the state (Greenwald, 2014). In the global war against terrorism, it is tempting for governments to use AI to look for potential threats. But surveillance of this sort raises a number of questions for any democracy, such as how the need for public safety can be balanced with civil liberty concerns about invasion of privacy. At a time when China is using algorithms to compile information about all citizens' lives in order to calculate a 'social credit' score that will impact on their ability to access public services and obtain loans (Zeng, 2018), there is an urgent need for discussions about the limits to what data can be gathered, how and by whom.

If democracy in a nation state is posited on the legitimacy of its government to regulate aspects of the society, and to be held accountable by the population for that, then there is a serious democratic concern about the collective power of the five big tech companies—Apple, Amazon, Google, Facebook and Microsoft. These companies have become so successful that they now provide things that no one can do without. In earlier times, they would have been seen as public goods, owned and controlled by governments. But when private companies operate them globally, it is difficult for any one nation-state to regulate and control them and address issues such as 'fake news' (Aldrick, 2018). Relying on private companies to act in the public interest rather than their own self-interest is fraught with danger. As the power of the large technology companies grows, so the legitimacy of governments starts to weaken. This raises important questions for any democracy.

Similarly, the emerging field of AI is largely in private hands. Since every technology can be used for good or ill, it is important that democratically elected governments can ensure that AI developments are used to benefit humanity. This means creating incentives for companies to use the power of AI to address such big challenges as climate change, poverty and inequality, rather than focus on such developments as lethal autonomous weapons to wage war, including killer robots, drones and automated machine guns. At the same time, it will be important not to fall prey to 'AI solutionism'—the belief that, if given enough data, machine learning algorithms can solve all the world's major problems—thus creating unrealistic expectation about what AI can really do (Polonski, 2018).

It also means tackling the ethical dilemmas attached to the deployment of nearly every new technology, and ensuring that there are appropriate regulations and controls (Harland, 2017; Sample, 2017). The community must contribute to the development of the criteria that can be used to test for suitability—not leave these decisions in the hands of private companies who have a financial stake in the final decision.

In short, the fourth industrial revolution doesn't just involve neutral digital technology. It has the potential to enhance our democracy and, at the same time, contains the seeds of its destruction. This section has highlighted some of the trends that appear more likely to result in the latter outcome. They are exacerbated by the challenges of globalisation, the dominance of neoliberal ideology and the commercialisation of the public sphere (Sandel, 2012).

Every year, Freedom House compiles an authoritative report on the state of democracy around the world, using a range of criteria. In 2017 its report claimed that democracy faced its most serious crisis in decades as the fundamental conditions of free and fair elections, the rights of minorities, freedom of the press and the rule of law came under attack around the world. This is consistent with the slide over the last twelve years, in which time 113 countries have shown a net decline in political rights and civil liberties, and only 62 have shown an improvement (Freedom House, 2018).

Australia continues to be one of the countries described in the Freedom House report as being 'free' and characterised by the elements of a healthy democracy. And yet each of the dangers to democracy highlighted in this section are also emerging in Australian society, and capable of doing harm to our polity (Camilleri, 2014), and trust in government and satisfaction with democracy is declining (Triffitt, 2018). What is needed to prevent such damage from occurring?

What capacities for citizenship are needed to handle the impact of the fourth industrial revolution?

The previous section argued that the digital revolution is one of the factors that has contributed to the decline of key elements of democratic life. But it pointed out that the new technologies have the power to enhance democracy, provided certain conditions are met. The central feature of a democratic recovery must be a knowledgeable and active citizenry with the capacity to use technological tools for the common good, rather than their own narrow self-interest. What are the capacities needed for such a democratic citizenry? The following suggestions are drawn from the analysis above.

- *Knowledge about democratic life:* If some of the fundamental tenets of democracy are under threat, the first step in overcoming the dangers is for the citizenry to understand what needs to be defended and why. This suggests that all citizens understand our democratic system, its origins, history, institutions, processes and values. This should not be a static understanding, but one that enables citizens to recognise how to improve democratic processes or institutions in ways that are consistent with the basic principles of democracy.
- *Capacities for civic and political engagement:* A number of capacities for civic and political engagement are needed if the dangers to democracy described in this section are to be avoided or overcome. These include capacities for:
  - *Discernment and scepticism*—if factors such as fake news and hyper-individualised targeting at elections are prevalent through social media, citizens need strategies to recognise and resist them (Susaria, 2018). This suggests that citizens should have the skills to be able to discern propaganda, identify the authority of any source, weigh up evidence, and be sceptical about claims. It underlines the importance of media literacy, given that recent studies demonstrate that the majority of young people aged 8–16 years do not feel they possess the awareness or skills to detect fake news (e.g., Notley et al., 2017).

- *Engagement with different views and beliefs*—if social media is driving people into echo chambers where their own biases are confirmed, citizens in a democracy need the capacity and commitment to seek out alternative views and to engage in respectful discussion about them. As Michael Sandel (2010) suggests in the US context, 'we need to rediscover the lost art of democratic argument'.
- *Local and global thinking*—if global surveillance via big data, and the power of the big tech companies, poses a threat to democracy at the local and global levels, citizens need to have the skills to recognise what is happening and work with others at a local and global level to devise and take action to effect change.
- *Reflection and action*—if the speed of the 24-hour news cycle is causing superficial consideration of disparate issues, then citizens need to develop strategies that allow them to discern big trends, reflect on them in depth and take appropriate action.
- *Dispositions for civic and political engagement:* In the previous section I argued that various developments in the social media and the use of big data are contributing to a heightened sense of self-interest and individualism. Since a sense of society is important in a democracy, citizens must possess such dispositions as:
  - *A commitment to the common good*—if strategies such as hyper-personalised targeting at election time are based on appeals to self-interest, it is crucial that in a democracy citizens have an ability to recognise propaganda, and a commitment to thinking beyond themselves and considering benefits to the wider community—particularly those who are most disadvantaged in our society.
  - *Ethics of artificial intelligence including computational ethics*—if the development of AI raises a number of

ethical issues and dilemmas, and the resolution of these will have long-lasting consequences, it is crucial that all citizens—not just a few researchers—have the capacities to understand the dilemmas and are equipped to consider the ethical dimensions of any mooted solutions.

The implications for individual, social and cultural life[12]

The digital revolution has had a remarkable impact on individuals and on the social and cultural life of many societies. Much of this impact has been positive—people have instant access to the world's knowledge; can talk to family and friends at anytime and anywhere in the world; make financial transactions; purchase books, films and music; express ideas freely in a multitude of forums for debate and discussion; and much more.

Notwithstanding these many advantages, there are a number of emerging concerns about the adverse impact that the new technologies are having on individuals and society. However, as was argued in the previous sections, just as the possible dystopian effects on work and democracy of the digital revolution can be minimised or excised by human action, so too does this apply to the possible effects on individual, social and cultural life. This section will describe, in no particular order, a few of the issues that need to be addressed.

One concern relates to the issue of data and privacy (Keen, 2018). Search engines and recommendation platforms now provide us with personalised suggestions for products and services based on our search history and our social interactions on places like Facebook and Instagram. Often the suggestions

---

12 The individual and social and cultural purposes of education have been combined in this section owing to the overlap of implications for these arenas with this topic.

being offered so closely match our choices that it is hard to detect that we are being manipulated. In fact, the more information we unconsciously cede to search engines and social media platforms, the more we are being controlled, as each of us becomes the target of hyper-individualised marketing. Indeed, the eminent scholar Shoshana Zuboff claims that we are living through the rise of a new variant of capitalism—what she calls 'surveillance capitalism'—where our behavioural data produces prediction products that are traded in a behavioural futures market (Zuboff, 2019).

Many people say that this predictive assistance can be quite helpful. However, when it begins to shape the nature and cost of a product or service we seek, it may become more sinister. Insurance companies, for example, are starting to use data from social media and other sources to assess an individual's risk, and thus the cost of her/his insurance premiums (Boyd, 2017). The point is that as the Internet of Things expands, so too does the capacity to generate more and more data about each of us. It is becoming ever more urgent that our society debate the extent and limits of individual privacy, and how data can be protected from hacking.

Another pragmatic issue is the increasing awareness of the negative effects of social media use. These range from the growth of cyberbullying, which can leave its victims deeply psychologically scarred, to the fact that people feel always contactable and so can never break from work, to the growth of addictive behaviours whereby people experience withdrawal symptoms or anxiety when they are separated from their smartphone or online games for even a few minutes (Gillespie, 2019). There is some evidence that social media platforms like Facebook, Twitter or Instagram can make people perceive themselves to be more socially isolated (Primack et al., 2017), and even cause depression as people unfavourably compare their lives with the life story of others. Others, such as Anne Manne (2014), fear that the idea of 'curating the self' through social media can lead to a narcissism incompatible with the notion of Rifkin's collective commons.

White et al. (2018) agree that such dangers exist, but point to research that shows that it is possible to use the internet to reduce conflict by fostering friendships and bringing people together. That is, just as technology can be part of the problem, so too can it be part of the solution if people have the skills, awareness and dispositions to use it in that way.

Allied with the issue of privacy is the question of what the fourth industrial revolution is doing to our humanity. We are now living in a society where even the everyday things we use—fridges, phones, toothbrushes, coffee machines, televisions and so on—are all equipped with communicating sensors that are generating data about us all the time. Some people use some of this information to help them make decisions. For example, people can self-quantify by using various devices such as smart phones and Fitbits to monitor their moods, sleeping patterns, activity levels, heart rates, how much alcohol they drink and so on, for purposes of self-improvement. Most of us allow technology to make decisions for us, without thinking much about it. Thus, the GPS in cars tells us where to drive to get to a particular destination, and algorithms make predictive decisions in many areas of human activity such as watching a movie, or buying books, music or a house—all based on the data that has been collected about our previous actions, choices and interests. In this way we are becoming inputs into a process as algorithms take on human responsibilities. Instead of humans programming computers, it is the computers programming us. The danger is that, over time, humans will lose the capacity to make decisions and solve problems, thus ceding our autonomy to machines.

Yuval Harari (2016) argues that there are two trends coming out of Silicon Valley. The first he calls 'dataism', which involves information and algorithms eventually taking the place of our human instincts for the purposes of decision-making. The second he labels 'techno-humanism', whereby, as humans, we try to protect and lengthen human life by upgrading ourselves biologically.

Harari cites such examples as nanorobots patrolling our blood stream looking for pathogens to destroy, or human brains being connected to the internet, or to other brains, to make an internet of minds. Both these trends may contribute to the development of a sort of super life form that is more techno-based than human—a new machine species. While at the end of the second decade of the 21st century scenarios like these sound far-fetched, Harari argues that the digital revolution is proceeding at such a speed that within three decades the trends may be so advanced that they are irreversible. If humans want to maintain their autonomy and their humanity, we need to recognise now what is possible and make decisions about how far we want AI to extend.

Walsh (2017b) is more optimistic, but agrees that humans must take control now. He argues that the AI revolution gives us the chance to rediscover the things that make us human. Thus, although machines may be able to produce amazing art and music, we will still prefer works that are produced by humans and speak to the human experience.

> No machine will truly experience love like we do. As well as the artistic, there will be a re-appreciation of the artisan. Indeed, we see the beginnings of this already in hipster culture. We will appreciate more and more those things made by the human hand. Mass-produced goods made by machine will become cheap. But items made by hand will be rare and increasingly valuable. Finally as social animals, we will also increasingly appreciate and value social interactions with other humans. So the most important human traits will be our social and emotional intelligence, as well as our artistic and artisan skills. The irony is that our technological future will not be about technology but all about our humanity. (Walsh, 2017b)

The digital revolution will also have an impact on the cultural and social life of our society. Two examples relating to the important diversity of Australian society will be given to demonstrate this point. The first example highlights the hidden dangers of AI. With machine learning, the ability of computer programs to interpret language has improved significantly. Machines can acquire human-like language abilities by interpreting the patterns contained in the vast amounts of online data they absorb. Researchers in England and the US have found that AI tools can absorb the biases contained in these patterns and exhibit significant racial and gender biases (Devlin, 2017; Eubanks, 2017; Noble 2018). On reflection, this is not surprising. Algorithms are mathematical models based on data constructed by humans, and so reflect all the prejudices that exist in our society. Cathy O'Neil (2016) calls them 'weapons of math destruction' that are 'important, secret and destructive' and which simply automate the status quo. O'Neil gives examples of an increasing number of decisions that are being taken by AI—such as who gets a job interview, a loan or parole—and that reinforce existing prejudices and social inequalities.

Far from being objective and neutral, the algorithmic models in which we place so much trust are no more than 'opinions embedded in mathematics' (O'Neil, 2016). Of course, as Fry (2018) points out using a number of examples, these issues are not the fault of the technology per se. If biases like this exist and are identified, it is possible to reconstruct the algorithms to remove the causes of the bias. At this stage, it depends on humans with the capacity to recognise injustice and the commitment to work to rectify it.

The second example relates to the possibilities for social disruption. The earlier section on the impact of the digital revolution on work described some of the less-work or no-work scenarios that are possible in the coming decades. Ryan Avent (2016) fears a society comprising a small number of highly paid workers, and a large number of unemployed or very poorly paid workers, as robots replace humans and productivity increases. Such a society, he argues, must consider policies based on redistribution—such as through a universal basic wage and job sharing—if there is not to be social dysfunction. However, he points out that redistributive policies like these inevitably exacerbate tensions between groups, heightening the suspicion of outsiders. Those with well-paid jobs who see themselves as the 'makers', are reluctant to subsidise the poor, including immigrants, who they see as the 'takers'; and in turn the poor are aggrieved by the growing gap between themselves and the rich, and the indignity of having to accept hand-outs.

These social fractures can be seen already in many countries around the world, as the industrialised economies of the second industrial revolution unravel, and those who lose their jobs begin to look for reasons, often blaming outsiders such as immigrants for their situation. People turn to populist leaders, who milk the grievances by providing simplistic explanations for the problems and make promises that are impossible to keep. In such an environment, the broad social consensus evaporates as society loses its tolerance of diversity, its sense of community and its social wealth. In a number of countries, separatist and fiercely nationalist groups have already started to pull up the drawbridges and argue that social cohesion can only be achieved by excluding outsiders and reducing difference.

This scenario, even if only partly accurate, poses a huge threat to Australia's successful multicultural society. It means that citizens must not only understand what may happen, but be committed to devising strategies for the new economic and social contexts based on a deep appreciation of the social and cultural benefits of diversity and a commitment to the common good.

What are the implications of the impact of the fourth industrial revolution for individual, social and cultural capacities?

The previous section described some of the issues emerging from the fourth industrial revolution that are having adverse effects at the level of the individual and the society. Like the areas of work and democracy, these issues can only be dealt with by human action, and so require individuals with the capacities to understand what is happening, change their individual behaviour where necessary and work with others to address the challenges to the wider society. The following suggestions about the nature of these capacities are drawn from the analysis above.

- *Knowledge for individual and cultural life:* If the technological developments of the fourth industrial revolution are raising significant ethical dilemmas related to privacy, human autonomy and agency, then individuals must have some foundational knowledge about these philosophical concepts in order to recognise the problems and work out strategies to deal with them. They also need a practical understanding about the basis of the technological developments that are challenging human freedoms. For example, people will need to be able to understand, and develop views about, concepts and ideas such as:
  - the relationship between the individual and society
  - individual freedom and human agency
  - the tension between a right to individual privacy and social action to protect groups in society
  - the balance between diversity and social cohesion
  - basic computational concepts and how they are employed in algorithms
  - how big data works and is used in our society.
- *Capacities for digital awareness:* If the new technologies of the digital revolution are creating the kinds of personal and social issues described in this section, then individuals will need to develop strategies to deal with such matters as:
  - recognising and dealing with cyberbullying, addictive technological behaviours and social isolation
  - ensuring that technology usefully augments our lives

rather than ceding agency to it by meekly accepting the decisions made by algorithms
- understanding that algorithms are based on human prejudices and can be questioned, resisted or altered
- continuing to develop the skills and passions that make us human, such as art and music, making things by hand, and emotional intelligence.

- *Dispositions for ensuring that technological development serve the common good:* As described above, developments like AI have the potential to result in social dysfunction. If so, citizens will need to have dispositions that will help to ensure that the developments don't widen inequality and foster discrimination and mistrust between social, cultural, racial and ethnic groups. These dispositions will include empathy, compassion, caring and social justice.

Summary: The case study so far

Chapter 8 proposed a six-step process for exploring the educational implications of a major societal trend. It was suggested that the reference point for the analysis should be the purposes of education, a detailed consideration of which has been a missing element in contemporary educational policy-making. This chapter used the concept of the fourth industrial revolution as a case study to model the first three steps of the process.

The suggestions from the case study about the capacities needed to handle the impact of the fourth industrial revolution are not exhaustive, but serve an illustrative purpose to demonstrate the process in action. And, of course, the speed of change in this trend means that nothing will stay the same. But, in a way, that is the point. If the purposes of education are to assist children and young people to have the capacities to not only handle change but to shape it, then educators need to keep abreast of key societal changes. A process such as the one described provides an essential framework of understanding that enables the ongoing monitoring needed for appropriate and relevant curriculum change.

Back to the Learning District

At the start of the chapter, an imaginary school district—the Learning District—was suggested as a strategy to make the process come to life. The reader will recall that the Learning District had decided to make the fourth industrial revolution its professional development focus for eighteen months, with Steps 1–3 of the model being covered in Terms 1–3 of the first year. The whole-of-district and site-based investigations conducted into the topic during this time, culminated in a district PD day at the end of Term 3 where insights from the process were discussed. In particular, the focus was on the suggestions for the kinds of capacities needed to handle the impact of the fourth industrial revolution for individuals and society in the arenas of work, democratic, social, and cultural life. At the end of the conference the district agreed on a list of the capacities, and was now in a position to plan Steps 4–6, which involves looking at the educational implications. This would be the major whole-of-district interest for the rest of the year and the first two terms of the following year.

Since the educational implications of the case study can influence change at all levels, the technique of using the Learning District as an example of the process at work will not be modelled for Steps 4–6. Rather it will be assumed that the insights derived from the case study and described in the next three chapters (Part 4) can be applied in a number of settings ranging from modifying, adapting or expanding aspects of curriculum, pedagogy or culture at the level of classrooms, individual schools and districts, through to taking collective system-wide action to effect change. Importantly, the educational implications of the case study will also suggest some possible features for a new educational narrative.

Part 4

New policy directions for Australian education

Overview

The six-step process proposed in Chapter 8 assumes that if educational responses to the challenges of the future are to be appropriate, they must be based on a thorough understanding of those challenges. Guesswork won't do the job. Thus, the first three steps of the proposed six-step model quite deliberately steer clear of a detailed consideration of education. Chapter 9 modelled this through an investigation of the nature and impact of a key societal trend—the fourth industrial revolution.

In **Part 4**, the next three steps of the model explore the educational implications of what was unearthed in Chapter 9. Each step involves exploring the changes or modifications to current policy and practice that might be needed as a result of what the case study demonstrates. Any modifications need to be more systematic than simply listing some of the capacities that emerged from the case study and devising new policy to accommodate them. For a start, it means looking at more than just one aspect of educational policy and practice, such as the official curriculum. The weakness of having a single focus is that it fails to acknowledge that, since aspects of schooling are interdependent, change in one aspect may be contradicted by another. Thus, in **Part 4**:

Chapter 10 investigates the implications for the official curriculum (what is taught).

Chapter 11 looks at the implications for pedagogy (how it is taught).

Chapter 12 explores the implications for school and system-wide culture (the environments that impact on teaching and learning). That is, a new narrative in education must address the question of how to create an environment in which genuine, deep and thoughtful consideration is given to complex educational issues.

Since proposals for change often founder on the rock of entrenched practices, each chapter also canvasses the blockages to change and how these might be overcome. The key point is that there should be consistency and compatibility between various aspects of schooling.

Chapter 10

New curriculum directions

What are the implications of the case study for the intended curriculum?

In Australia, the official (intended) curriculum is represented nationally in the compulsory years of schooling by the Australian Curriculum, and in the senior secondary years in the states and territories by separate certificates.[13] Each of these reflects a particular view about what is valued knowledge in our society and is organised upon beliefs about child development and learning theories. Thus, identifying what knowledge the official curriculum should contain and how it should be constructed is a value-laden task that results in fierce debates. Although what is intended to be taught doesn't necessarily translate into what is enacted in the classroom, the official curriculum influences and constrains educators, and so it is an important aspect to consider.

---

13 Part 4 will discuss the implications for curriculum, pedagogy and the educational environment without reference to specific year levels. That is, the proposals that follow would apply both to the end of the compulsory years of schooling, and to the senior secondary years. However, they may be translated into practice differently depending on year level and jurisdiction.

Step 4 of the model looks at the implications of the case study for the intended curriculum, including the blockages to change. At the level of a school or school district, educators may decide— on the basis of what their investigation into a key societal trend has identified—to modify, adapt, reinforce or rebalance how they have been using the official curriculum. This may lead into professional development or sharing of current practice focusing on specific aspects. If their investigation has revealed what is broadly agreed to be a glaring gap in the official curriculum, then that information can be fed into the relevant curriculum authority for consideration during the next curriculum review.

At the level of a curriculum agency which has overall responsibility for the official curriculum, the investigation into a key societal issue will have been conducted more widely, and may indicate the need for broader changes to the official curriculum. This chapter will explore some of the insights that the case study has generated in relation to our national curriculum, called the Australian Curriculum. These insights confirm aspects of the Australian Curriculum, but also suggest a number of changes or modifications that could be made to better address the challenges of the future.

What did the case study tell us, and what curriculum changes are suggested by it?

Chapter 9 examined the effects of the fourth industrial revolution on work, democracy, individuals, and social and cultural life. Each of those sub-sections suggested a number of capacities that people might need to engage successfully with the changes in each arena. If it is the role of education to develop these capacities, then the next task is to consider them together and try to discern patterns and common elements.

There are many possibilities for organising the capacities

identified. In this chapter they have been grouped under four kinds of interrelated knowledge categories: discipline-based learning, interdisciplinary learning, general capabilities and meta-learning. Table 3 (see next page) provides a summary of how these categories have been arrived at from the case study.

From a curriculum perspective, the key point is that each of the four components should not be seen in isolation but rather as connected parts of a coherent whole. That is, each curriculum component is reliant on a dynamic relationship with the other components. To what extent are these curriculum components already represented in the Australian Curriculum which covers the compulsory years of schooling? The good news is that aspects of each component are present. However, on the basis of what the case study reveals, there are some significant gaps, not only within the components but in the lack of interrelatedness between them.

Disciplinary learning: Disciplines are the foundation blocks of knowledge in our society and are therefore central to learning. School subjects/learning areas are selections from disciplines by educators who organise and sequence them on the basis of what is known about students. The other three curriculum components enrich the curriculum by working in and through the disciplines.

In the Australian Curriculum, disciplinary learning, as represented through the learning areas and subjects, is the most prominent of the four components. There are always ways in which these can be improved (see Reid & Price, 2018), and indeed the ongoing questions about which disciplines and subjects should be represented in the official curriculum, what knowledge is essential, and which disciplines should be core and which elective will continue to be a central part of educational debates. It is important however that curriculum discussion is not confined to disciplines and learning areas.

Table 3: What did the case study tell us?

Curriculum aspect	What did the case study show?	Examples from the case study
Disciplinary learning	The case study suggests a number of capacities that are about knowing facts, concepts and ideas, most of which are contained in the knowledge located in academic disciplines.	Areas of knowledge suggested by the case study include: • knowledge about our democratic system, its origins, history, processes and values • understanding key concepts such as the meaning of individual freedom, human agency, privacy, computation, big data, diversity and social cohesion.
Interdisciplinary learning	The case study provides a number of examples of the need for people to be able to grapple with contemporary issues, problems and dilemmas by moving across disciplinary boundaries in order to see the whole rather than its parts.	The case study provides many examples of tensions and dilemmas for democracy, work, and social and cultural practices brought about by the fourth industrial revolution that can only be addressed by working across disciplinary silos.

Curriculum aspect	What did the case study show?	Examples from the case study
General capabilities	The case study suggests a number of capabilities—skills, dispositions and values—that people need to meet the demands and challenges produced by the fourth industrial revolution.	The capabilities suggested by the case study include: • creative and critical thinking • innovation • ethical thinking and dispositions • thinking locally and globally • using information and communication technologies (ICTs) • discernment and scepticism • intercultural understanding • a disposition for the common good.
Meta-learning	The case study demonstrates that in an information society where knowledge is expanding at an exponential rate, it is important to be able to understand oneself as a learner and the process of learning, and have the ability to develop these understandings throughout life. It is wider than metacognition and so has been termed meta-learning.	The case study shows that having the ability to reflect on one's strengths and weaknesses as a thinker and learner includes: • strategies for thinking about thinking (metacognition) • understandings about one's own learning capacities • learning *about* learning, as well as learning *to* learn • a love of learning.

Interdisciplinary/multidisciplinary/transdisciplinary learning:[14] As demonstrated by the case study, increasingly new knowledge is generated through the synthesis of knowledge from different specialised disciplinary fields. Indeed, ways of understanding and dealing with societal issues and problems can only be achieved if the fundamental 'unity of knowledge' (Wilson, 1998) is appreciated, and people are able to work across disciplinary boundaries. Thus, the capacity to combine disciplines (interdisciplinary), draw from a number of disciplines (multidisciplinary) or blend disciplinary knowledge (transdisciplinary) is a fundamental capacity in the 21st century. Interdisciplinary knowledge has a symbiotic relationship with disciplinary knowledge.

The problem is that interdisciplinary learning is weakly represented in the official Australian Curriculum. The three cross-curriculum priorities are important,[15] but they represent just one element of interdisciplinary learning. Although ACARA would claim that interdisciplinary study is always possible with a discipline-based curriculum, the reality is that is not easy for teachers to organise the curriculum this way without significant support. For example, there is no mechanism in the Australian Curriculum that signals where an interdisciplinary approach might be used, nor are there resources to assist teachers to develop such approaches. In the past few years, interdisciplinary work has achieved some curriculum prominence through official support for an emphasis on science, technology, engineering and mathematics (STEM). This is to be applauded, but it is important that an emphasis on STEM does not lead to a neglect of other curriculum areas such as the social sciences and humanities. As the case study demonstrated, the fourth industrial revolution

---

14 From this point, the single term 'interdisciplinary' will be used to convey the general aims of these cross-disciplinary forms of investigation.

15 The three cross-curriculum priorities are Aboriginal and Torres Strait Islander histories and cultures, Asia and Australia's engagement with Asia, and Sustainability.

means that citizens are exposed to what US Professor Mishra calls 'the "dark arts" of fake news, social media and online distortion . . . [and so] we need to educate ourselves and our children to learn to disbelieve, to question' (Baker, 2019). There is an important role for the social sciences to integrate with the sciences in this work.

General capabilities: There are a number of key skills, values and dispositions without which people could not function adequately in our society. In the Australian Curriculum these have been called general capabilities. They are key to the enactment of disciplinary and interdisciplinary study, and to individual and social practice. General capabilities are certainly present in the Australian Curriculum, and to a lesser extent in senior secondary curricula around Australia. The problem is that they tend to exist more in name than in practice, and they are often treated in isolation from the learning areas.

Meta-learning: Meta-learning is the capacity to understand oneself as a learner and the process of learning. It goes beyond metacognition, taking in new understandings in fields as disparate as neuroscience and the functioning of the brain, emotional and social learning, cognitive psychology, and the link between physical movement and learning. Meta-learning is fundamental in an information/knowledge society where knowledge is expanding at an exponential rate, and where technology is causing us to ask questions about which aspects of our humanity we want to retain rather than cede to machines. That is, if learning is central to living in the 21st century, and to preserving our humanity in an age of AI, then understanding the many aspects of learning is crucial. In curriculum terms, meta-learning involves deep reflection on learning as students work with disciplinary, interdisciplinary and capability-based knowledges.

In the Australian Curriculum, meta-learning is present, but in a diluted form. Thus, metacognition—which is a key aspect of meta-learning but not the only one—is named only as one of a number of aspects of the 'critical and creative thinking' general capability. The time has come to recognise the broader concept of meta-learning as a separate and key component of the official curriculum.

In summary, from the perspective of the case study, these four broad curriculum components—disciplinary learning, interdisciplinary learning, general capabilities, and meta-learning—are the key elements of a contemporary curriculum. Importantly, the four components cannot be seen or developed in isolation—the deep essence of each can only be fully realised when it is in a dynamic relationship with the other components. Figure 2 tries to capture the synergy derived from this interrelatedness.

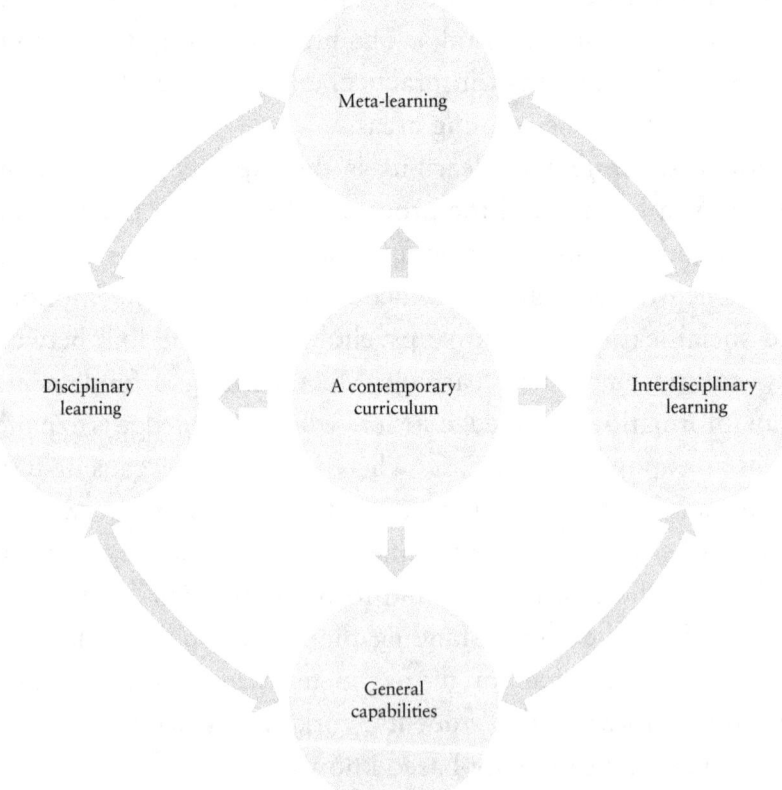

Figure 2: The dynamic relationship between key components of the contemporary official curriculum

Although they are present in the Australian Curriculum the four components identified by the case study exist mainly in isolation, and three of them—interdisciplinary learning, general capabilities and meta-learning—are each seriously underdeveloped. That is, the case study has alerted us to some significant shortcomings with current curriculum approaches. What should be done?

Given that the four curriculum components already exist, albeit in an emaciated form, the first step is to identify the problems that are holding them back. In other words, what are the embedded blockages hindering the development of a well-theorised model of the official curriculum comprising all four aspects in a dynamic relationship? There are at least four major blockages.

What are the blockages to change?
Blockage 1: The binary of disciplinary and interdisciplinary knowledge

A key blockage to keeping the four elements of the curriculum in productive tension is the singular dominance of the disciplines in the public debate and in the Australian Curriculum. The case study demonstrates that having the capacity to think and work across disciplinary boundaries is fundamental in the 21st century, if people are to understand and participate in addressing social, political, cultural and environmental problems. And yet any proposal to introduce the idea of interdisciplinary learning is rejected by those who hold that attempts to integrate the established disciplines will 'dumb down' the curriculum.

According to many conservative commentators, unless the curriculum comprises disciplinary-based knowledge about our shared cultural heritage, it is not rigorous. The argument, which resides firmly within the revert camp described in Chapter 7, makes a fundamental error: it assumes that those arguing for an interdisciplinary approach are antagonistic to disciplinary-based knowledge. Such an argument draws a false binary between discipline-based and interdisciplinary-based study.

Speaking at a STEM conference in 2018, Australia's Chief Scientist Alan Finkel told his audience that the current attempts in education to introduce students to interdisciplinary learning—he calls it 'generalist learning'—are misguided because

> a discipline is like a ladder. You have to put in the effort to climb it, step by step, with structure and sequence, accepting the guidance of your teachers. Learn the principle. Do the practice. Apply the skills. Repeat . . . Mastering a discipline is mastering your destiny. (Finkel, 2018)

Apart from the traditional approach to didactic pedagogy, Dr Finkel is creating a false dichotomy. In fact, the relationship between these knowledge forms is symbiotic: interdisciplinary work cannot be achieved without the existence of the disciplines, and disciplinary study is sterile if key disciplinary concepts from different disciplines are not combined in the service of addressing key societal issues. A central curriculum question is when and how to study disciplinary-based knowledge in isolation, and when and how to combine the knowledge across disciplines to understand big issues, problems and dilemmas.

A singular discipline-based approach fails to grapple with the application of knowledge. Thus the knowledge, skills and dispositions identified in Chapter 9 demand an ability to understand an issue holistically and a capacity to integrate key concepts drawn from a number of learning areas. Disciplinary silos are a necessary but insufficient means to face up to the challenges of the 21st century. As Fadel et al. (2015) argue, more innovative knowledge maps and an understanding of the interrelatedness of knowledge are needed for deep learning.

The binary thinking that assumes that to introduce students to interdisciplinary knowledge is to downgrade the importance of disciplinary knowledge is a stumbling block to creating a contemporary curriculum. It has prevailed for too long in the public arena, and needs to be challenged. In the absence of support from curriculum agencies, it is up to educators to lead the public debate by showcasing some of the dynamic interdisciplinary work in which students in many schools around the country are engaged, and demonstrating how such work confirms, consolidates and builds on the disciplines. This could be done not only through printed and online resources, but also through community exhibitions and workshops.

In addition, more assistance with approaches to interdisciplinary programs could be provided to teachers. For example, the Australian Curriculum is organised around learning areas that select and sequence knowledge from specific disciplines. However, although ACARA claims that there is nothing to prevent interdisciplinary study, the reality is that there is no mechanism in the official curriculum to signal where an interdisciplinary approach might be used, nor are there resources to assist teachers to develop such approaches. An important task in the next phase of the Australian Curriculum is for ACARA to conduct a close examination of the ways in which interdisciplinary work can be facilitated through its learning areas.

Blockage 2: The dominant understanding about how an official curriculum can cater for all students.

Another blockage involves the disputes about how educational disadvantage is best addressed in the official curriculum. The dominant view maintains that since disciplines comprise the best knowledge that has been produced by communities of specialist disciplinary researchers over time, then it is the 'entitlement of all pupils' (Young, 2014).[16] That is, it is claimed that the

---

16 It is important to remember that school subjects/learning areas are not disciplines, they are selections of knowledge from disciplines that are organised and sequenced in the official curriculum.

disciplinary-based learning areas represent the 'powerful knowledge' of any society to which all students should have the same access. This is the view of the connection between equity and the curriculum upon which the Australian Curriculum is based.

The problem is that the same-curriculum-for-all approach ignores the extent to which the selected valued knowledge of the official curriculum is socially and culturally bound, and reflects the values and interests of the groups that design it. Many curriculum scholars argue that this official knowledge is the 'knowledge of the powerful', rather than 'powerful knowledge', because it favours those students who have the largest helpings of the dominant social and cultural capital (e.g., Apple, 1993, 2004). At the same time, it alienates students from educationally disadvantaged backgrounds, whose lifeworld knowledge is not represented in the official curriculum. If all students are entitled to have access to society's powerful knowledge, then a fundamental educational challenge today—made even more urgent by the kinds of issues outlined in the case study in Chapter 9—is to involve students from educationally disadvantaged backgrounds in a curriculum that gives them access to powerful knowledge, but doesn't marginalise their social and cultural knowledge.

Taking account of the culturally diverse knowledge of students from educationally disadvantaged backgrounds is not to ignore disciplinary knowledge, as is commonly claimed. The fact is that lifeworld knowledge can be powerfully connected to disciplinary knowledge, making the learning experience both more interesting and more meaningful to students. Zipin (2017) makes a cogent argument for what he calls a problematic-based curriculum approach, where students engage in projects exploring problematic conditions in their everyday lives, such as ecosystem damage or increasing youth unemployment, informed by disciplinary-based study. Far from marginalising disciplinary knowledge, such an approach contextualises it to produce more powerful learning. But if such approaches are to move into the mainstream they need research and resources; and they also need advocacy. As Brennan and Zipin (2018) argue:

> Curriculum that includes 'all'—equivalently in terms of empowerment, but respectful of meaningful diversity within the empowered 'all'—cannot emerge if an assimilative 'same' is distributed to all. The trend toward a false 'equity' in the name of 'the same' must be contested. (Brennan & Zipin, 2018, p. 186)

Put another way, redistribution of powerful knowledge is an impoverished social justice principle unless it is accompanied by both the 'recognition' of the community values and knowledges of diverse student groups, as well as the 'representation' of these groups in the decision-making processes that produce the official curriculum (Fraser, 2009). The Australian Curriculum is based on an inadequate understanding of equity that needs to be addressed urgently.

Blockage 3: Undeveloped understandings about the nature, role and purposes of the general capabilities

One of the four aspects of a 21st-century curriculum that emerged from the case study is a number of capabilities. These are skills, dispositions and values that people need to meet the demands and challenges produced by the fourth industrial revolution. In the Australian Curriculum they are known as general capabilities.[17] Some of those suggested by the case study, such as creative and critical thinking, ethical behaviour and intercultural understanding, are already represented in the Australian Curriculum,

---

17 At the time of writing, there are seven general capabilities in the Australian Curriculum: literacy; numeracy; information and communication technology capability; critical and creative thinking; personal and social capability; ethical understanding; and intercultural understanding.

while others, such as the ability to be discerning and sceptical and to have a disposition for the common good, might be considered in the future. Given the importance of the general capabilities to 21st-century learning, adding to or modifying them should be a regular process based on the kind of analysis of contemporary societal trends suggested in this book. For example, consideration of whether or not the current list of general capabilities is still fit for purpose could be part of the process when the national goals of schooling are developed each decade.

However, for at least two decades the official attitude to what are now called general capabilities has been too cavalier. They have tended to operate with what has been described as a 'name and hope' approach, comprising a list of generic capabilities accompanied by an exhortation to teachers to incorporate them into teaching and assessment across education systems (Reid, 2006). The Gonski Review, aimed at achieving educational excellence in Australian schools, is an example of this approach. Although its report (2018, pp. 38–40) argues that the general capabilities should be taken seriously, the discussion in the report about the ways in which the status of the general capabilities can be raised in the curriculum through professional development and the provision of resources ignores the issues that have impeded their take-up. Thus, the report jumps from an identification of the problem of lack of take-up, to its solution—without exploring the reasons for the problem. This leads to its Recommendation 7—to strengthen the general capabilities through developing 'learning progressions' (Gonski, 2018, p. 41)—a recommendation that can only diminish, if not destroy, the power and potential of the general capabilities. I will explain this claim by reference to some of the current blockages.

There are at least two important conceptual issues that must be addressed if the potential of the general capabilities is to be realised. The first issue relates to understanding the ontology of capabilities and their *purposes* in the curriculum. There is a widely held but misguided view that the idea of capabilities somehow signals the end of a discipline-based curriculum. From England, Daisy Christodolou asserts that 'the movement for twenty-first century skills is a codeword for removing knowledge from the curriculum' (2014, p. 52). And in Australia, as soon as the Gonski Report was released, some commentators attacked it on the basis that strengthening the general capabilities meant abandoning the disciplines (e.g., Ashman, 2018; Donnelly, 2018b). But the argument that knowledge and capabilities cannot coexist is to establish another false dichotomy—a problem that can only be addressed by clarifying the ontology and purpose of capabilities.

There are many ways to think about the essence and purpose of capabilities, with most of them focusing solely on education. For example, one report argues that the overarching purpose of the capabilities is to develop skills and dispositions that, in concert with disciplinary and interdisciplinary knowledge, enable individuals to act in and on the world through creating knowledge, making decisions, taking action and assuming responsibility (Lucas & Smith, 2018). In other words, the capabilities are part of a package. They provide the glue for a 21st-century curriculum by contributing the kinds of generic skills and dispositions that enable disciplinary and interdisciplinary knowledge to be used in the world. Put another way, capabilities cannot exist or be taught in a vacuum, they can only be taught through a relationship with knowledge.

Another approach, initially developed by Sen (2001) and Nussbaum (2011), has a broader sweep, starting from the perspective of development studies and welfare economics. Sen argues that economic growth is too narrow an indicator for judging the quality of life in a developing society. It doesn't, for example, tell us about those aspects of life that go to making up a quality of life; and nor does it help in understanding the barriers to equity and wellbeing. Instead, Sen argues for the importance of what he calls *capabilities to function*—that is focusing on what people are able to do and be, on the quality of their life, and on removing obstacles in their lives so that they have more freedom to live the kind of life they find valuable.

Sen suggests that there are four aspects of 'capabilities to function': *commodities* (goods and services), which provide the means to achieve; *capabilities*, which offer the opportunity to achieve; *agency freedom*, which is the ability of individuals to choose and pursue goals that one values and the freedom do to so; and *functioning*, which is the actual achievement of a capability (the beings and doings). All of this is, of course, circumscribed by the social, cultural and political environment, as well as by individual characteristics. Education's role from this perspective is largely focused on *capabilities*, which are a combination of knowledge (disciplinary and interdisciplinary) and skills (what are currently called general capabilities). But the approach also implies that educators need to be involved in the social and political considerations that contribute to 'functionings' within schools and in the wider community.

These two very different approaches to understanding the capabilities have been described in order to demonstrate that there is a lot of important conceptual work to do before the potential of capabilities can be realised. It should be noted that while both approaches come from very different ideological stables, they both assume a symbiotic relationship between knowledge and capabilities. The point is, how can we expect general capabilities to be taught in the Australian curriculum in the absence of this prior theoretical work?

The reason that capabilities are identified and named separately from learning areas is to ensure that their development is not a haphazard or hit-and-miss affair. It means that educators can ensure that capabilities are systematically developed across the curriculum with increasing levels of sophistication. Thus, agreeing on the purposes of capabilities will help to deflect the binary thinking holding back their role in the curriculum. At the same time, there is some important explanatory work needed in the education and wider communities. This could be achieved by ACARA producing and disseminating an accessible resource that clarifies the relationship between disciplinary/interdisciplinary knowledge and capabilities. Until such work is done, proposals about developing the general capabilities will continue to meet opposition based on a false premise.

The second conceptual matter relates to the *meaning* of each of the specific general capabilities. ACARA has made an effort to describe and sequence a continua of each of the seven general capabilities across the levels of the Australian Curriculum for each learning area (ACARA, 2018). The Gonski Report (2018) has taken this approach much further, recommending that a number of progression levels for each capability be developed. Unfortunately, breaking each capability up into a number of small pieces can only diminish their potential to be used holistically. That is, while it is important for educators to decide how to increase the sophistication of capabilities across year levels, atomising them through many progression levels is to lose their essence. A more productive approach would be to conduct a professional conversation about the meaning of each capability, informed by the latest research and writing. Such a conversation would enable educators to hold a coherent picture of the whole, even while they focus on aspects of a specific capability.

The example of the general capability *critical and creative thinking* can be used to demonstrate this point. There have been many books and articles written about the nature of creativity and critical thinking (e.g., Brandt & Eagleman, 2017; Sternberg, 2003). Each provides intriguing insights into the nature of creativity, and its relationship to critical thinking. Some suggest that creative and critical thinking are complementary, others that they are very different entities and that it is unhelpful to combine them in the way the Australian Curriculum has done. Some offer fascinating insights into ideas for teaching for both. For example, a recent book (Brandt & Eagleman, 2017) on creativity explores what is happening in the brain when people are being creative and suggests, on the basis of analysing hundreds of instances of creativity, that there are three common creative processes across many fields of endeavour: bending (changing shape), breaking (taking apart and reassembling) and blending (combining).

Such studies deepen our understanding of the capability *creativity* and, at the same time, spark ideas about relevant, appropriate and interesting learning activities across all learning areas. Thus, deeper, research-informed discussions across learning areas about the meaning of each general capability would enhance the possibility of developing a consistent, whole-of-school approach to teaching them, and would enable each capability to be taught as a coherent whole, rather than broken into dozens of pieces.

Apart from the lack of conceptual clarity that is blocking the potential of the capabilities from being realised, there are some important practical matters. Developing the general capabilities through the learning areas is easier said than done. It requires teachers to identify what role their learning area might have in the development of specific capabilities, and share this across learning areas so that there is a consistent and coherent school-wide approach. It also means paying attention to the question of whether capabilities should be assessed separately or in conjunction with content knowledge, or both; and how capability development can be reported on through mechanisms like portfolios.

If the capability agenda is to advance—as the case study in Chapter 9 suggests it must—teachers will need support in the form of professional development and resources. But before that can happen, there is an urgent need to grapple with the kinds of prior conceptual questions that have been described in this section. If the Gonski Report (2018) referred to earlier had done this, it would not have fallen into the trap of proposing progression levels, which are a technocratic, lock-step approach to the general capabilities that can only stunt their transformative potential. Rather than opt for such a narrow approach, it is to be hoped that the Education Council will support some trials across Australia of approaches to teaching for, and assessing and reporting on, the general capabilities in ways that capture the transformative spirit and purpose of the capability approach.

Blockage 4: The fragmented approach to understanding learning, and the predilection for silver bullets

If the case study shows anything, it is that in the 21st century people must have the capacity to learn, transfer knowledge to different contexts, relearn on the basis of new knowledge or experience, and keep on learning. However, there is little point in talking about the need for people to be lifelong learners if they don't have the capacity to learn new things in new contexts. The speed of knowledge production makes an understanding of the processes of learning the sine qua non of the future.

For some time now, there has been general agreement among educators that learning to learn is fundamental to the knowledge society. And yet there hasn't been a strong focus on clarifying the concept. Indeed, as Gert Biesta (2016) argues, learning has become a catch-all term for education, emptied of meaning because it seldom relates to what is learned and the purpose of learning. Since it is based on the purposes of education, the process proposed in this book has cleared that obstacle, but in so doing has laid bare the need for deeper understandings of learning.

Of course, there have been some serious efforts to grapple with the concept of learning to learn. For example, the Australian Curriculum includes metacognition in the critical and creative thinking general capability, describing it in the following way:

> Students think about thinking (metacognition), reflect on actions and processes, and transfer knowledge into new contexts to

create alternatives or open up possibilities. They apply knowledge gained in one context to clarify another. In developing and acting with critical and creative thinking, students:
- think about thinking (metacognition)
- reflect on processes
- transfer knowledge into new contexts. (ACARA, 2018)

However, although this approach does some of the work needed, if an understanding of learning is as central as the case study suggests, then it needs to be expanded beyond its current position as a small part of one of seven capabilities and become one of the key curriculum components. In so doing, account should be taken of some of the most recent insights into cognition. For these reasons, it is suggested that a focus on *learning to learn* be elevated to become one of the four central components of the official curriculum, and be named *meta-learning*.[18]

One of the earliest users of the term meta-learning was the Australian John Biggs, who described it as a state of being aware of, and taking control of, one's learning, including the learner's conceptions of learning, epistemological beliefs, and learning processes and skills (Biggs, 1985). According to him, the meta-learner is able to evaluate the effectiveness of their learning approaches, and regulate them for the learning activity. Of course, Biggs was writing more than 30 years ago, so his understanding of meta-learning did not take into account some of the developments in learning that have occurred over that time.

More recently, Charles Fadel and colleagues (2015) resurrected the concept of meta-learning, arguing that it should be one of the central pillars of a 21st-century curriculum. They proposed

---

18 The term 'meta-learning' is now being used in the artificial intelligence field, with approaches being developed where machines rely less on a huge amounts of data, and more on the capacity to learn how to learn. Given some of the insights in Chapter 9 (including the challenges to our humanness), it is perhaps more urgent that humans develop the capacity!

expanding 'metacognition' by adding the idea of 'growth mindset'—a concept developed by the psychologist Carol Dweck (2016) about the importance of beliefs about one's capacities to learn. However, this version of meta-learning omits a number of important elements of learning and needs further extension.

In the past few years, there have been some significant advances in such areas as cognitive psychology, with new insights into metacognition, cognitive neuroscience and research into the links between the functioning of the brain and learning, and the collapse of Freud's division of brain and mind (Hardiman, 2017). In addition, the role of emotions in learning, sensory learning, the relationship between learning and physical movement, epistemological beliefs and learning, interpersonal and intrapersonal learning and play-based learning are extending our understandings about learning. These and other areas of research demonstrate that an understanding of the processes of learning involves a range of aspects such as the social, emotional, physical and sensory, which go beyond a focus on metacognition.

In my view, an important future project for education is to combine the insights from these various fields into a coherent program/framework designed to help students to reflect on and understand processes of learning in particular contexts and for particular purposes, and to assist teachers with their planning. Given that researchers are just starting to scratch the surface of understandings about the brain, it would need to be a tentative and ongoing project. It would require collaboration between researchers who represent a number of the research fields that look at different aspects of learning, and educators with a knowledge of pedagogy and curriculum design. The developed program—which would focus on teaching students to understand, develop, monitor, regulate and evaluate approaches to learning—would span the year levels of schooling and connect to the other three components of the curriculum, and be continuously updated as new research comes in.

Such a project would have to surmount a number of barriers. The biggest of these is the predilection for education systems to grab the latest passing fad and promote it as a silver bullet. For example, springing from one or more of the learning research fields listed above are educational programs and approaches such as *mindfulness, growth mindset, brain-based learning* and *multiple intelligences*. Based on empirical research, each approach claims that it will boost learning and leave students with a lifelong capacity to learn new things in new contexts. Often the approaches are well packaged and marketed, and taken up with enthusiasm, if not zeal, by educators looking for ways to enhance student learning.

However, all is not as it seems. The speed with which these programs are adopted often leads to problems. Sometimes there is unease about the efficacy of the approaches themselves and the research upon which they are based; and sometimes the developers of the idea itself become concerned about the approach being oversimplified, or distorted beyond recognition. The well-known mindset theory can be used as an example.

Carol Dweck's mindset theory was developed from her research in cognitive psychology and, over the past twenty years, has become one of the most popular and well-known approaches in education (Dweck, 2016). Based on the idea that intelligence is not fixed but can grow through effort and perseverance, Dweck's views have spread across the world through professional development programs, conferences and packaged resources. Many education systems have urged teachers to adopt growth-mindset approaches.

The problem is that the missionary zeal with which the idea has been embraced has masked some basic issues. A key concern is the questions being asked about the mindset research itself, with some researchers casting doubt about the methodology and the statistics that were used to produce the findings, and others claiming that the results have not been replicated in similar studies. Some researchers, like John Hattie, ask whether a growth mindset is needed for all tasks, or whether it might not be more desirable to have a fixed mindset in some circumstances (Hazell, 2017). A further concern is that the idea allows deep-seated structural factors such as poverty, socioeconomic status and ethnicity to be ignored simply by blaming students or teachers for not having growth mindsets. This academic debate will continue as the idea is tested for its rigour.

However, there is also a practical problem related to mindset theory in use, with claims that many teachers have oversimplified the idea. Carol Dweck herself is worried about this, saying that some teachers are adopting what she calls a 'false mindset':

> Often when we see kids who aren't learning well, we might feel frustrated or defensive, thinking it reflects on us as educators. It's often tempting to not feel it is our fault. So we might say the child has a fixed mindset, without understanding instead that, as educators, it is our responsibility to create a context in which a growth mindset can flourish.
>
> Yes, another misunderstanding [of growth mindset] that might apply to lower-achieving children is the oversimplification of growth mindset into just [being about] effort. Teachers were just praising effort that was not effective, saying 'Wow, you tried really hard!' But students know that if they didn't make progress and you're praising them, it's a consolation prize. They also know you think they can't do any better. So this kind of growth-mindset idea was misappropriated to try to make kids feel good when they were not achieving. (Dweck, quoted in Gross-Loh, 2016)

Indeed, Dweck is so concerned about what she sees as misuse of her work that she has republished her original book and included a new section on 'false mindset' (Dweck, 2016).

None of this is to denigrate the concept of mindset, or those who are using it. Similar stories could be told about educational programs based on mindfulness, or multiple intelligences, or the use of brain-based theory—each of which promises much but is also the subject of considerable criticism. But it does provide a salutary lesson about picking up the latest idea as a silver bullet, and running with it, rather than placing the idea within a broader theoretical framework, rigorously checking out the research and engaging teachers in ongoing professional development.

Based on this experience, if the idea of meta-learning has some merit, then there are some important tasks to be undertaken before it can be introduced. These include doing a synthesis of the latest research about meta-learning, and turning this into a holistic framework spanning its various cognitive, emotional, physical, sensory and epistemological dimensions. Given the current stage of development, such work would need to be ongoing with the framework amended as knowledge expands.

One way to avoid the silver bullet syndrome that has plagued some of the earlier simplistic attempts to translate the results of brain research into pedagogical proposals would be to have educators working with researchers in other fields, and in other projects. An example of the latter is the Australian Brain Initiative, which includes an aim to 'harness the plasticity of the brain to improve teaching and learning outcomes', and to 'transform the way we teach and learn' (Australian Brain Alliance Steering Committee, 2016). Clearly educators need to get in on the ground floor of such projects, not only to provide educational expertise to them, but also to add to the sum of professional knowledge about learning.

Summary of the implications of the case study for the official curriculum

In this chapter, having considered the case study in Chapter 9, a number of possibilities for modifications and additions to the official Australian Curriculum have been suggested. These are summarised in Table 4 below. It has been argued that a contemporary curriculum would comprise four interrelated elements—disciplinary knowledge, interdisciplinary teaching, capabilities and meta-learning. Each of these elements is present, to a greater or lesser extent, in the current curriculum, with meta-learning representing the biggest change.

However, there are a number of blockages to the successful implementation and integration of the four elements, not the least of which is the tendency to treat them in isolation and to think about them in 'either-or' terms. Perhaps the biggest lesson to emerge from this analysis is that key curriculum concepts have been under-theorised. There is an urgent need for policy-makers to engage with educators and researchers in deeper conversations about the official curriculum, rather than to marginalise professional expertise and impose standardised, narrow and superficial curriculum policy dictates.

Table 4: Summary of implications for the intended curriculum

Sub-questions	Aspect: Curriculum
What did the case study tell us, and what curriculum changes are suggested by it?	There are four components to a 21st-century curriculum: • Disciplinary knowledge • Interdisciplinary capacities • Capabilities • Meta-learning
What are some blockages to change happening?	• The binary of disciplinary and interdisciplinary knowledge • Disputes about how an official curriculum can cater for all students • Disputes about the nature, role and purposes of the general capabilities • The fragmented approach to understanding learning and the predilection for silver bullets

Chapter 11

New pedagogical directions

Apart from guidance about what should be taught, the case study of the fourth industrial revolution undertaken in Chapter 9 also unearths a number of implications for pedagogy.[19] Obviously it doesn't specify the teaching approaches to use, but it does suggest the kinds of learning outcomes that should guide this choice. Such outcomes include developing people who are able to learn both independently and collaboratively, who are open-minded and critical thinkers with the capacity to transfer knowledge and apply their skills to different contexts, who understand the processes of learning and the strengths or weaknesses they bring to them, and who have a disposition for the common good. The challenge for all educators is to select teaching approaches that nurture these outcomes. The approaches must be flexible to suit a range of contexts, and be able to cater for individual as well as collaborative group learning. So Step 5 of the model proposed in Part 3 asks the question: what are

---

19 Pedagogy in this section is understood to mean the theory and practice of teaching in order to influence student learning. It includes approaches to teaching as well as the environment in which teaching occurs.

the implications for pedagogy, and what blockages need to be removed?

It is proposed that the key to pedagogies, now and in the future, is held by teachers who come to a learning situation with a toolkit of teaching approaches from which they will select—often in conjunction with students—a teaching and assessment approach. That approach will be one they believe best suits the purpose of the topic or program; the context of the study; student—individual and group—interests, readiness and needs; and the resources available. Now this may sound like an obvious proposal, but it will be argued that much of the contemporary debate about teaching assumes there to be just one teaching approach or a limited range of them; or offers a disparate set of variables that are claimed to promote best practice no matter the context or situation.

Put another way, the argument is that pedagogies of the future hinge on the development of a framework for teaching that enables teachers to use their professional knowledge by selecting approaches appropriate to the students in their care. Such a framework should not be imposed or set in stone, but refined and improved through practice, research and professional conversations. In this way, teachers would genuinely be curriculum and learning designers, rather than technicians implementing an imposed pedagogy organised through, say, online generic resources designed by technology companies.

In order to illustrate this idea, Table 5 represents a possible framework containing a number of elements that are described below. The idea is that the teacher(s) will move across the columns, broadly from left to right, piecing together an approach to teaching a particular aspect of the official curriculum such as a concept, theme or topic, for a particular group of students.

The selection will be informed by teaching principles, which sit atop the framework. The principles being suggested include that the pedagogy will be inclusive, rigorous, personalised, relevant, collaborative and engaging; enable knowledge integration; and promote higher-order thinking and deep understanding. It is important to note that the framework is posited on the understanding that learning is both an individual and a social process.

At the foot of the framework are a list of the values and practices that are established and nurtured in the classroom and school environment. These have been separated out because, unlike much of the teaching framework, they are not a matter of choice but are developed and practised in an ongoing way. The examples listed are ones that are suggested by the case study and are consistent with beliefs about the purposes, values and principles described in Chapter 8. They include respectful relationships, trust, democratic practices, an appreciation of diversity, equity, and an intolerance of discrimination and bullying. Given the power of the hidden curriculum, these cultural values should be transparent and worked on continuously.

In the framework itself, the first column covers the broad learning philosophy that underpins the teaching and assessment approaches represented in the next four columns to the right. Thus:

View of learning/orientation: Clearly any pedagogy is based, consciously or sub-consciously, on a view about how people learn best in particular situations. It is on the basis of this view that teachers make decisions about how the teaching will be conducted, including the role of the teacher. For example, two of the best-known theories of learning are instructivism and constructivism. The former is teacher-centred, with the teacher devising strategies to convey knowledge to students; and the latter more student-centred, with students actively constructing their own knowledge by connecting new ideas to existing ideas, with the teacher as a facilitator of learning. Despite claims by some commentators that to adopt one view of learning is to reject the other (e.g., Donnelly, 2018c), this framework suggests that different learning theories can be used at different times,

Principles of teaching e.g., inclusive, rigorous, personalised, relevant, collaborative, engaging, knowledge integration, promote higher-order thinking and deep understanding.

Orientation (based on views of learning)	Teaching Approaches and Models	Teaching Strategies	Assessment		Class Organisation
Student-centred ⇅ **Teacher-centred**	**Process approaches** e.g. • information processing • personal • social • play-based **Directive approaches** e.g. • explicit / transmission • demonstration • direct instruction • mastery learning	**Examples:** • role play • teacher exposition • group work • debates • performances • field work • use of ICT • flipped classroom	**Reference** e.g. • self • standard • criterion • norm **Reporting** e.g. • marks • grades • descriptions	**Technique** e.g. • portfolios • tests • essays • multiple-choice	**Examples:** • *across year levels* (small or large groups depending on purpose) • classes organised in *group formation* • year-level classes in *formal class structure*

Classroom and school environment: e.g., respectful relationships, trust, democratic, appreciation of diversity, equity, intolerance of discrimination and bullying.

with the selection dependent on the purpose and context of the learning and the stage of readiness of the learners. This is not to say that there should not be a particular emphasis—indeed, the case study shows the importance of student-centred approaches. But it makes the point that it is not inconsistent for example, to combine some directive teaching for a specific purpose with a largely student-centred approach.

Teaching approaches and models: Once the general learning orientation has been determined, the next step is to decide on the model of teaching to be used, which will be consistent with the orientation and the purpose of the topic being studied. At the teacher-centred end of the continuum are more directive approaches, which include behaviourist models, such as direct instruction and mastery learning, and directive models, such as explicit teaching. Common to all of them is a process of presenting content, getting students to internalise the content through activities and then assessing to check for understanding (I do, we do, you do). At the student-centred end are process approaches to teaching (Joyce et al., 2017). These include information process models, such as concept attainment or inquiry; personal models, such as negotiated/co-design models of project-based learning; and social models, such as the controversial social issues model. The selection of the model will depend on the purpose of the topic being studied. Common to each of the process models is an intention that students develop metacognitive understandings about how to use the process in a different setting, as well as gaining content knowledge.[20]

Teaching strategies: Once teachers have decided on the model of teaching, the next step is to plan the teaching strategies to be employed during the steps of the model. These are not tied to any particular orientation and include such standard practices as

---

[20] The use of teaching models like this might be a way of grounding some of the pedagogical frameworks like 'deep learning' (Fullan, Quinn & McEachen, 2018), which emphasise student agency, collaboration, and structured learning tasks, but tend not to use many of the well-developed models of teaching that exist.

role play, group work and debates, through to more possibilities enabled through ICTs, such as flipped learning and online investigations. The way in which each strategy is used depends on the model of teaching being used.

Assessment: Teachers will then determine the approach to assessment. This will be influenced by the purpose of the assessment—for example, whether it is formative, summative or diagnostic—and by the teaching orientation. The other important consideration is the reference point against which assessment judgements are to be made, spanning such approaches as criterion-, standards-, self- or norm-referenced assessments; and using a range of techniques (e.g., tests, essays, performance, portfolios, multiple choice, online) and feedback mechanisms (e.g., marks, grades, descriptions).

Organisation: A key practical consideration is the organisation of the school and classrooms. The dominant organisational model is year level–based classes, although within this model there are many practices depending on the orientation. For example, teacher-centred classes are more likely to have a formal classroom seating structure, while student-centred approaches lend themselves to more flexible group-based arrangements. The advent of new technologies has led to practices that break the traditional model, with students sometimes organised into large groups, or working individually online, or spending time in the community or in the school's outdoor environment, depending on the particular purposes of the teaching. Increasingly, the year–level model is breaking down with students being grouped variously across traditional year levels depending on progress and interests.

Some advantages of the proposed framework

It is important to note that the framework is not exhaustive or complete. Its main purpose here has been to make four key points. First, it demonstrates the serious limitations of the current debates about teaching quality and standards. There has been a tendency to assume that decisions about pedagogy are an either/or proposition. Take, for example, the pronouncement by Kevin Donnelly in *The Weekend Australian* that

> Australian students have suffered as a result of a constructivist approach to education, which favoured student-centred learning in a democratic interactive environment over explicit teaching and firm discipline . . . we need a greater focus on more effective pedagogy and what happens in the classroom. Teachers need to be in control. (Urban, 2018, p. 7)

Assertions like this not only misrepresent the approaches they counterpose, but incorrectly assume there is one fixed best approach to teaching. In contrast, the framework demonstrates that pedagogies of the future depend on teachers selecting an approach, from a toolkit of approaches, that best suits the purpose of the topic or program, the context of the study, and students' interests, readiness and needs. At times this may be a student-centred teaching model; at other times it could involve explicit teaching. By widening the pedagogical options for teachers, the framework will contribute to deepening student learning.

Second, the framework demonstrates that pedagogical work is theoretical as well as practical, and that it is important to have a sound and consistent theoretical basis upon which to plan teaching approaches. The case study suggests that giving students agency and encouraging them to develop as independent as well as collaborative learners means building learning skills slowly and methodically during their time at school. It enables teachers to decide when students are ready to move to a more student-centred approach, while still allowing for teacher instruction when needed.

Third, a framework like this could be the basis of an ongoing professional conversation about teaching and learning, not only for professional development purposes but also to establish some agreed understandings across the profession about the meaning of key pedagogical concepts. It is on the basis of these discussions, as well as the outcomes of evaluation of practice and research, that the framework could be developed and refined. In this way it would be owned by the profession.

Fourth, the framework shows how new technologies can be used to expand the range of teaching strategies, without assuming that the presence of a new technology is itself a different approach to teaching. Virtual reality headsets, flipped classrooms or Chromebooks can be just as teacher-centred as traditional instructive approaches. However, the new technologies can extend the reach and scope of learning and so, as Greg Whitby argues, they offer ways by which the grip of traditional directive teaching models can be loosened if informed by a strong pedagogical rationale (Whitby, 2013). More than this, it offers a way to ensure that robots developed to support teachers (Sommer & Boden, 2018) do not replicate the standard transmission version of education but, rather, are sufficiently flexible to be able to change to suit the decisions teachers have made about the appropriate learning orientation, teaching model, and strategies decided on for a specific child, class or study program.

In summary, it is argued that pedagogies for the future should be about teachers, increasingly in partnerships with students, deciding on an orientation to learning and selecting a teaching model and strategies consistent with the aim of the topic/unit and the needs and readiness of the students.

What are the blockages?
Blockage 1: The dominant tendency to view teaching approaches as a choice between explicit instruction or inquiry

One of the major blockages to implementing a framework like the one described above is the dominant dichotomy between teacher-directed instruction and inquiry. This dichotomy is pushed by influential organisations like the OECD, and repeated by international consultancy groups like McKinsey and Company, and think tanks such as the Centre for Independent Studies. A full explanation of the problem, requires a description of what is actually involved in inquiry-based learning.

When first designed, inquiry approaches were prominent in the teaching of science (e.g., Schwab, 1962), but slowly they spread to other areas of the curriculum. Over time a number of different models of inquiry learning have developed, such as inductive and deductive inquiry, discovery learning and problem-solving. Common to each is the focus on individual or group investigations of problems, scenarios, puzzles and dilemmas. However, approaches vary in such matters as purpose, method and sequence of steps; and in terms of the extent to which teachers are in control of topic choice and process (e.g., structured and controlled inquiry) or students have greater agency (e.g., guided and free inquiry). In other words, there is no homogeneous inquiry model of teaching. Those using the term need to be explicit about the approach to which they are referring.

Apart from variations within inquiry approaches, it is important to understand that while they have a student-centred emphasis, they were never considered to be the only teaching model with that emphasis. Well-known books on models of teaching describe many other models of teaching that are student-centred, but each has a very different purpose (e.g., Joyce et al., 2017). Thus, the concept attainment model is specifically structured so that students learn the process of understanding and applying key concepts, while the controversial issues model is designed to assist students to learn how to understand and develop a stance on an important social or political issue (Moore et al., 1991, Chapter 2). In summary, the inquiry model can take a number of different forms and is just one of a number of models in the teaching toolkit. However, this is not how inquiry teaching is represented in the public arena. A recent example will be used to demonstrate the extent of confusion that exists.

In the 2015 PISA tests, the OECD interviewed fifteen-year-old students about the extent to which they experienced inquiry teaching in their science classes. The questions seemed to be based on the idea that inquiry in science involved students in practical experiments, class debates, and the teacher giving them time to explain ideas and use the scientific method. As argued above, this is a very limited idea of what constitutes inquiry learning, and in any case the questions only related to science teaching. This notwithstanding, the OECD then aggregated the responses and correlated them with the PISA test scores to come up with an index of inquiry-based instruction purporting to show that, for many countries, there was a negative correlation between inquiry-based teaching and success in the science tests (OECD, 2016b).

Despite the distorted view of inquiry and the inadequate methodology upon which the OECD report was based, once the report hit the public domain its findings were further distorted. Commentators and consultants turned the results—remember, they were based on interviews about science teaching with fifteen-year-olds—into generalisations about teaching in all subjects across all year levels. At the same time, they reinforced the misconception that there are only two forms of teaching. Thus, a recent McKinsey and Company report argues:

> There are two dominant types of teaching practices. The first is 'teacher-directed instruction,' in which the teacher explains and demonstrates ideas, considers questions, and leads classroom discussions. The second is 'inquiry-based teaching,' in which students are given a more prominent role in their own learning—for example, by developing their own hypotheses and experiments. We analyzed the PISA results to understand the relative impact of each of these practices. In all five regions, when teachers took the lead, scores were generally higher, and

the more inquiry-based learning, the lower the scores. (Mourshed et al., 2017)

In *The Australian*, two researchers from the Centre for Independent Studies used the same study to claim that:

> Consistent with decades of research ... OECD findings indicate that teacher-directed instruction is highly beneficial for student learning. Inquiry-based teaching, which in some ways is the opposite of teacher-directed instruction, is characterised by class-led learning activities and encouragement of discovery through group collaboration. This style of teaching is associated with less student achievement. (Joseph & Buckingham, 2018)

In both examples, the authors rely on flawed research, lack understanding about what is entailed in inquiry teaching, and construct teaching as a simple either/or proposition between direct instruction or inquiry. Unfortunately, ill-informed views like these have become dominant in public discussions about education. They are a significant impediment to the possibilities of developing richer and deeper pedagogies capable of meeting the challenges of the future. The proposal for a framework like the one suggested above may help the profession to speak back to those who simplify pedagogical work.

Blockage 2: The appropriation of progressive ideas for instrumental purposes

The Introduction to this book described the standardising influence of the global education reform movement (GERM) in shaping education policy around the world through high-stakes testing and intrusive forms of accountability. If the case study shows anything, it is that standardising education in this way is incompatible with the kind of pedagogy needed for the 21st century. However, it is sometimes not immediately apparent that GERM-like policies are being proposed, because recently there has been a tendency to connect them to an idea, or clothe them in a language, that appears to be consistent with 21st-century learning. This masks the instrumentalism at the core of the policies. The report of the Gonski Review into ways to 'achieve excellence in Australian Schools' is an example of this process at work (Gonski, 2018).

The central proposal in the Gonski 2.0 report relates to 'personalised learning' (Gonski et al., 2018). Using the well-rehearsed argument that all students should be able to demonstrate a year's learning growth every year, the report recommends that schools move from a curriculum based on year levels to one expressed as 'learning progressions' independent of year or age. It claims that this move will enable schools to better meet the individual learning needs of students.

The report says that the straitjacket of organising by year levels is a remnant of the industrial era and must change if schools are to come into the 21st century. The idea of scrapping year levels potentially creates a greater flexibility for students and teachers. Rather than aiming curriculum at the average of a cohort of students at a particular age, teachers are able to 'personalise' the curriculum by making an individual student's readiness for learning the key criterion for curriculum planning. Of course, a number of schools already do this, and in many other schools where year levels are still used teachers use adaptive or differentiated teaching to cater for individual interests.

There is always a danger that removing year levels will result in a return to streaming if teachers group students according to perceived ability levels rather than age, but this is not an automatic outcome and can be guarded against. However, the question of removing year-level structures cannot be separated from the issue of what is taught and how. And it is here that it seems the report has taken a progressive idea like *personalisation* and colonised it with the *standardisation* agenda.

There are many different approaches to personalising learning. Some approaches enable teachers and students to negotiate learning programs based on students' interests and learning needs. For example, in the Big Picture schools in Australia and the US, students investigate topics or issues individually or in groups and report on their findings (e.g., Washor & Mojkowski, 2014). The key to the learning involves skilled teachers assisting students to make connections across the curriculum as understandings about key concepts and discipline-based knowledge are built through negotiation and collaboration. It is an approach that prizes student agency and group as well as individual activities, and recognises that learning is not a linear and scripted activity.

But that is not the version of personalised learning proposed in the Gonski Report (2018). It recommends an approach where content and skills across every area of the curriculum are atomised into bite-sized chunks of knowledge, and then sequenced into progression levels. Students work on their own and, at regular points, use online assessment tools to test their readiness for the next chunk of knowledge. Once one level is mastered, they move onto the next.

The report recommends that, over the next five years, the recently developed and implemented Australian Curriculum should be rewritten so that *every* learning area and *every* general capability is written up as a number of progression levels. It offers an example of 'spelling' being broken into a 16-level progression, with students mastering each step before moving lock-step onto the next level (Gonski et al., 2018, p. 33).

The Gonski version of personalised learning is not unlike the model of direct instruction developed in the 1960s (Bereiter & Englemann, 1966). That model is a tightly scripted, step-by-step approach that follows a predetermined sequence through packaged resource materials. Assessment follows each instruction phase with tests aligned to the behavioural goals of the program.

The results are fed back to the teacher and student and the stage is then set for the next phase (Luke, 2014).

The direct instruction process bears an uncanny resemblance to what the Gonski Report is proposing, whereby students 'advance incrementally' (p. 31) through progression levels and at regular intervals are assessed by an online formative assessment tool, which is 'calibrated against the learning progressions—that measures student attainment and growth in attainment levels over time' (Gonski et al., 2018. p. 63). The description of the online assessment tool is revealing.

> Critically, the tool should hold a large store of validated assessment items and tasks in multiple learning areas, mapped across the learning progressions to enable teachers to measure a student's attainment. Teachers could select items of their choice from the pool of appropriate assessment tasks, in order to identify the level of attainment of a student in a particular subject or learning area prior to tailoring teaching or developing their learning unit. The student would then undertake those tasks, either electronically or as an open-ended task set by the teacher. The task could be marked via the online tool, or the teacher could validate or mark the task and enter the scores. On the basis of the evidence provided about the student's current level of attainment, the teacher could then personalise the next challenge in learning for the student, assisted by suggestions made by the learning tool. (Gonski et al., 2018, p. 64)

Although there is an apparent nod in the direction of teacher decision-making, it is inevitable that the tightly scripted nature of the process would result in the use of online resources. The recent manifestation of this model in the US has been a financial bonanza for private technology companies such as Summit, owned by Facebook Founder Mark Zuckerberg. These companies have developed online tests and learning resources capable of tracking the progress of, and devising programs for, individual students. By redefining the purposes of education, minimising the role of the teacher and constructing education as a consumer product, these companies have made personalised learning a form of 'customised privatization' (Sen 2016).

With such programs, students become individual automatons moving through standardised progression levels. Creativity and critical thinking are stifled as students are steered down a path '. . . that has already been laid out with pavement, guardrails and penalties for daring to wander further' (Greene, 2019). And teachers are increasingly excluded from the process, as planning and decision-making is done by algorithms. The result is a narrow and highly individualised learning experience that is unlikely to prepare students adequately for the challenges of the 21st century. After reviewing a number of personalised learning programmes in the United States, a report by the National Education Policy Center concludes that they

> reflect a hyper-rational approach to curriculum and pedagogy that limits students' agency, narrows what they can learn in school, and limits schools' ability to respond effectively to a diverse student body. (Boninger, Molner & Saldana, 2019, p. 4)

The point is that 'personalised learning' can take many forms. Some approaches will liberate learners, some will tightly constrain them. The model being proposed by the report is more likely to do the latter, and thus work against the benefits that could accrue from abandoning the organisation of schools by year levels. In this way, a progressive idea like personalised learning is enlisted to serve a highly instrumentalist agenda. Far from moving schools away from an industrial model, it would entrench such a model. It is not claimed that this is the intention of the proposal, but surely, at the very least, the idea of progression levels and online formative assessment tools needs to be trialled and be the subject of widespread professional discussions, rather than imposed by decree. More than this, if personalised learning is the goal, then why not evaluate a number of different models of personalised learning rather than sanction an immediate overhaul of the Australian Curriculum based on one narrow and untried approach?

At the time of writing, the Gonski Report (Gonski, 2018) is still under consideration by education ministers from around the country. It is hoped that they will look closely at the version of personalised learning it proposes, and ensure that the approach they support is one that nurtures a love and a passion for learning, not one that reduces learning to a checklist.

Summary

In this chapter, having considered the case study in Chapter 9, a number of suggestions have been made about the key features of a contemporary pedagogy. Table 6 provides a summary of these. The central point is that an education that aims to prepare young people for a world where they will have to be ready to adapt and change to meet new challenges must itself be flexible. It is time to jettison the tiresome and outmoded discourse that insists that there is only one best approach to teaching. It should be replaced by an understanding that the key to pedagogies of the future lies in enabling teachers to use their professional knowledge to select approaches appropriate to the learning context, including the needs and interests of students in their care.

Rather than imposing on teachers scripted, narrow and ready-made 'solutions', the focus of a new educational narrative should be on professional conversations about such matters as values and principles, theories of learning, teaching approaches and models, teaching strategies, assessment and so on. In this way, teachers would genuinely be curriculum and learning designers, rather than technicians. Of course, if such a model was to work, there would need to be some supportive conditions. It is to this matter that Chapter 12 will turn.

Table 6: Summary of implications for pedagogy

Sub-questions	Aspect: Pedagogy
What did the case study tell us, and what pedagogical changes are suggested by it?	Pedagogies of the future depend on teachers selecting an approach, from a toolkit of approaches, which best suits the purpose of the topic or program, the context of the study, and students' interests, readiness and needs. This means that the profession requires a framework for teaching and learning which includes principles, views of learning, models of teaching, strategies of teaching, assessment and class organisation.
What are some blockages to change happening?	• The dominant tendency to view teaching approaches as a choice between explicit instruction or inquiry. • The appropriation of progressive ideas for instrumental purposes.

Chapter 12

New directions in system-wide and school-based cultures

It is pointless attempting to introduce a new narrative into an educational environment that is dominated by policy and practice inconsistent with it. Parts 1 and 2 of this book described a number of aspects of the current policy regime that would need to change if the new ideas are to have any chance of success. But it is not enough to just remove the impediments to planned change. If the change is to occur in more than name only, then there must also be a set of supporting conditions. These range from physical resources, to human resources, to the culture of an organisation—and they need to be tailored to suit the demands of the change. For example, if new skills and understandings for staff are required, then appropriate professional development programs are needed. The role of Step 6 of the proposed model is to identify the conditions and practices that will support the change.

The most important element of the supporting conditions is consistency between the changes and the culture into which they are introduced. This means ensuring that the values and practices of schools and systems do not exude characteristics that are incompatible with the changes. Even the most dynamic change ideas will founder on the rock of an incompatible culture. Thus, a key step is to identify what kind of cultures will help to build and sustain the changes suggested by the new narrative, rather than work against them. I have chosen to examine the question of cultural consistency as an example of what is involved.

What conditions and practices are consistent with the new narrative?

In 1968, Philip Jackson coined the term 'the hidden curriculum' to describe the unofficial or unintended lessons, values and perspectives that students learn in schools. They are hidden because they are not a part of the formal curriculum, as lessons and learning activities are. Rather, students absorb lessons through, for example, school rules about what behaviours are considered unacceptable. The lessons are hidden because they are unexamined. They may reinforce the formal curriculum or they may contradict it by revealing inconsistencies between what a school says are its purposes and values of education, and what students actually learn (Jackson, 1968).

Just as Jackson exposed the hidden curriculum in a school, so too is there a hidden curriculum in education systems as a whole. The policies and practices of systems reveal a lot about what is valued and not valued. And, like schools, the ways in which education systems operate can contradict the fine-sounding mission statements and strategic plans that invariably litter the organisational landscape.

In general terms, there must be consistency between purposes and aims, policies and practices, and culture in the context of education systems as well as schools. There are a number of aspects of a culture compatible with the curriculum and pedagogical changes suggested in Chapters 10 and 11, and this chapter will deal with two of them. Since public education systems and schools comprise the largest proportion of educational providers in Australia, they will be the reference point where examples are needed. However, many of the ideas are just as relevant to private schools, although they need to be interpreted in the different context of private schooling.

A culture of research and inquiry[21]

Many of the issues facing educators today are context-bound: they are not amenable to universal solutions. The case study demonstrates that educational systems and schools in the future must have cultures that eschew certainty and dogmatism. This doesn't mean that decisions are never made but, rather, that decisions are provisional, based on the best available evidence and always open to review. In other words, there needs to be a culture of open-minded discussion and debate wherein the participants can systematically review and inquire into questions, problems and dilemmas that face them in their specific contexts. This is very different to an approach involving the wholesale transport of strategies or programs developed elsewhere, or the imposition of ideas labelled as 'best practice' with the insistence that no other ideas can entertained.

In the contemporary environment, educators face the considerable challenge of designing curricula for local contexts that are flexible enough to address the rapid growth of knowledge and that recognise the increasing religious, cultural and ethnic diversity of their student populations. This means that, in the 21st century, educators need to be inquirers into educational practice who can question their routine practices and assumptions and

---

21 This section is based on a paper written for the South Australian Department of Education (Reid, 2004).

who are capable of individually and collaboratively investigating the effects of their teaching on student learning (e.g., Darling-Hammond, 2000; Farrell, 2004; Reid, 2004; Campbell & Groundwater-Smith, 2010; Nichols & Cormack, 2017). From this perspective, educators are people who learn from teaching, rather than people who have finished learning how to teach (Darling-Hammond, 2000).

This is not something that is done only at the level of individual classrooms: it should be a culture that permeates the school and education system. Not only will it result in better decision-making at these levels, but it will serve as an important pedagogical tool. After all, if it is the task of educators to develop in children and young people the learning dispositions and capacities to think critically, flexibly and creatively, then educators must possess and model these capacities.

The need to create a culture of research and inquiry[22] is one of the most important challenges facing educational institutions, their systems and their leaders in the future. How much more productive would it be for education systems to put resources into developing and sustaining cultures of inquiry and research, than into instruments of measurement and surveillance?

There are many fine examples of inquiry-based practices in schools. And yet the administrative/bureaucratic arms of most

---

22 This section draws a distinction between research as a formal peer-reviewed activity, and inquiry as a systematic investigation into practice that does not need to conform to the accepted conventions of research. All educators should be inquirers into educational practice; and some educators may be researchers. This distinction emphasises the importance of the one to the other, but removes from practitioners the unrealistic expectation that whenever they embark on a process of inquiry they must conform to the widely accepted conventions of research. The distinction between inquiry and research also points to the centrality of research to a culture of inquiry. Published research should be a rich source of information for those engaged in reflecting on their work practices or in developing policy, provided that it is not simply transferred unproblematically, but is read in the context of the issues being explored through inquiry. It ensures that inquiry is open, not closed; expansive, not constrained. In this way inquiry and research can be seen as different sides of the same coin.

education systems don't function in the same way. Unless the operations of the central offices in education systems are also consistent with research and inquiry, they can actually work against it. This can only be avoided by shifting from the dominant managerial model of educational organisation and change to an authentic inquiry-based model.

Challenging the dominant managerial model

Most education systems operate through a model that constructs teachers as technicians whose job it is to implement plans, policies and products developed by others. In this dominant organisational model, a policy, plan or product is developed in a central office—usually as a response to emerging needs or a government priority—and the task of schools is to implement that policy. Ironically, one of the responses to the speed of change has been to strengthen this view. Thus, often the reaction to the challenges of the new environment has been to devise and implement more policy, produce more packages and construct more accountability mechanisms. It is an old response to a new challenge.

Of course, the extent to which this happens in isolation from schools varies depending on the system. Sometimes there are processes of consultation. But invariably the common element of a consultation is a focus on the detail—it rarely involves conceptualising the key ideas. In addition, the consultation process itself is usually in relation to the product or policy at a particular point in time: it stops when the development phase is over.

This managerial model does not of itself prevent practitioner inquiry in schools. However, there is no *systematic* way by which the knowledge and insights that emerge from inquiry, or the issues that are identified as a consequence of it, are fed into the policy-making process on a regular basis. Inquiry is confined largely to the school; improving classroom practice but contributing only marginally to the wider professional knowledge in the system.

There are a number of problems with this dominant managerial model. First, the model impoverishes the knowledge base for educational policy-making. By foregrounding bureaucratic knowledge, the model marginalises arguably the most consequential knowledge in an education system: school-based knowledge produced by educators in the context of working with children and young people.

Second, the model promotes a façade of change. All that has been discovered about educational change over the past twenty years tells us that change occurs when those whose practice is the focus of change are involved in the process of challenging and rethinking the assumptions and theories upon which their practice is based (e.g., Fullan, 2015). Unless this happens, imposed change in the form of a new product is simply filtered through the lens of established beliefs and practices, and is colonised by that practice. The same things are done with new labels.

Third, the model limits the possibilities for real improvement, because it does not encourage educators to focus on deepening their understanding about teaching and learning. It implies that new products (a new resource, curriculum or off-the-shelf model) can solve teaching issues or problems. This is not to denigrate the use of quality resources but, rather, to make the point that the use of these resources is most powerful in the context of inquiring into possible answers to teaching and learning issues, not as something to be seen as a magic elixir for all contexts.

Finally, the model promotes superficial forms of external accountability. It understands accountability to mean closing the gap between what is developed (or aspired to) centrally and the outcomes in schools. When the gap refuses to close, the fault is invariably located with schools. This is a spurious form of accountability because it encourages educators to hide issues and problems, rather than discuss them openly. In so doing, it contributes to the privatisation of professional practice. Real accountability comes from genuine attempts to deepen understandings about teaching and learning through inquiry and research, in an atmosphere of collaboration and trust. Imposed accountability encourages smoke screens; real accountability is transparent.

In summary, the dominant model of system organisation establishes a dislocation between the central office and schools. The model creates its own logic and dynamic. On the basis of this model, the response to the new demands of the contemporary environment is to develop another product or policy to meet the challenges of new times. Invariably, inside the new approach beats the heart of the old model of change. Is there an alternative? How else might a system operate?

Towards an inquiry-based approach to educational change and improvement

A culture of research and inquiry represents a different way to think about the system and its approach to educational change and improvement. Here, inquiry is added to the mix in a way that alters the dynamics and logic of the system. It is the fuel that makes the system work. In this model, educators are engaged in inquiry and research into the issues, problems, puzzles and dilemmas associated with their educational practice. The new knowledge and the issues that emerge from this process feed back into classrooms and schools, deepening learning and reinvigorating professional discussion and debate. But, more than this, there are structures and processes in place that enable these insights and issues from inquiry to be aggregated and responded to by the central office, such as in the form of changing policy or providing resources to meet emerging demands.

It is important to understand that this model is not a bottom-up approach. Rather, it is constructed upon an iterative dynamic between the various layers of the system. This dynamic doesn't obviate the need for the central identification of systems' priorities. Governments will continue to express priorities, although they may be affected by the knowledge that is being produced, and issues that are being identified, by schools. But much of the work of the central office will involve responding to the implications of what is emerging from inquiry and research *in relation to these priorities*—meeting the needs identified by schools for learning and professional development resources, providing arenas in which the new professional knowledge can be shared and debated, altering policies to reflect new insights and so on.

It is also important to understand that the model is not suggesting that the only worthwhile knowledge is that produced in schools. Far from it. The sort of inquiry being argued for here must draw on innovative ideas and the latest research that is produced elsewhere, in other contexts and other countries. The difference is that these ideas would not be imposed or seen as best practice. They would be treated as part of the inquiry mix, examined systematically by those engaged in the business of educating.

In summary, contemporary challenges demand educators who practise inquiry and research as a way of professional being. However, such an aspiration cannot be realised unless a system-wide culture is established that is consistent with inquiry and research. It means rethinking dominant forms of educational organisation at a system-wide level. This is a leadership challenge of some magnitude, but models consistent with research and inquiry have the potential to:

- foster deeper understandings about teaching and learning and thus enhance student learning outcomes
- generate excitement and enthusiasm as educational ideas are discussed and new professional knowledge is shared within schools, and across education systems as a whole

- lead to genuine forms of accountability that are based on collaborative efforts to identify problems and their causes
- make central office policy, plans and products responsive to the needs of schools
- contribute to the breaking down of the 'them and us' culture that has developed in education systems in recent years
- lead to genuine change because it is consistent with what is known about the factors that promote change
- unite public education systems around a focus on student learning, while enabling a great deal of flexibility within schools
- contest the limited and instrumental notion of evidence-based policy by replacing it with an approach that is rigorous and context-specific.

But just as there are many advantages, so too are there dangers. A key one of these is the danger of superficiality, where the concept of inquiry is embraced enthusiastically but applied uncritically to many activities and issues without a deep understanding of the conditions that are needed for it to flourish. It is crucial that an education system moves gradually, thoughtfully and systematically to build a culture of research and inquiry. There are a number of conditions that must exist to foster such a culture.

First, it demands an environment—at the school or system-wide level—that encourages discussion and debate involving the widest range of voices possible, and insists on dialogue that is respectful, open-minded, tolerant, wholehearted and civil and rejects certainty and dogmatism. A key component of such an environment is trust, with educators feeling free to talk about difficulties and concerns in their teaching without being penalised. The features of an environment conducive to inquiry and research could be made explicit in each institution or education system through the development of a charter or manifesto which becomes the touchstone for the organisation.²³

Second, there must be a willingness to commit resources to enabling a culture of research and inquiry. Given that practitioner inquiry involves a range of skills and approaches, there is a need for ongoing professional development to assist educators to enhance their inquiry skills and understandings throughout their careers. Becoming skilled at professional inquiry should be seen as an ongoing project.

Third, there must be processes and structures within schools and across systems, that enable the knowledge gained from inquiry to be shared. This might involve sharing new insights about teaching and learning with colleagues, collaborating with neighbouring schools on inquiry into common concerns, and identifying issues that need to be addressed at the school or system level. In this way, education systems based on a culture of research and inquiry are alive with discussion and debate as fresh ideas and new knowledge is circulated.

The standardising approach to education policy is almost the opposite of what is needed today. It fosters a culture of blame, fear, competition, certainty and dogmatism, where professional debate is stifled and the 'answers' to complex educational issues are imposed. Such an environment is the antithesis of what is needed for 21st-century education and is in stark contrast to a culture of open-minded research and inquiry.

---

23 There are many examples which might guide the development of such a manifesto. One brilliant example written as far back as 1951 is Bertrand Russell's *Liberal Decalogue,* which summarised his vision for the responsibilities of a teacher. The Decalogue synthesised many of the themes from Russell's writing over the years, including the purpose of education, the value of uncertainty, and the importance of critical thinking and intelligent criticism (Russell, 1967, p. 71—72).

A culture that promotes and sustains the characteristics of public education

One of the key insights emerging from the case study in Chapter 9 is that all citizens should possess the understandings, skills and dispositions to promote the common/public good in our society. That is, so many of the challenges today demand that people have a commitment to the collective good, rather than an interest solely in what will benefit the individual. As Robert Reich describes it:

> (The) common good . . . is a set of shared commitments—to the rule of law, and to the spirit as well as the letter of the law; to our democratic institutions of government; to truth; to tolerance of our differences; to equal political rights and equal opportunity; to participating in our civic life, and making necessary sacrifices for the ideals we hold in common. We must share these commitments if we are to have a functioning society. They inform our judgments about right and wrong because they constitute our common good, Without them, there is no 'we'. (Reich, 2018, p. 182)

But how is a disposition for the common good nurtured?

If the common good is arrived at through rational, respectful and critical deliberation among the public, then the quality of that participation in the public sphere is a function of the skills, understandings and dispositions that the public can bring to bear. And how is this quality assured? Our systems of education are the primary mechanisms through which the public is renewed (Feinberg, 2012). If they place a greater emphasis on the individual purposes of education than they do on its public purposes, then the public sphere can only be weakened as people lose the capacity to exchange views respectfully with each other and to think beyond individual interests. From a common-good perspective, the role of education is to maintain and improve the conditions for deliberation and debate in the public sphere.

It is this role that has been most neglected in educational discourse. As was argued in Parts 1 and 2 of this book, the prevailing neoliberal ideology emphasising choice in an education market has downgraded education to a commodity largely benefiting individuals. As a consequence, it has reduced public education to being perceived as a safety net. A push back against this dominant trend requires a clear articulation of what it means for public education to serve the common good. This will provide a reference point for policy and practice that foregrounds the public benefits of public education and resists the trend to privatise it.

There are at least two key aspects to consider. The first is to create and maintain a system of education that itself models a commitment to the common good. This includes ensuring that education is available free to all on a comparatively equal playing field and on a non-exclusionary basis, and has policy and practices consistent with, and promoting, the common good *in* education. The second aspect relates to the role of education *for* the common good. This involves schools developing the skills, dispositions and understandings of children and young people, such that they can engage—respectfully and thoughtfully—with others in deliberation about the common good in the broader society.

There are a number of characteristics that are consistent with developing an education in and for the common good. The fact is that public schools are well positioned to sustain and build each of them because the characteristics are embedded in the very essence of public education. However, in many countries there have been various attempts over the past two decades to dismantle public education through overt privatisation programs, or through policies designed to make public schools behave as though they are private (Bonnor & Caro, 2007; Watkins, 2012; Katz, 2013; Reid, 2016). Such policies are counterproductive because they are destroying the very qualities and characteristics needed for education systems to meet the challenges of the future. Thus, a new educational narrative would understand the importance of ensuring that public schools retain their publicness, and protect and enhance the characteristics that lie at the essence of being public (Reid, 2016 & 2017). These characteristics include the following.

An ethical and socially just system and culture

Education is one of the most fundamental of human rights—it should not be apportioned according to parents' financial capacity. Thus, while there will always be differences in educational outcomes, these should not be as a result of differences in parental wealth or influence. This means that there must be a relentless focus on addressing equity in education in public systems. This has, of course, been the rhetorical aspiration of educational institutions for decades. But it assumes a greater urgency in an era of a knowledge society where success, in school and beyond, will be largely determined by the capabilities students possess. An educational institution taking this task seriously will build into its culture an ongoing interrogation of its programs and activities against the central criterion of social justice.

A public education for the common good must create the conditions in which all children and young people can flourish. In particular, there should be strategies that accommodate those children and young people who have arrived at school from educationally disadvantaged backgrounds and require particular forms of support. This support will often be additional to that offered to more advantaged students in an effort to establish an environment where educational outcomes are determined by effort and capacity, not birth. In a public system promoting the common good, issues would always be looked at from the perspectives of the least advantaged by giving them a genuine say in developing the policies and practices of schools and systems.

In addition, it is important to ensure that the formal and informal curriculum of schools models and practises a commitment to equity, and so develops young people with the understandings and commitments needed to work towards a more ethical, sustainable and socially just world.

A democratic system and school culture

The case study demonstrates the importance of capacities for democratic participation. As one of the key sites in Australian society for the development of these capacities, public schools and their systems must exemplify and practise democracy at all levels by ensuring that there are structures and processes that give an authentic voice to all. Sometimes, democratic decision-making in educational institutions is constructed as though it were an optional extra, something that can be tried once the bigger decisions have been made and things have settled down. And even then, watered-down versions of democracy are often established whereby a modicum of consultation conceals where the real power lies. But establishing democratic institutions can no longer be a matter of choice, or done half-heartedly. Surely, in conditions of uncertainty, a deliberative democracy that encourages deep and respectful dialogue from multiple perspectives is more likely to result in sound decision-making than one that assumes that wisdom resides in a person holding a position of responsibility.

If schools are to develop citizens who can participate actively in the public sphere; if they are to cultivate people who can work collaboratively with and respect others from diverse cultures; and if they are to foster the sort of trust that comes from genuine engagement by all those who are affected by decisions, particularly those with the weakest and most marginalised voices, then educational leaders must work to establish the conditions that allow democracy to flourish in their institutions. This commitment to democracy should also permeate the school, classroom and curriculum so that students develop the capabilities to play active roles in decision-making in civil society. Fostering student agency is an important component of a new educational narrative.

A culture of diversity and cohesion

Since public schools exist in every local community and are accessible to all, they are microcosms of that community, reflecting a rich diversity of cultures and backgrounds. There are a number of benefits that flow from diversity being stitched into the fabric of every public school. For a start, local and international research demonstrates that the greater the social mix of a school, the better the academic outcomes (Teese, 2011; Wells et al., 2016; Ayscue et al., 2017). But beyond academic outcomes are the rich social and cultural learnings that accrue from students doing the hard work of learning from and through the diversity that is part of the daily life of a public school. This experience serves to stretch personal horizons beyond the familiar, encouraging the capacity to appreciate and respect difference, even while it contributes to enhancing the cohesiveness of a multicultural society. In brief, public schools provide spaces in our society where young people can be inducted into a civic culture of recognising and vigorously engaging with their differences. Rather than simply educating individuals, they turn a group of people with a host of differences into a civic entity called a public.

If, as the case study demonstrates, schools must prepare young people for an increasingly global and mobile world, then it is important to maintain the diversity that comes naturally to public schools. It would be contradictory to cocoon students from diversity, as happens in more homogeneous educational settings. And yet if Australia embraces educational choice through market-based approaches and vouchers in its public school systems, it would face an increasing social and cultural stratification of our public schools (Ho, 2017, 2019). This must not happen to public education in Australia, as it has in countries like the US and England, which have been captured by the choice agenda.

A collaborative and community-based culture

The common good demands that people not only coexist peacefully but actually work together to achieve benefits for the whole community, rather than just for individuals or special interest groups. This makes collaboration a central feature of a public education system focused on the common good. Public schools collaborate to achieve success and to build the strength and quality of the whole public system. In such a system, the failure of one school diminishes all schools. This means that, rather than hiding good practice or ideas in order to preserve market advantage, the emphasis is on disseminating and sharing within and across schools. Such an approach also models to students how and why to collaborate for the common good. It would be inconsistent for a public education system to urge its schools to develop collaborative skills in its students, while forcing the same schools to engage in fierce competition.

Public schools also have the advantage of existing within the local communities from which their student population is drawn, and so there is a strong bond between schools and their communities. Such close links enable each community to use the facilities and resources of its public school to enhance local community life; and each public school to use the resources of the community in its learning programs—to the benefit of both school and community. Policies that ignore community links—such as those that allow choice between public schools and so promote people travelling across communities to get to their chosen school—destroy the considerable learning and community benefits that accrue from the localness of public schools.

A culture of innovation

One of the biggest challenges facing educators today is how to develop a curriculum (including approaches to teaching and learning) that meets the individual needs of students by personalising curriculum, as well as ensuring that all students are prepared for the demands of the contemporary world. The challenges include the rapidity of technological change, the creation of new economies, the increasing mobility of people, and the fact that communities are more culturally and ethnically diverse than they have ever been. The scale and pace of this change means that schools must constantly adapt to meet the new demands, making creativity and innovation in designing for the future important aspects of education. As a result, approaches to innovation need to be more systematic and extensive than they have ever been. Given that public schools serve the vast bulk of students in our community (including the vast majority of students who are educationally disadvantaged), it is the public sector that must take the lead in developing, trialling and implementing innovative practice in such areas as teaching and learning, school organisation and community interaction. That is, public systems should be at the cutting edge of innovation in educational practice, while also seeking to develop capabilities for innovation in students. A more privatised public system is less likely to promote innovation. The pressure of market competition can often lead to a culture of copying those schools that appear to be successful, which leads to homogeneity and conformity of practice.

Summary

It is pointless attempting to introduce a new educational narrative into environments where existing policies and practices work against the proposed changes. However, just as important as removing impediments to change is the idea of introducing and sustaining the kind of environments that will help the change to grow and flourish (Step 6). This chapter has suggested two significant school and system cultural attributes—a culture of research and inquiry, and a culture that promotes the characteristics of public education—that are not only sympathetic to, but would positively promote, the new approaches to education policy suggested in this book. There are other such attributes that would contribute, and it is up to schools and systems to decide on those they believe would best advance the purposes, values and principles of the new educational narrative in their specific contexts. Without taking this step seriously, no amount of new strategies will disrupt entrenched educational practices.

Epilogue

Towards a new narrative for Australian education

The challenge

This book began with the assertion that the dominant discourse in Australian education is standardising and favours certainty, uniformity, individualism, competition and quantification in education policy. The case study of the technological disruption wrought by the fourth industrial revolution (Chapter 9) makes it clear that the standardising agenda goes nowhere near what is required of an education system that aims to equip people to meet the challenges of the future. Indeed, it is counterproductive to achieving such outcomes. If that is so, then ways must be found to shift our educational discourse from one based on certainty to one that embraces the complexity, ambiguity and uncertainty of contemporary times. In short, Australia needs a new educational narrative.

Such an aspiration slips easily off the tongue, but is not so easy to deliver. It requires more than simply removing or modifying those policies that are causing damage. Unless the core elements of the neoliberal discourse in education—choice, the education market, competition, self-interest and a neglect of the common good and so on—are challenged and removed, new policies will simply be subsumed by the same ideological baggage: old wine in new bottles. Challenging neoliberalism in education demands more fundamental change. In particular it means making sure that a new educational narrative comprises features that contest the key elements of neoliberalism in education.

Responding to the challenge: Elements of a new educational narrative

The book has proposed that there are three elements of a new narrative for Australian education. Each has a part to play, and they are also interrelated.

Element 1—Purposes

Educational purposes establish why education is needed in the contemporary world. They are the bedrock of the wider educational narrative. It has been proposed that there are four major purposes of education. The first assumes education to be important in its own right, and aims to develop individuals to their fullest potential. The other three purposes are social and utilitarian and involve developing individuals for the work force, as citizens in a democracy, and as members of social and cultural communities.

Being clear about 'purposes', rather than simply assuming them, is important for a new educational narrative because it protects policy and practice from becoming narrow and pinched. Keeping all four purposes in productive tension ensures that policy responds as much to the democratic, individual, social and cultural purposes as it does to the economic purpose that has been dominant in the past two decades. That is, in a new educational narrative, purposes play a key role in charting the territory to be covered by policy while also marking out the boundaries.

Element 2—Values and principles

It is pointless clarifying the purposes of education without fleshing out the detail that is covered by each purpose. When that work is done, policy enters the domain of values and principles. That is, what is aimed to be achieved by each purpose cannot be a value-free exercise since it is fundamentally about the kind of society we want. For example, decisions about how to develop citizens for our democracy depend on such issues as the version of democracy being used, beliefs about the extent and nature of citizen participation required, and understandings about the arenas in which democratic practices can occur. The judgements about each of these matters are inescapably informed by a set of prior values and principles that must be developed through wide-ranging professional and community discussion, and must always be open to review.

The book has made the case for a number of values and principles that are in opposition to those contained in a neoliberal discourse. The central one has been the belief that the challenges of living in the contemporary world demand a commitment to the common good, whereby people look out for others, think about the effects of individual and social actions on the wider community, and are not obsessed with how they can advance their individual interests. This might include such values as social justice, care, compassion, empathy, collaboration, equity, community, generosity, integrity, respect and so on.

Once articulated in a new educational narrative, the values, as well as the principles that give practical expression to them, play the role of a reference point or benchmark against which policy and practice can be judged. Their existence does not remove debates about policy—obviously there are many different strategies that can be consistent with a common set of values and principles; rather, they help to identify those strategies that would work against the broad intent of the narrative.

Element 3—A process

A fundamental task of education is to help people develop the capacities they need to shape, rather than passively accept, future societal trends. But if the future is really unknown and unknowable, what does this mean for devising educational programs? This book has argued that the best way to plan an education program is to use a process that enables educators and policy-makers, in an ongoing way, to understand, monitor, evaluate and assess broad societal trends and the changes they are bringing in the various arenas covered by the purposes of education. Thus, the third element of a new educational narrative involves building a process into the rhythms of an educational organisation or system.

The key role of the process is to identify changes, at the level of schools and education systems, that could be made to such things as curriculum, pedagogy, school structures and culture in response to the societal changes being investigated. That is, rather than being reliant on the traditional stop–start approach to curriculum and organisational development, change is ongoing. In addition, such a process could break the stranglehold of the standardising approach to education policy by providing the evidence needed to substantiate policies and practices that are better suited to the changing environment of the 21st century.

Combining the elements to create a new educational narrative

All three elements of the new educational narrative—purposes, values and principles, and an agreed process—are interrelated and must be addressed. Thus the purposes, values and principles serve as reference points for deciding on the kinds of strategies that are suggested by the process.

Reflecting on the new narrative

Chapter 8 proposed a six-step process that employed the three elements of the new educational narrative, and the rest of the book then modelled the process using a case study of the fourth industrial revolution. The process helped to identify the contours of an official curriculum and pedagogy that meets the challenges of the future; and it clarified the kinds of obstacles that need to be addressed, and cultures that need to be fostered, if the change proposals are to be more than wishful thinking. Obviously, there are any number of ways in which a similar process might be developed and refined over time, so the six-step process proposed in this book is illustrative only. Nonetheless, the experience of trialling it suggests that there are a number of advantages of using such a process.

First, not only did the analysis of the fourth industrial revolution help to identify the kinds of capacities needed for the 21st century, but it provided a very strong case for the educational strategies that are best placed to develop the capacities. For example, in the face of the evidence revealed by the case study, it would be difficult for policy-makers to deny the importance of interdisciplinary learning, meta-learning, or a range of teaching approaches. Vague assertions about rigour or the need for a single approach to teaching would not suffice. Indeed, in the face of the information from the case study about the effects of technological disruption on work, the economy and social and cultural life, the standardising agenda looks emaciated, if not lifeless.

Second, the process does not assume a curriculum tabula rasa. It highlights the need for some additions, modifications or changes to what is currently taught and how, rather than the wholesale changes that often occur with the traditional model of curriculum change every five to ten years, which are so disruptive and onerous for teachers. Within this process there could be a stimulating school or system-wide focus on a specific societal trend for a period of time, say a year. During the course of this discussion (conferences, circulation of papers, seminars, research projects etc.) the information and insights gained could contribute to teaching programs. Importantly, as the discussion moved to Steps 4–6 of the model, there could be sharing across the school or system about how particular capacities are currently accommodated, as well as what might need to change. In this way, change becomes an organic process growing out of educational discussion and debate and resulting in ongoing adaptation or modification.

Third, the process demonstrates a way by which educators can be brought back into the heart of decision-making about education, rather than being the marginalised recipients of policies and strategies developed by those divorced from the classroom. It could revitalise the profession with the stimulation and the fun of discussion and debate about key ideas; and, at the same time, offer means by which parents and students can be involved, sharing insights and experiences and so building a real sense of a learning community. In short, the process is consistent with the values and principles suggested for a new educational narrative. After all, it is pointless to aspire to develop values such as trust, collaboration, respect and empathy, if the top-down decisions of policy-makers treat educators and their school communities with disdain.

Fourth, the process could contribute to a new way for education systems to function and plan. Thus, at the school level it could be used as the basis for a discussion about curriculum and pedagogy, with policy and/or practices being modified or changed as a result. At the system-wide level, there could be an aggregation of ideas emerging from schools, with the system responding by providing resources, offering relevant professional development programs, changing policy or altering the official curriculum. In other words, the process suggests a way to establish a more dynamic relationship between schools and systems—one based on partnership, rather than the current model of top-down imposition. In this way, the fulcrum of the standardising model would shift from schools serving policy-makers, to the other way around.

Using the new educational narrative: An alternative policy agenda

It is important to recognise that a new educational narrative does not remove policy disagreement. Rather it changes the terrain on which the disagreement is based. If there is largely bipartisan agreement about the sorts of purposes, principles and values described in this book, and these are genuinely used as reference points for policy debates, then the zeitgeist of Australian education policy will have shifted from its current myopic focus on standardisation to one that embraces uncertainty and complexity.

Within a new educational narrative, disagreement about specific policies would involve debate about which policy best realises the agreed values and principles, with participants using research and experience to make their judgements. In order to see how this plays out, it might be useful to look at how the new educational narrative would change some key areas of education policy. The term 'futures-focused' has been used to describe the new narrative, and the examples will assume the values and principles suggested in Chapter 8.

Choice, competition and public education

A neoliberal policy narrative involves individuals choosing between schools, thus creating competition between schools. Flowing from this logic, public schools are independent and in competition, with 'customers' provided with data from standardised test results to help them make their choice.

In contrast, a futures-focused narrative would recognise that 'choice' of schools is an illusion, since choice is constrained or non-existent for most. In free market education systems, some schools succeed and many are residualised. Thus the logic of the new narrative would be to ensure that every local community has properly funded, well-resourced public schools that collaborate and share in order to maximise the strength of each school and the public system as a whole. From this perspective, policies promoting 'independent public schools' make little sense. Instead, policy would aim to enhance the public characteristics of public schools and resist attempts to privatise them, overtly or by stealth.

Accountability

A neoliberal logic believes that education quality can be measured through standardised testing in a narrow range of areas, usually literacy and numeracy. Associated with this is a belief in the infallibility of the test scores. The results of these tests are made public, league tables are often created, and there are consequences for schools that don't 'improve' test results, such as 'naming and shaming' schools or moving staff.

A futures-focused logic understands the importance of the public accountability of schools to the community. However, it is concerned that a focus on one test (such as NAPLAN) inevitably makes it high stakes, with all the associated negative outcomes, including narrowing what is valued in the curriculum. In addition, it recognises the deep-seated problems of validity and reliability associated with standardised tests (Wilson, 1997, 2007). A new educational narrative would support an approach to accountability that is much wider, richer, more diagnostic and less intrusive than the current method. Devising approaches that support student learning, assist teachers, and inform the community about the breadth and quality of what is being achieved in our schools is a priority for Australian education.

Some possibilities for alternative approaches already exist. For example, the Australian Curriculum is organised around achievement standards which are used by teachers to report student progress to parents and students, and yet these are ignored when systems seek to assess education standards. It is puzzling that teacher judgment is good enough for students but not for politicians and bureaucrats. Why not use the millions of dollars currently being expended on NAPLAN in a scheme which samples one or two learning areas each year using teacher judgment that has been assured through processes of teacher moderation? In one stroke Australia would have an approach to accountability that recognises the breadth of student learning across the curriculum, respects teacher professional judgment, and, through moderation, provides ongoing professional development and curriculum conversation.

Equity

The neoliberal policy narrative understands equity to involve 'closing the gap' in standardised test results between groups of students. Social and cultural factors are considered to be immaterial and are often described as being 'excuses' for poor educational outcomes. The focus is on using strategies such as direct and explicit instruction and scripted 'evidence-based' programs to drive up test results.

In contrast, a futures-focused narrative would recognise that achieving educational equity is a complex, long-term goal that can't be achieved by quick-fix 'solutions' that ignore the causes of inequalities in education. It would ensure that education policy is informed by a well-theorised understanding of equity, promotes ongoing research into curriculum and pedagogical approaches that factor in social and cultural factors in student learning, and ensures that the voices of those who are least advantaged in our education system are represented in decision-making (e.g., Laing et al., 2019).

Student assessment

A neoliberal narrative assumes that the fundamental purpose of student assessment is to compare students against one other. This informs students about where they are placed in a student cohort, fosters competition between students, aids the process of selection for various purposes, and, as it does this work, bestows student identity. In order to achieve this multiplicity of tasks, the favoured assessment approach is norm-referenced or standardised where marks, percentages or grades are allocated, so providing the precision needed for things like selection and awards. It is possible to see here all the key ingredients of the neoliberal philosophy at work—individualised, competitive, quantified and certain.

A futures-focused approach to assessment charges that norm-referenced assessment—although it is rarely admitted—is shot through with error (Wilson 2007), and anyway starts from the wrong educational assumptions. By contrast, it views assessment first and foremost as making an important contribution to student learning. Thus:

- assessment *as* learning involves students taking responsibility for their own learning by developing the capacities to judge the extent of their learning individually or with their peers;
- assessment *for* learning usually involves teachers and/or students using evidence from student work for feedback and to make decisions about the next stage of the learning journey;
- assessment *of* learning involves teachers and/or students making judgments about what has been learned and at what standard, using an agreed point of reference, such as standards or criteria.

From a futures-focused perspective, it is the professional judgement of teachers made in the context of their teaching that not only provides the best way to support student learning, but also the best evidence for system-wide accountability.

Decision-making and evidence

A neoliberal narrative assumes that 'best practice' in education can be identified and will suit all contexts. Thus, it promotes 'evidence-based' policy and practice that primarily uses the results of randomised control trials, or correlates a range of variables with the results of standardised tests. The sense of 'certainty' that is created by this approach flows across into the decision-making practices that are adopted in the neoliberal policy world. Thus, teachers are seen as people who must put into practice the 'knowledge' created by the evidence base. As a result, teachers are usually excluded from decision-making as policy is imposed on them, and associated accountability mechanisms monitor the extent of their compliance. Despite the fact that it is teachers' work that is the focus of policy, the professional expertise and judgement of teachers is not trusted.

A futures-focused policy narrative would understand that educational work is far more complex and context-specific than is appreciated by the standardising discourse. In particular a new educational narrative would place the practice-based knowledge created everyday by teachers at the heart of policy-making. This knowledge would be supported by research—both qualitative and quantitative—and effort would go into supporting teachers to be systematic about inquiring into the effects of their teaching. A new policy narrative would look for ways to support teachers in making professional judgements in their specific contexts, rather than handing them the 'answer' derived from one narrow approach that purports to be applicable to all contexts.

The five examples described above give a brief glimpse into what is entailed in adopting a new educational narrative. However, it is enough to demonstrate that when educational purposes, values and principles are articulated and then taken seriously rather than ignored, broad policy settings are established. After that, of course, the policy process will take its usual form, with debates about which particular strategies will produce the best results. The difference is that the new narrative establishes the terrain on which these debates occur, suggests who is involved in these debates and what constitutes 'evidence', and continues to act as a reference point for decision-making.

What is needed to establish a new educational narrative?

The installation of a new educational narrative will take some work, it won't just happen by agreeing to it. This last section of the book makes four suggestions about what is needed to establish a new educational narrative.

Bipartisan political agreement about the purposes, principles and values upon which Australian education is based.

The proposal highlights the need for there to be a vehicle for establishing the purposes, values and principles. Fortunately, such a vehicle exists—it is currently called the *Melbourne Declaration on Educational Goals for Young Australians* (MCEETYA, 2008).[24] At the time of writing the current version is under review. It is hoped that the next document will be developed through genuine community-wide and professional discussion and will involve a consideration of purposes, values and principles that has been largely absent in previous versions. Since the document should effectively represent the contemporary educational settlement, then ten years is a suitable time frame for its refreshment.

---

24 The national Goals for Schooling document is updated every decade. It began in 1989 as the Hobart Declaration, in 1999 it became the Adelaide Declaration, and in 2008 it was called the Melbourne Declaration.

A commitment to using the agreed purposes, principles and values as the reference point for policy-making and practice.

Expressing and updating the purposes, values and principles underpinning the educational settlement is only the first step in shaping a new narrative. It is a pointless exercise if the document is developed and then ignored. Commonwealth, state and territory governments must ensure that there are mechanisms at hand to enable the document to be expressed in both the spirit and the letter of education policy. That is, the document must become the light on the hill for Australian education—not only an aspiration to aim for, but a resource that will help guard against a retreat to a regressive standardising agenda.

The development of processes—at the level of systems and schools—that will enable Australian education to deal with the rapidity of societal change.

If the first two suggestions for implementing a new narrative involve using an existing policy instrument, the third suggestion means developing a new one. The book has argued that an agreed process for enabling ongoing consideration of educational policy and practice is needed—to be used in schools, in state and territory jurisdictions, and at the national level. The six-step model proposed in Chapter 8, involves a detailed investigation of a key societal trend (the case study example in Chapter 9 looked at the fourth industrial revolution) and its educational implications. If the idea is taken seriously, it will need time and resources for development and trialling. It may be that a number of different models could be developed for use in different contexts and settings. The obvious group to initiate, resource and supervise such activity is the Education Council, comprising the ministers for education at state and national levels.

A recognition of the importance of involving educators (teachers, principals, professional associations and unions) in policy-making.

If the case study in this book showed anything, it was that, like it or not, education is a highly political activity—not least because it deals in knowledge, which is a precious currency and therefore strongly contested. There are many groups that want to exert influence on governments to shape education policy in ways that serve their interests. And yet educators have tended not to engage in the political process. This is no longer tenable. At a time when international comparisons are being made; education policies are being constructed on the basis of test results; and state and territory governments are trying to work out how best to structure and organise educational systems to meet contemporary challenges, it has never been more important for educators to engage in the public and wider professional debate at the state, national and global levels.

In the first instance—given that people working in system-based bureaucracies are directly beholden to their ministers and, in any case, are often not educators themselves—the onus will fall on school-based educators and their professional associations and unions to act. However, rather than wait and then react, educators must become involved in shaping public opinion and policy directions. This sort of political engagement starts at the school and local community level. Educators must not only keep abreast of contemporary trends and debates, but also develop ways by which the school community can contribute to these on a regular and systematic basis. Since the decisions that are made at various levels of policy affect what happens in schools and classrooms, it is an educational act to participate in the political process, not a politically partisan one.

For these reasons, and on the basis of what the case study reveals, in the 21st century school leaders—not only those formally designated as school leaders, such as principals, but all those educators who see leadership as a set of capacities rather than a position—must be able, democratically and collegially, to:

- understand and lead discussions involving educators, students and school communities about broader social, political and cultural trends, and identify the implications for schools
- be curriculum and pedagogical leaders who can use the curriculum expertise residing in their school communities to generate informed, lively, respectful and ongoing curriculum discussion and debate
- lead the creation and maintenance of a culture of research and inquiry
- identify, and work democratically to address, blockages to agreed curriculum and policy changes
- understand and contribute to system-wide policy development
- advocate for and model the values and principles consistent with a new educational narrative, including a commitment to equity, diversity and cohesion, collaboration, democracy and innovation
- be politically aware enough to know how to work collectively to put their case and place political pressure where it is needed.

In other words, the impetus for the development and implementation of a new educational narrative for Australian education must come from its educators. These are the people who have been marginalised and excluded by the standardising discourse in education, and who must now take the lead if we are to reverse the years of damage that has been wrought by policy-makers in the thrall of neoliberal philosophy. It will require collegial and resource support, political skill, educational expertise and a not inconsiderable amount of courage. But it must be remembered that educators are members of school communities, and so the task does not have to be borne by educators alone if they are able to bring these communities into the conversation. More than this, there are school communities in every local community in Australia, which makes for an incredibly powerful voice.

Breaking the domination of the standardising discourse in Australia education will be hard work, but the rewards will be great. Australia could lead the world not only in exposing the damage caused by neoliberal domination of education policy, but also in demonstrating that there is a better way. A new narrative for education offers the best hope Australian society has of dealing with the kinds of environmental, economic, technological, democratic and social challenges that we face at the national and global levels.

Glossary

aggregate – data that are combined from several measurements.

correlation – the process of determining the strength of an association or relationship between two or more things or variables.

cross-correlation – a measurement that tracks the movements of two variables or sets of data relative to each other to determine if a correlation exists.

diagnostic assessment – a form of pre-assessment that is used to identify student difficulties and to guide lesson and curriculum planning.

disaggregated – data that, after being collected and aggregated, is broken down into component parts or smaller units to reveal underlying trends, patterns or insights that are not observable from aggregated data sets.

empirical research – research that is based on observed and measured phenomena and derives knowledge from actual experience rather than from theory and belief.

field research – qualitative method of data collection that aims to observe, interact with and understand people while they are in their natural environment.

formative assessment – a range of formal and informal assessment procedures conducted by teachers during the learning process in order to adapt teaching and learning activities to improve student learning.

high-stakes testing – any test which has important consequences for students, educators, schools or systems. The results are used to punish, reward, advance or promote.

ICSEA – Index of Community-Socio-Educational Advantage. Each school in Australia has an ICSEA value which is worked out by looking at certain factors such as parents' occupations and education, and a school's geographical location. It is devised for use by the Australian Curriculum, Assessment and Reporting Authority (ACARA) to enable fair comparisons of schools on the My School website.

Inductive and deductive inquiry – different models of inquiry teaching. Inductive inquiry moves students from the specific to the general. Students seek information by gathering facts, determining and pursuing relevant questions, and developing and testing hypotheses. Deductive inquiry moves students from the general to the specific. They test hypotheses and generalisations by gathering information and applying it to specific examples.

negative correlation – a relationship between two variables in which one variable increases as the other decreases, and vice versa.

qualitative data – non-numerical data which are descriptive and include attributes, characteristics, properties and meanings of a thing or phenomenon. Data are collected through such methods as observations, interviews, and focus groups.

quantitative data – measures of values or counts that are expressed as numbers, where each data set has a unique numerical value associated with it. These are used for mathematical calculations and statistical analysis which answer such questions as 'how many?', 'how often?', and 'how much?'.

randomised control trial – a trial in which subjects are randomly assigned to one or two groups: one (the experimental group) receiving the intervention being tested, and the other (the control group) receiving an alternative (conventional) treatment or placebo.

raw score – unaltered data from a test or observation.

representative sample – a subset of a population that seeks to accurately reflect the characteristics of a larger group.

sampling processes – methods used to assess probability, such as random sampling, systematic sampling and stratified sampling.

standard deviation – a measure that is used to quantify the amount of variation or dispersion of a set of data values relative to the mean.

summative assessment – refers to the assessment of students where the focus is on the outcome of the program, usually by comparing it against a benchmark. It usually takes place at the end of, rather than during, a unit of work or program, to assess student progress.

triangulated – using more than one method to collect data on the same topic, thus assuring the validity of the research.

validity and reliability – considered to be the two most important characteristics of a well-designed assessment procedure. Validity refers to the degree to which a method assesses what it claims to assess. Reliability refers to the extent to which an assessment method or instrument measures consistently the performance of students, with consistent standards over time, and between different learners and examiners.

variables – anything that has a quality that can exist in differing amounts or types, and that can be controlled or changed.

Acknowledgements

I would like to acknowledge three significant professional associations with whom I have been associated in the past decade, and thank them for granting permission to include some sections of texts I have published with them.

The Australian Association for Research in Education (AARE) (and Springer) granted permission to use sections of the following two articles published in the journal the *Australian Educational Researcher*:

- Reid, A., 2013, 'Renewing the public and the role of research in education' in the *Australian Educational Researcher*, vol. 40, no. 3, pp. 281–97.
- Reid, A., 2016, 'The use and abuse of research in the public domain' in the *Australian Educational Researcher*, vol. 43, no. 1, pp. 75–91.

The Australia Government Primary Principals' Association (AGPPA) granted permission to include parts of the publication they invited me to write on the funding debates in education:

- Reid, A., 2016, *Building the nation through public education*, January 2016, Melbourne: Australian Government Principals Association.

The Australian Secondary Principals' Association (ASPA) granted permission to include parts of the publication they asked me to write on education and the future:

- Reid, A., 2018, *Beyond certainty: A process for thinking about futures for Australian education*, August 2018, Brisbane: Australian Secondary Principals' Association.

It was an honour to work with each of these important professional associations, and to meet so many of their members at the various state and territory conferences at which I was invited to share my ideas. Their commitment and their passion to make Australian education the best it can possibly be despite the constant policy interventions into their work, inspired me to write this book.

Finally I would like to acknowledge and thank my wife, Liz, for her unstinting love and support, as well as her interest in the project, during the time I was so absorbed by the book.

References

Abbott, T., 2019, 'Covert brainwashing of our kids is taking its toll', *The Weekend Australian*, 9–10 March, <www.theaustralian.com.au/nation/inquirer/covert-brainwashing-of-our-kids-is-taking-its-toll/news-story/f0ba78a349f7c4e2cbbf0e9c0448b632>, accessed 30 May 2019.

Abdullah, A., Doucouliagas, H. & Manning, E., 2015, 'Does education reduce income inequality? A meta-regression analysis', *Journal of Economic Surveys*, vol. 29, no. 2, pp. 301–16.

Acemoglu, D. & Restrepo, P., 2017, 'Robots and jobs: Evidence from US labor markets', *NBER Working Paper*, no. 23285, <www.nber.org/papers/w23285>, accessed 27 November 2018.

ACOSS, 2018, *Inequality in Australia 2018*, Strawberry Hills: Australian Council of Social Services and the University of New South Wales.

Aldrick, P., 2018, 'Living in a smartphone world: New thinking needed to control big tech's power', *The Times*, 23 April (republished in *The Australian*, 4 May 2018), <www.theaustralian.com.au/news/world/the-times/living-in-a-smartphone-world-new-thinking-needed-to-control-big-techs-power/news-story/0597e9aa81124956ebf996a51f80ad62?nk=6f46d0b24200f4e9cf9b4cd022aa52b4-1525676345>, accessed 7 May 2018.

Ainley, J. & Gebhardt, E., 2013, *Measure for Measure: A Review of Outcomes of School Education in Australia*, Melbourne: Australian Council of Educational Research (ACER), pp. 1–93.

Airoidi, M., 2018, 'Intolerance on social media: #refugeeswelcome and the Paris terrorist attacks', *The Conversation*, 13 November, <https://theconversation.com/intolerance-on-social-media-refugeeswelcome-and-the-paris-terrorist-attacks-106795>, accessed 4 December 2018.

Apple, M., 1993, 'The politics of official knowledge: Does a national curriculum make sense?', *Teachers College Record*, vol. 95, no. 2, pp. 222–41.

Apple, M., 2004, *Ideology and Curriculum*, 3rd edn, New York, NY: RoutledgeFalmer.

Apple, M., 2006, *Educating the 'Right' Way: Markets, Standards, God and Inequality*, 2nd edn, New York, NY: Routledge.

ASA, 2014, *ASA Statement for Using Value-added Models for Educational Assessment*, 8 April, Alexandria, Virginia: American Statistical Association.

Ashman, G., 2018, 'Inquiry learning fashion has us running in a wheel', *The Australian*, 27 April, p. 14.

Au, W. & Ferrare, J.J., 2015, 'Introduction: Neoliberalism, social networks, and the new governance of education' in W. Au & J.J. Ferrare (eds), *Mapping Corporate Education Reform: Power and policy networks in the neoliberal state*, New York: Routledge, pp. 1–22.

Australian Brain Alliance Steering Committee, 2016, 'Australian Brain Alliance', *Neuron*, vol. 92, no. 3, pp. 597–600.

Australian Curriculum and Assessment and Reporting Authority, 2018, *General Capabilities: Learning Continua*, Sydney: ACARA, <www.australiancurriculum.edu.au/f-10-curriculum/general-capabilities/>, accessed 9 April 2018.

The Australian Editorial Board, 2012, 'A salutary lesson from the world's top school systems', *The Australian*, 17 February, <www.theaustralian.com.au/opinion/editorials/a-salutary-lesson-from-the-worlds-top-school-systems/news-story/f92c20f653c4b342cc9c079851ea5a8d>, accessed 24 January 2019.

Autor, D., 2015, 'Why are there still so many jobs? The history and future of workplace automation', *Journal of Economic Perspectives*, vol. 29, no. 3, pp. 3–30.

Avent, R., 2016, *The Wealth of Humans: Work and Its Absence in the Twenty-First Century*, New York, NY: St Martin's Press.

Ayscue, J., Frankenberg, G., & Siegel-Hawley, G., 2017, *The Complementary Benefits of Racial and Socioeconomic Benefits in Schools*, Research Brief No. 10, Washington, D.C.: National Coalition on School Diversity.

Baker, J., 2019, 'Stem focus leaves kids vulnerable to the "dark arts" of "fake news"', *Sydney Morning Herald*, 29 January, <www.smh.com.au/education/stem-focus-leaves-kids-vulnerable-to-the-dark-arts-of-fake-news-expert-20190125-p50tmp.html>, accessed 29 January 2019.

Ball, S., 2008, *The Education Debate*, Bristol: Policy Press.

Ball, S., 2016, 'Neoliberal education? Confronting the slouching beast', *Policy Futures in Education*, vol. 14, no. 8, pp. 1046–1059.

Ball, S. & Junemann, C., 2012, *Networks, New Governance and Education*, Bristol: Policy Press.

Ball, S. & Youdell, D., 2008, *Hidden Privatisation in Education*, Brussels: Education International.

Barber, M. & Mourshed, M., 2007, *How the World's Best-Performing School Systems Came Out On Top*, London: McKinsey and Company.

Bellenca, J. & Brandt, R. (eds), 2010, *21st Century Skills: Rethinking How Students Learn*, Bloomington, IN: Solution Tree Press.

Beregron, P-J. & Rivard, L., 2017, 'How to engage in pseudo-science with real data: A criticism of John Hattie's arguments in *Visible Learning* from the perspective of a statistician', *McGill Journal of Education*, vol. 52, no. 1, <http://mje.mcgill.ca/article/view/9475/7229>, accessed 1 April 2018.

Bereiter, C. & Engelmann, S., 1966, *Teaching Disadvantaged Children in the Preschool*, Englewood Cliffs, NJ: Prentice-Hall.

Betts, J. & Tang, E., 2011, *The Effect of Charter Schools on Student Achievement: A meta-analysis of the literature*, Seattle, WA: National Charter School Research Project.

Biesta, G., 2010, 'Why what works still won't work: From evidence based education to value-based education', *Journal of Studies in Philosophy of Education*, vol. 29, no. 5, pp. 491–503.

Biesta, G., 2012, 'Giving teaching back to education: Responding to the disappearance of the teacher', *Phenomenology & Practice*, vol. 6, no. 2, pp. 35–49.

Biesta, G., 2016, *The Beautiful Risk of Education*, London: Routledge.

Biggs, J., 1985, 'The role of metalearning in study processes', *British Journal of Educational Psychology*, vol. 50, no. 3, pp. 185–212.

Bishop, M., Green, M., 2008 *Philanthrocapitalism: How the Rich Can Save the World*, New York, NY: Bloomsbury Press.

Blanden, J. & McNally, S., 2014, 'Reducing inequality in education and skills: Implications for economic growth', *EENEE Analytical Report*, No. 21, prepared for the European Commission.

Bolton, R., 2018, 'Private school fees outstrip inflation as technology costs hit', *Australian Financial Review*, 21 January, <www.afr.com/news/policy/education/private-school-fees-outstrip-inflation-as-technology-costs-hit-20180118-h0k3rv>, accessed 10 July 2019.

Boninger, F., Molnar, A. & Saldana, C., 2019, *Personalized Learning and the Digital Privatization of Curriculum and Teaching*, University of Colorado, Boulder: National Education Policy Center.

Bonnor, C., 2019, *Separating Scholars: How Australia Abandons Its Struggling Schools*, Sydney: Centre for Policy Development.

Bonnor, C. & Caro, J., 2007, *The Stupid Country: How Australia is Dismantling Public Education*, Sydney: University of New South Wales Press.

Bonnor, C. & Shepherd, B., 2015, 'Private school, public cost: How school funding is closing the wrong gaps', *Australian Policy* (online), 23 July, <http://apo.org.au/node/56111/>, accessed 29 January 2019.

Bonnor, C. & Shepherd, B., 2017, *Losing the Game: State of Our Schools in 2017*, Sydney: Centre for Policy Development.

Borland, J., 2017, 'Why we are still convinced robots will take our jobs despite the evidence', *The Conversation*, 26 November, <https://theconversation.com/why-we-are-still-convinced-robots-will-take-our-jobs-despite-the-evidence-87188>, accessed 8 April 2018.

Bosworth, D., 2011, 'The cultural contradictions of philanthrocapitalism', *Society*, vol. 48, no. 5, p. 382.

Boyd, A., 2017, 'Could your Fitbit data be used to deny you health insurance?', *The Conversation*, 17 February, <https://theconversation.com/could-your-fitbit-data-be-used-to-deny-you-health-insurance-72565>, accessed 9 April 2018.

Bracewell-Worrall, A., 2018, 'All New Zealand Charter schools now approved to become state integrated', *NewsHub*, 17 September, <www.newshub.co.nz/home/politics/2018/09/all-nz-charter-schools-now-approved-to-become-state-integrated.html>, accessed 30 May 2019.

Bradshaw, T., 2011, 'Murdoch signals push into education', *Financial Times*, 25 May, <www.ft.com/content/ed72924c-8630-11e0-9e2c-00144feabdc0>, accessed 28 May 2019.

Brandt, A. & Eagleman, D., 2017, *The Runaway Species: How Human Creativity Remakes the World*, Edinburgh: Canongate.

Bregman, R., 2018, *Utopia For Realists*, London: Bloomsbury.

Brennan, M. & Zipin, L., 2018, 'Curriculum for all? Exploring potentials for (in)justice in the Australian Curriculum', in A. Reid & D. Price (eds), 2018, *The Australian Curriculum: promises, problems and possibilities*, Canberra: Australian Curriculum Studies Association, pp. 179–88.

Brown, K., Lipsig-Mumme, C. & Zajdow, G., 2003, *Active Citizenship and the Secondary School Experience: Community Participation Rates of Australian Youth*, LSAY Research Reports, Melbourne: ACER.

Cadwalladr, C. & Graham-Harrison, E., 2018, 'How Cambridge Analytica turned Facebook "likes" into a lucrative political tool', *The Guardian*, 18 March, <www.theguardian.com/technology/2018/mar/17/facebook-cambridge-analytica-kogan-data-algorithm>, accessed 8 April 2018.

Cahill, D. & Toner, P. (eds), 2018, *Wrong Way: How Privatisation and Economic Reform Backfired*, Melbourne: La Trobe University Press.

Caldwell, B., 2015, *School Autonomy and Student Achievement: Case Studies in Australia*, Melbourne: Educational Transformations, <www.educationaltransformations.com.au>, accessed 29 March 2019.

Camera, L., 2017, 'Gates Foundation to shift education focus', *US News*, 19 October, <www.usnews.com/news/education-news/articles/2017-10-19/gates-foundation-pledges-17-billion-to-k-12-education-will-focus-on-building-school-networks>, accessed 30 March 2019.

Camilleri, J., 2014, 'Democracy in crisis', *Sydney Morning Herald*, 14 December, <www.smh.com.au/opinion/democracy-in-crisis-20141214-126quk.html>, accessed 21 June 2018.

Campbell, A. & Groundwater-Smith, S., 2010, *Connecting Inquiry and Professional Learning in Education*, London: Routledge.

Campbell, C., Proctor, H. & Sherington, G., 2009, *School Choice: How parents negotiate the new school market in Australia*, Sydney: Allen & Unwin.

Campbell, C. & Proctor, H., 2014, *A History of Australian Schooling*, Crows Nest: Allen & Unwin.

Carnoy, M., 2015, *International Test Score Comparisons and Educational Policy: A Review of the Critiques*, Boulder, CO: National Education Policy Center, Stanford University.

Carnoy, M. & Rothstein, R., 2013, *What Do International Tests Really Show About American Student Performance?*, Washington, DC: Economic Policy Institute.

Cavill, A., 2014, 'Pyne launches 'independent' public schools plan', *SBS News*, 3 February, <www.sbs.com.au/news/pyne-launches-independent-public-schools-plan>, accessed 30 March 2019.

Choi, P-K., 2005, 'A critical evaluation of education reforms in Hong Kong: Counting our losses to economic globalization', *International Studies in Sociology of Education*, vol. 15, no. 3, pp. 237–56.

References

Christian, D., 2004, *Maps of Time: An Introduction to Big History*, Berkeley, CA: University of California Press.

Christian, D., 2018, *Origin Story: A Big History of Everything*, New York, NY: Little, Brown & Company.

Christian, D., Stokes-Brown, C. & Benjamin, C., 2014, *Big History: Between Nothing and Everything*, New York, NY: McGraw-Hill.

Christodoulou, D., 2014, *Seven Myths About Education*, London: Routledge.

Cobbold, T., 2015, *Fighting For Equity in Education*, speech delivered at the AEU Federal conference on 27 February 2015, <www.saveourschools.com.au/equity-in-education/equity-or-privilege-in-education>, accessed 30 March 2019.

Cobbold, T., 2016, 'Australia's unfair school funding system must be overhauled', *SOS Australia* (posted 15 February), <www.saveourschools.com.au>, accessed 29 January 2019.

Cobbold, T., 2017a, 'Private schools are over funded by $4–6 billion per year', *SOS Australia* (posted 5 April), <www.saveourschools.com.au/funding/private-schools-are-over-funded-by-4-6-billion-a-year>, accessed 29 January 2019.

Cobbold, T., 2017b, 'Resource gaps between advantaged and disadvantaged schools among the largest in the world', *SOS Australia* (posted 12 February), <www.saveourschools.com.au>, accessed 27 January 2019.

Cobbold, T., 2018, 'New figures show states have cut funding to private schools', *John Menadue—Pearls and Irritations* (posted 31 May), <https://johnmenadue.com/trevor-cobbold-new-figures-show-states-have-cut-funding-to-public-schools-2/>, accessed 29 January 2019.

Cobbold, T., 2019, 'Funding increases for private schools continue to outstrip increases for public schools', *SOS Australia* (posted 20 March), <http://saveourschools.com.au/funding/funding-increases-for-private-schools-continue-to-outstrip-increases-for-public-schools/>, accessed 30 March 2019.

Coffield, F., 2012, 'Why the McKinsey reports will not improve school systems', *Journal of Education Policy*, vol 27, no. 1, pp. 131–49.

Colby, L., 2015, 'Rupert Murdoch's $1 billion education failure', *Financial Review*, 10 April, <www.afr.com/business/media-and-marketing/rupert-murdochs-1-billion-education-failure-20150410-1micbs>, accessed 27 March 2019.

Connell, R., 1995, 'Transformative labour: Theorizing the politics of teachers' work' in M. Ginsburg (ed.), *The Politics of Educators' Work and Lives*, New York, NY: Garland Publishing, pp. 91–114.

Connell, R., 2013, 'The neoliberal cascade and education: An essay on the market agenda and its consequences', *Critical Studies in Education*, vol. 54, no. 2, pp. 99–112.

Connors, L. & McMorrow, J., 2015, *Imperatives in Schools Funding: Equity, Sustainability and Achievement*, Camberwell: ACER Press.

CREDO, 2009, *Charter School Performance In 16 States*, Stanford, CA, Centre for Research on Education Outcomes, <https://credo.stanford.edu/>, accessed 24 January 2019.

CREDO, 2013, *National Charter School Study*, Stanford, CA Centre for Research on Education Outcomes, <https://credo.stanford.edu/>, accessed 24 January 2019.

CREDO, 2017, *Charter Management Organization Study*, Centre for Research on Education Outcomes, Stanford, CA: Stanford University.

CREDO, 2019, *Charter School Performance in Ohio: 2019*, Stanford, CA: Centre for Research on Education Outcomes, pp. 1–52.

Creighton, A., 2018, 'There's so much robots can't do—like take our jobs', *The Australian*, 12 November, <www.theaustralian.com.au/nation/politics/theres-so-much-robots-cant-do-like-take-our-jobs/news-story/8c991980af795708db1b9660a3b83f6e>, accessed 10 July 2019.

Darling-Hammond, L., 2000, 'How teacher education matters', *Journal of Teacher Education,* vol. 51, no. 3, pp. 166–73.

Darling-Hammond, L., 2006, 'Securing the right to learn: Policy and practice for powerful teaching and learning', *Educational Researcher*, vol. 35, no. 7, pp. 13–24.

Dawkins, J., 1988, *Strengthening Australia's Schools*, Canberra: AGPS.

Denniss, R., 2018, 'Dead right: How neoliberalism ate itself and what comes next', *Quarterly Essay*, vol. 70, pp. 1–137.

Devlin, H., 2017, 'AI programs exhibit racial and gender biases, research reveals', *The Guardian*, 14 April, <www.theguardian.com/technology/2017/apr/13/ai-programs-exhibit-racist-and-sexist-biases-research-reveals>, accessed 9 April 2018.

Dodd, T., 2017, 'OECD expert reads Australian schools the riot act', *Financial Review*, 6 October, <www.afr.com/leadership/oecd-expert-reads-australian-schools-the-riot-act-20171006-gyvgq0>, accessed 30 March 2019.

Donnelly, K., 2009, 'Chairman Rudd's Education Revolution', *Quadrant Online*, 28 February, <https://quadrant.org.au/magazine/2008/12/chairman-rudd-s-education-revolution/>, accessed 20 February 2015.

Donnelly, K., 2012, *Educating Your Child: It's Not Rocket Science*, Brisbane: Connor Court Publishing.

Donnelly, K., 2014a, 'Greater flexibility and better results will follow the move to independent public schools', *The Australian*, 24 May, p. 22.

Donnelly, K., 2014b, 'School equity experts barking up the wrong tree', *The Drum*, 20 June, <www.abc.net.au/news/2014-06-17/donnelly-school-equity-experts-barking-up-the-wrong-tree/5527358>, accessed 24 January 2019.

Donnelly, K., 2015, 'Back to school: Why we should embrace autonomy', *The Drum*, 28 January, <www.abc.net.au/news/2015-01-28/donnelly-back-to-school/6049562>, accessed 24 January 2019.

Donnelly, K., 2016, 'Grattan school funding report ignores voucher system option', *The Australian*, 28 November, <www.theaustralian.com.au/commentary/opinion/grattan-school-funding-report-ignores-vouchersystem-option/news-story/d521034fef1a800a92116fdb4f75b250>, accessed 10 July 2019.

Donnelly, K., 2018a, 'The battle of ideas is being lost in our classrooms', *The Australian*, 4 January, p. 10.

Donnelly, K., 2018b, 'Creativity can't be taught or learned in a vacuum', *The Weekend Australian*, 5–6 May, p. 7.

Donnelly, K., 2018c, 'Better education for our teachers', *The Australian*, 24 April, p. 6.

Donnelly, K., 2018d, *How Political Correctness Is Destroying Education*, Melbourne: Warriewood Wilkinson.

Donnelly, K., 2019, 'Progressive fads promote cultural illiteracy in schools', *The Weekend Australian,* 19–20 January, p. 9.

Dunlop, T., 2018, *The Future of Everything: Big Audacious Ideas for a Better World*, Sydney: NewSouth Publishing.

Dweck, C., 2016, *Mindset: The New Psychology of Success*, 2nd edn, New York, NY: Ballantine Books.

Eacott, S., 2015, 'Evidence for success of independent schools is flawed', *The Conversation*, 20 August, <https://theconversation.com/evidence-for-success-of-independent-public-schools-is-flawed-46382>, accessed 29 March 2019.

Eacott, S., 2017, 'School leadership and the cult of the guru: The neo-Taylorism of Hattie', *School Leadership & Management*, vol. 37, no. 4, pp. 413–26.

Eubanks, V., 2017, *Automating Inequality: How High-Tech Tools, Profile, Police and Punish the Poor*, New York, NY: St Martin's Press.

Fadel, C., Bialik, M. & Trilling, B., 2015, *Four-Dimensional Education: The Competencies Learners Need to Succeed*, Boston, MA: Center for Curriculum Redesign.

Farrell, T., 2004, *Reflective Practice In Action*, Thousand Oaks, CA: Corwin Press.

Feinberg, W., 2012, 'The idea of public education', *Review of Research in Education*, vol. 36, pp. 1–32.

Fernandez-Cano, A., 2016, 'A methodological critique of the PISA evaluations', *Relieve*, vol. 22, no. 1, art. M15.

Fiel, J., 2015, 'Closing ranks: Closure, status competition and school segregation', *American Journal of Sociology*, vol. 21, no. 1, pp. 126–70.

Finkel, A., 2018, 'Finkel: Students, focus on your disciplines then you'll see your options expand', *The Conversation*, 28 November, <https://theconversation.com/finkel-students-focus-on-your-discipline-then-youll-see-your-options-expand-107440>, accessed 30 May 2019.

Flynn, D. & Robu, V., 2017, 'The new industrial revolution: Robots are an opportunity, not a threat', *The Conversation*, 9 April, <https://theconversation.com/the-new-industrial-revolution-robots-are-an-opportunity-not-a-threat-81792>, accessed 8 April 2018.

Ford, M., 2015, *Rise of the Robots: Technology and the Threat of a Jobless Future*, London: Oneworld Publications.

Foundation for Young Australians, 2015, *The New Work Order: Ensuring Young Australians Have Skills and Experience for the Jobs of the Future, Not the Past*, Melbourne: Foundation for Young Australians.

Foundation for Young Australians, 2016, *The New Work Mindset: Seven New Job Clusters to Help Young People Navigate the New Work Order*, Melbourne: Foundation for Young Australians.

Frankenberg, E., Siegel-Hawley, G. & Wang, J., 2011, 'Choice without equity:

Charter school segregation', *Educational Policy Analysis Archives*, vol. 19, no. 1, DOI: <https://doi.org/10.14507/epaa.v19n1.2011>.

Fraser, N., 2009, *Scales of Justice: Reimagining Political space in a Globalizing World*, New York, NY: Columbia University Press.

Fray, C. & Osborne, M., 2013, *The Future of Employment: How Susceptible Are Jobs to Computerisation?*, working paper, Oxford: University of Oxford, <www.oxfordmartin.ox.ac.uk/publications/view/1314>, accessed 8 April 2018.

Frayne, D., 2015, *The Refusal of Work: The Theory and Practice of Resistance to Work*, London: Zed Books.

Freedom House, 2018, *Freedom in the World 2018: Democracy in Crisis. Annual Freedom House Report on Democracy in the World*, <https://freedomhouse.org/report/freedom-world/freedom-world-2018>, accessed 9 April 2018.

Friedman, M., 1962, *Capitalism and Freedom*, Chicago, IL: University of Chicago Press.

Fry, H., 2018, *Hello World: How to Be Human in the Age of the Machine*, New York, NY: Norton & Co.

Fuchs, T. & Woesmann, L., 2007, 'What accounts for international differences in student performance? A re-examination using PISA data', *Empirical Economics*, vol. 32, no. 2, pp. 433–64.

Fullan, M., 2015, *The New Meaning of Educational Change*, 5th edn, New York, NY: Teachers College Press.

Fullan, M., Quinn, J. & McEachen, J., 2018, *Deep Learning: Engage the World Change the World*, Thousand Oaks, CA: Corwin Press and the Ontario Principals' Council.

Gallant, A. & Riley, P., 2017, 'Early career teacher attrition in Australia: Inconvenient truths about new public management', *Teachers and Teaching: Theory and Practice*, vol 23, no. 8, pp. 896–913.

Garratt, P., 2012, 'Opening address AITSL professional learning conference', *The Australian* [online], 23 February, <www.theaustralian.com.au/opinion/editorials/a-salutary-lesson-from-the-worlds-top-school-systems/news-story/f92c20f653c4b342cc9c079851ea5a8d>, accessed 24 January 2019.

Gates, B., 2008, *Bill Gates—A Forum on Education in America*, <https://www.gatesfoundation.org/media-center/speeches/2008/11/bill-gates-forum-on-education-in-america>, accessed 26 March 2019.

Giddens, A., 1998, *The Third Way: The Renewal of Social Democracy*, Cambridge: Polity Press.

Gillard, J., 2008a, *Address to UBS dinner for Joel Klein*, Canberra: Ministers' Media Centre, <https://ministers.jobs.gov.au/gillard/address-ubs-dinner-joel-klein>, accessed 25 January 2019.

Gillard, J., 2008b, *Education Revolution in Our Schools*, Ministers' statement, 27 August, Canberra: Minister's Media Centre, <https://ministers.employment.gov.au/gillard/education-revolution-our-schools>, accessed 29 March 2019.

Gillespie, D., 2019, *Teen Brain: Why Screens Are Making Your Teenager Depressed, Anxious and Prone to Life-Long Addictive Illnesses—And How to Stop It Now*, Sydney: Pan Macmillan.

Gittins, R., 2017, 'Why the robot revolution won't play out as predicted', *Sydney Morning Herald*, 12 September, <www.smh.com.au/opinion/why-the-robot-revolution-wont-play-out-as-predicted-20170912-gyfk82.html>, accessed 27 November 2018.

Gobby, B., 2019 'Competitive entrepreneurship and community empowerment', in J. Wilkinson, R. Niesche & S. Eacott (eds), *Challenges for Public Education*, London: Routledge, pp. 59–72.

Gonski, D., 2011, *Review of Funding for Schooling—Final Report*, Canberra: Department of Education, Employment and Workplace Relations.

Gonski, D., Arcus, T., Boston, K., Gould, V., Johnson, W., O'Brien, L., Perry, L. & Roberts, M., 2018, *Through Growth to Achievement: The Report of the Review to Achieve Educational Excellence in Australian Schools*, Canberra: Commonwealth of Australia.

Goodlad, J., 2008, 'A non-negotiable agenda', in J. Goodlad, R. Soder & B. McDaniel (eds), 2008, *Education and the Making of a Democratic People*, London: Paradigm Publishers, pp. 9–28.

Goss, P., 2019, 'Lopsided funding gives more to schools that need it least', *The Age*, 16 May, <www.theage.com.au/education/lopsided-funding-gives-more-to-private-schools-that-need-it-least-20190514-p51ndt.html>, accessed 26 May 2019.

Goss, P., Sonnemann J., Chisolm, C. & Nelson, L., 2016, *Widening Gaps: What NAPLAN Tells Us About Student Progress*, Melbourne: Grattan Institute.

Grayling, A.C., 2017, *Democracy and Its Crisis*, London: Oneworld Publications.

Greene, P., 2019, 'Can personalized learning actually deliver', *Forbes*, 2 May, <www.forbes.com/sites/petergreene/2019/05/02/report-can-personalized-learning-actually-deliver/#2559e4f42020>, accessed 30 May 2019.

Greenwald, G., 2014, *No Place to Hide: Edward Snowden, the NSA and the Surveillance State*, London: Hamish Hamilton.

Gross-Loh, C., 2016, 'How praise became a consolation prize', *The Atlantic*, 16 December, <www.theatlantic.com/education/archive/2016/12/how-praise-became-a-consolation-prize/510845/>, accessed 18 May 2018.

Gunter H., Hall, D. & Mills, C., 2014, 'Consultants, consultancy and consultocracy in education policy-making in England', *Journal of Education Policy*, vol. 30, no. 4, <www.tandfonline.com/doi/full/10.1080/02680939.2014.963163?src=recsys>, accessed 20 April 2019.

Hanushek, E., Link, S. & Woessmann, L., 2013, 'Does school autonomy make sense everywhere? Panel estimates from PISA', *Journal of Development Economics*, vol. 104, pp. 212–32.

Hanushek, E., Woessmann, L. & Link, S., 2012, 'Allowing local schools to make more decisions may work in developed countries, but is questionable in developing countries', *VOX (CEPR Policy Portal)*, 9 January, <www.voxeu.org/article/independent-schools-luxury-developed-world>, accessed 20 February 2012.

Harari, Y., 2016, *Homo Deus: A Brief History of Tomorrow*, London: Harvill Secker.

Harari, Y., 2018, *21 Lessons for the 21st Century*, London: Jonathon Cape.

Hardiman, O., 2017, 'Freud's divide between psychiatry and neurology is redundant—here's why', *The Conversation*, 25 March, <https://theconversation.com/freuds-divide-between-psychiatry-and-neurology-is-redundant-heres-why-74598>, accessed 21 May 2018.

Harland, J., 2017, 'Artificial intelligence researchers must learn ethics', *The Conversation*, 29 August, <https://theconversation.com/artificial-intelligence-researchers-must-learn-ethics-82754>, accessed 9 April 2018.

Harrington, M., 2011, *Australian Government Funding for Schools Explained*, Background Note, Canberra: Parliamentary Library.

Harris, A., 2013, *Young People and Everyday Multiculturalism*, Hoboken, NJ: Taylor and Francis.

Harrison, D., 2012, 'A class above', *The Sydney Morning Herald*, 17 February, <www.smh.com.au/national/a-class-above-20120216-1tbq7.html>, accessed 24 January 2019.

Harvey, D., 2005, *A Brief History of Neoliberalism*, Oxford: Oxford University Press.

Hattie, J., 2009, *Visible Learning*, Milton Park: Routledge.

Hattie, J., 2017, 'Time for a reboot: Shifting away from distractions to improve Australia's schools', in T. Bentley & G.C. Savage (eds), *Educating Australia: Challenges for the Decade Ahead*, Carlton: Melbourne University Publishing.

Hayek, F., 1944, *The Road to Serfdom*, New York, NY: Routledge.

Hazell, W., 2017, 'Hattie on Dweck: Sometimes pupils need fixed mindsets argues leading academic', *Times Educational Supplement*, 29 June, <www.tes.com/news/hattie-dweck-sometimes-pupils-need-fixed-mindsets-argues-leading-academic>, accessed 15 May 2018.

Heffernan, A., 2019, 'Exploring a school improvement initiative' in J. Wilkinson, R. Niesche & S. Eacott (eds), *Challenges for Public Education*, London: Routledge, pp. 73–86.

Hendrix, J. & Carroll, D., 2017, 'Confronting a nightmare for democracy: Personal data, personalized media and weaponized propaganda', *Medium*, 4 May, <https://medium.com/@profcarroll/confronting-a-nightmare-for-democracy-5333181ca675>, accessed 9 April 2018.

Hetherington, D., 2018, *What Price the Gap? Education and Inequality in Australia*, Sydney: Public Education Foundation.

Ho, C., 2017, 'Selective schools increasingly cater to the most advantaged students', *The Conversation*, 9 March, <https://theconversation.com/selective-schools-increasinglycater-to-the-most-advantaged-students-74151>, accessed 18 January 2019.

Ho, C., 2019, *Ethnic Divides in Schooling*, Melbourne: Centre for Policy Development, pp. 4–18.

Hockey, J., 2014, 'Federal budget 2014—full speech', *Sydney Morning Herald*, 13 May, <www.smh.com.au/national/federal-budget-2014--full-speech-20140513-3887i.html>, accessed 29 May 2019.

Hogan, A., Sellar, S. & Lingard, R., 2015, 'Commercialising comparison: Pearson puts the TLC in soft capitalism', *Journal of Education Policy*, vol. 31, no. 3, pp. 243–58.

Horn, B., 2015, 'How Amplify broke all the rules for innovators', *Ed Surge*, 11 November, <www.edsurge.com/news/2015-11-11-how-amplify-broke-all-the-rules-for-innovators>, accessed 27 March 2019.

Hull, G., 2017, 'Why social media may not be so good for democracy', *The Conversation*, 6 November, <https://theconversation.com/why-social-media-may-not-be-so-good-for-democracy-86285>, accessed 9 April 2018.

Illich, I., 1971, *Deschooling Society*, New York, NY: Harper & Row.

IMF, 2017, *Fiscal Monitor—Tackling inequality*, Washington, DC: International Monetary Fund.

Inglis, F., 2004, *Education and the Good Society*, London: Palgrave Macmillan.

Jackson, P., 1968, *Life in Classrooms*, Philadelphia, PA: Holt, Rinehart and Winston.

Janmaat, J., 2014, 'Do ethnically mixed classrooms promote inclusive attitudes towards immigrants everywhere? A study among native adolescents in 14 countries', *European Sociological Review*, vol. 30, no. 6, pp. 810–22.

Jensen, B., Hunter, A., Sonneman, J. & Burns, T., 2012, *Catching Up: Learning from the Best School Systems in East Asia*, Melbourne: Grattan Institute.

Jensen, B., 2012a, 'Shanghai success a lesson delivery', *The Australian*, 18 February, <www.theaustralian.com.au/opinion/editorials/a-salutary-lesson-from-the-worlds-top-school-systems/news-story/f92c20f653c4b342cc9c079851ea5a8d>, accessed 24 January 2019.

Jensen, B., 2012b, 'We have much to learn from education systems in Asia', *The Australian*, 23 November, <www.theaustralian.com.au/national-affairs/opinion/we-have-much-to-learn-from-education-systems-in-asia/news-story/3b895dfda385824b0f06059932dfbd9bI>, accessed 24 January 2019.

Jerrim, J., 2015, 'Why do East Asian children perform so well in PISA? An investigation of western-born children of East Asian descent', *Oxford Review of Education*, vol. 41, no. 3, pp. 310–33.

Jha, T. & Buckingham, J., 2015, *Free to Choose Charter Schools: How Charter and For-Profit Schools Can Boost Public Education*, research report, Sydney: Centre for Independent Studies.

Johnson, C., 2019, 'Win or lose the next election, it may be time for the Liberals to rethink their economic narrative', *The Conversation*, 26 February, <https://theconversation.com/win-or-lose-the-next-election-it-may-be-time-for-the-liberals-to-rethink-their-economic-narrative-110902>, accessed 31 March 2019.

Johnston, J., 2017, 'Australian NAPLAN testing: In what way is this a 'wicked' problem?' *Improving Schools*, vol. 20, no. 1, pp. 18–34.

Joseph, B. & Buckingham, J., 2018, 'Gonski 2.0 skims over key indicators such as discipline', *The Weekend Australian,* 5–6 May, <www.theaustralian.com.au/nation/inquirer/gonski-20-skims-over-key-indicators-such-as-discipline-in-schools/news-story/ab2c406240c9ac9afac2c8a37372464f>, accessed 28 May 2019.

Joyce, B., Weil, M. & Calhoun, E., 2017, *Models of Teaching*, London: Pearson.

Kadaras, N., 2017, *Glow Kids: How Screen Addiction Is Hijacking Our Kids—And How to Break the Trance*, New York, NY: St. Martin's Press.

Karmel, P., 1973, *Schools in Australia: Report of the Interim Committee for Australian Schools Commission*, Canberra: AGPS.

Katz, M. (ed.), 2013, *Public Education Under Siege*, Philadelphia, PA: University of Pennsylvania Press.

Keen, A., 2018, *How to Fix the Future: Staying Human in the Digital Age*, London: Atlantic Books.

Kessler, S., 2018, *Gigged: The End of the Job and the Future of Work*, New York, NY: St Martin's Press.

Knight, J. & Lingard, R., 1997, 'Ministerialisation and politicisation', in R. Lingard & P. Porter (eds), *A National Approach to Schooling in Australia? Essays on the Development of National Policies in School Education*, Canberra: Australian College of Education.

Koo, S., 2014, 'An assault upon our children', *New York Times*, 1 August, <www.nytimes.com/2014/08/02/opinion/sunday/south-koreas-education-system-hurts-students.html>, accessed 30 March 2019.

Koretz, D., 2017, *The Testing Charade: Pretending to Make Schools Better*, Chicago, IL: University of Chicago Press.

Kreiner, S. & Christensen, K., 2014, 'Analyses of model fit and robustness. A new look at the PISA scaling model underlying ranking of countries according to reading literacy', *Psychometrika*, vol. 79, no. 2, pp. 210–31.

Labaree, D., 1997, 'Public goods, private goods: The American struggle over educational goals', *American Educational Research Journal*, vol. 34, no. 1, pp. 39–81.

Ladwig, J., 2018, 'Here's what's going wrong with "evidence-based" policies and practices in schools in Australia', *Educational Research Matters* (posted 16 April), <www.aare.edu.au/blog/?p=2822>, accessed 30 March 2019.

Laing, K., Smith, L. & Todd, L., 2019, 'Using the concept of relational justice to apply fairness in schools', *The International Education Journal: Comparative Perspectives*, vol. 18, no. 1, pp. 128–42.

Larmer, B., 2015, 'China's cram schools', *New York Times*, 30 March, pp. 12–15.

Li, J. & Powdthavee, N., 2015, 'Does more education lead to better health habits? Evidence from the school reforms in Australia', *Social Science & Medicine*, vol. 127, pp. 83–91.

Lingard, B., 2015, 'Think tanks, policy "experts", and "ideas for" education policy making in Australia', *The Australian Educational Researcher*, vol. 43, no. 1, pp. 15–33.

Loveless, T., 2013, 'PISA's China problem', *Brookings Institute*, 9 October, <www.brookings.edu/research/pisas-china-problem/>, accessed 20 May 2018.

Lucas, B. & Smith, C., 2018, *The Capable Country: Cultivating Capabilities in Australian Education*, Mitchell Institute Policy Report No. 03/2018, Melbourne: Mitchell Institute.

Luke, A., 2014, *On Explicit and Direct Instruction*, Australian Literacy Educators' Association (ALEA) Hot Topic, May 2014, <www.alea.edu.au/publicresources/alea-hot-topics>, accessed 30 May 2019.

McGowan, M., 2018, 'Private education spending in Australia soars ahead of other countries', *The Guardian*, 11 September, <www.theguardian.com/

australia-news/2018/sep/11/private-education-spending-in-australia-soars-ahead-of-other-countries>, accessed 30 March 2019.

McGrath-Champ, S., Wilson, R., Stacey, M. & Fitzgerald, S., 2018, *Understanding Work in Schools: The Foundation for Teaching and Learning*, report to the NSW Teachers Federation, Sydney: NSWTF.

Mcloughlin, C., 2013, *Low-Cost Private Schools: Evidence, Approaches and Emerging Issues*, London: Economic and Private Sector PEAKS.

Macmillan, J., 2013, 'Parents pay up for the big business that is NAPLAN', *ABC News*, 14 May, <www.abc.net.au/news/2013-05-13/tutors-cash-in-on-naplan-as-parents-pay-out/4687012>, accessed 30 May 2019.

Madrigal, A., 2018, 'Against Big Philanthropy', *The Atlantic*, 27 June, <www.bing.com/search?q=against+big+philanthropy&src=IE-TopResult&FORM=IETR02&PC=UF03&conversationid=>, accessed 10 July 2019.

Manne, A., 2014, *The Culture of I: The New Culture of Narcissism*, Melbourne: Melbourne University Press.

Mannix, L., 2013, 'Making public schools more like private schools: Pyne's vision', *Indaily*, 9 May.

Marginson, S., 1993, *Education and Public Policy in Australia*, Cambridge: Cambridge University Press.

Martin, W., 2016, 'Nobel prize-winning economist Stiglitz tells us why "neoliberalism is dead"', *Business Insider Australia*, 19 August, <www.businessinsider.com.au/joseph-stiglitz-says-neoliberalism-is-dead-2016-8?r=US&IR=T>, accessed 31 January 2019.

Mason, P., 2015, *Postcapitalism: A Guide to Our Future*, London: Penguin Random House.

MCEETYA—see Ministerial Council on Education, Employment, Training and Youth Affairs.

Medina, J., 2010, 'Standards raised, more students fail tests', *The New York Times*, 28 July, <www.nytimes.com/2010/07/29/education/29scores.html>, accessed 25 January 2019.

Mencimer, S., 2011, 'Fox in the schoolhouse: Rupert Murdoch wants to teach your kids!', *Mother Jones*, 23 September, <www.motherjones.com/politics/2011/09/rupert-murdoch-news-corp-wireless-generation-education/>, accessed 28 May 2019.

Megalogenis, G., 2012, *The Australian Moment*, South Melbourne: Penguin.

Miller, P., 1986, *Long Division: State Schooling in South Australian Society*, Adelaide: Wakefield Press.

Ministerial Council on Education, Employment, Training and Youth Affairs, 2008, *Melbourne Declaration on Educational Goals for Young Australians*, Melbourne: MCEETYA.

Mitchell Institute, 2015, 'Senior school years: School completion uneven across Australia', *Fact Sheet 4: Education Opportunity in Australia 2015*, Melbourne: Mitchell Institute, Victoria University, pp. 1–2.

Mitra, S., 2005, 'Self-organising systems for mass computer literacy: Findings from the "hole in the wall" experiments', *International Journal of Development Issues*, vol. 4, no. 1, pp. 71–81.

Mitra, S., 2013, 'Build a school in the cloud', *TED Talk*, <www.ted.com/talks/sugata_mitra_build_a_school_in_the_cloud>, accessed 2 April 2018.

Mitra, S. & Rana, V., 2001, 'Children and the internet: Experiments with minimally invasive education in India', *British Journal of Educational Technology*, vol. 32, no. 2, pp. 221–32.

Moll, L., Amanti, C., Neffe, D. & Gonzalez, N., 1992, 'Funds of knowledge for teaching: Using a qualitative approach to connect homes and classrooms', *Theory into Practice*, no. 32, pp. 132–41.

Monbiot, G., 2017, *Out of the Wreckage: A New Politics for an Age of Crisis*, London: Verso.

Monbiot, G., 2016, 'Neoliberalism—the ideology at the root of all our problems', *The Guardian*, 15 April, <www.theguardian.com/books/2016/apr/15/neoliberalism-ideology-problem-george-monbiot>, accessed 30 May 2019.

Moore, B., Leask, B., Leverenz, P., Oliver, G., Reid, A. & Rutherford, M., 1991, *Issues in Australian Studies: People and Power*, South Melbourne: Macmillan.

Moore, M., 2018, *Democracy Hacked: Political Turmoil and Information Warfare in the Digital Age*, London: Bloomsbury.

Moreno, I., 2017, 'US charter schools put growing numbers in racial isolation', *AP News*, 3 December, <www.apnews.com/e9c25534dfd44851a5e56bd57454b4f5>, accessed 25 January 2019.

Mourshed, M., Chijioke, C. & Barber, M., 2010, *How the World's Most Improved School Systems Keep Getting Better*, London: McKinsey and Co.

Mourshed, M., Krawitz, M. & Dorn, E., 2017, *How to Improve Student Educational Outcomes. New Insights From Data Analytics*, New York, NY: McKinsey and Co., <www.mckinsey.com/industries/social-sector/our-insights/how-to-improve-student-educational-outcomes-new-insights-from-data-analytics>, accessed 30 May 2019.

Muller, J., 2018, *The Tyranny of Metrics*, Princeton, NJ: Princeton University Press.

Murdoch, R., 2008, 'Fortune favours the smart', *Golden Age of Freedom* (2008 Boyer lectures), <www.abc.net.au/radionational/programs/boyerlectures/lecture-4-fortune-favours-the-smart/3192470>, accessed 25 January 2019.

Netolicky, D., 2016, 'Performance pay for teachers will create a climate of fear and isolation', *The Conversation*, 23 May, <https://theconversation.com/performance-pay-for-teachers-will-create-a-culture-of-fear-and-isolation-59736>, accessed 10 April 2019.

Nghiem, H., Nguyen, H., Khanam, R. & Connelly, L., 2015, 'Does school type affect cognitive and non-cognitive development in children? Evidence from primary schools', *Labor Economics*, vol. 33, pp. 55–65.

Nichols, S., Glass, G. & Berliner, D., 2006, 'High stakes testing and student achievement: Does accountability pressure increase student learning?', *Education Policy Analysis Archives*, no. 14, pp 1–172.

Nichols, S. & Cormack, P., 2017, *Impactful Practitioner Inquiry*, Princeton, NJ: Princeton Teachers College Press.

Nichols, T., 2017, *The Death of Expertise: The Campaign Against Established Knowledge and Why It Matters*, New York, NY: Oxford University Press.

Noble, G., 2009, 'Everyday Cosmopolitanism and the Labour of Intercultural Community', in A. Wise & S. Velayutham (eds), *Everyday Multiculturalism*, London: Palgrave Macmillan, pp. 46–65.

Noble, S., 2018, *Algorithms of Oppression: How Search Engines Reinforce Racism*, New York, NY: New York University Press.

Notley, T., Dezuanni, L., Zhong, H. & Howden, S., 2017, *News and Australia's Children: How Young People Access, Perceive and Are Affected by the News*, Sydney: Western Sydney University, Queensland University of Technology and Crinkling News.

Nussbaum, M., 2011, *Creating Capabilities: The Human Development Approach*, Cambridge, MA: Harvard University Press.

OECD—see Organisation for Economic Co-operation and Development.

O'Neil, C., 2016, *Weapons of Math Destruction: How Big Data Increases Inequality and Threatens Democracy*, New York, NY: Crown Random House.

Orange, R., 2013, 'Swedish free school operator to close, leaving hundreds of pupils stranded', *The Guardian*, 1 June, <www.theguardian.com/education/2013/may/31/free-schools-education>, accessed 10 July 2019.

Organisation for Economic Co-operation and Development, 2010, *PISA 2009 Results: Overcoming Social Background—Equity in Learning Opportunities and Outcomes (Volume II)*, Paris: OECD Publishing.

Organisation for Economic Co-operation and Development, 2013, *PISA 2012 Results: What Makes Schools Successful? Resources, Policies and Practices* (vol. IV), Paris: OECD Publishing.

Organisation for Economic Co-operation and Development, 2015, *OECD Employment Outlook 2015*, Paris: OECD Publishing.

Organisation for Economic Co-operation and Development, 2016a, *Low-Performing Students: Why They Fall Behind and How To Help Them Succeed*, Paris: OECD Publishing.

Organisation for Economic Co-operation and Development, 2016b, *PISA 2015 Results (vol. 2): Policies and Practices for Successful Schools*, <https://read.oecd-ilibrary.org/education/pisa-2015-results-volume-ii_9789264267510-en#page73>, accessed 20 May 2018.

Organisation for Economic Co-operation and Development, 2018a, *The Future of Education and Skills: Education 2030*, Paris: OECD Publishing.

Organisation for Economic Co-operation and Development, 2018b, *Equity in Education: Breaking Down Barriers to Social Mobility*, Paris: OECD Publishing.

Organisation for Economic Co-operation and Development, 2019, *Balancing School Choice and Equity: An International Perspective Based on Pisa*, Paris: OECD Publishing.

Pak-Harvey, A., 2019, 'Nevada charter schools' successes aren't reaching everywhere', *Las Vegas Review Journal*, 13 January, <www.reviewjournal.com/news/education/nevada-charter-schools-successes-arent-reaching-everywhere-1572736/>, accessed 25 January 2019.

Pane, J., Steiner, E., Baird, M., Hamilton, L. & Pane, J., 2017, *Informing Progress: Insights on Personalized Learning Implementation and Effects*, Santa Monica, CA: Rand Corporation.

Pariser, E., 2011, *The Filter Bubble: What the Internet Is Hiding From You*, London: Viking/Penguin Books.

Peretti, J., 2017, *Done: The Secret Deals That Are Changing Our World*, London: Hodder & Stoughton.

Perry, A., 2017, 'How Charter schools are prolonging segregation', *Brookings Institution*, 11 December, <www.brookings.edu/blog/the-avenue/2017/12/11/how-charter-schools-are-prolonging-segregation/>, accessed 30 May 2019.

Perry, L., 2018, 'To reduce inequality in Australian schools, make them less socially segregated', *The Conversation*, 20 April, <www.abc.net.au/news/2018-04-20/inequality-in-australian-schools-ses-resources-poverty-ceda/9679028>, accessed 30 March 2019.

Perry, L. & McConney, A., 2010, 'School socioeconomic composition and student outcomes in Australia: Implications for educational policy', *Australian Journal of Education*, vol. 54, no. 1, pp. 72–85.

Pocock, B., 2009, 'The best of times, the worst of times: The Hawke and Rudd governments, employment and industrial relations', in G. Bloustein, B. Comber & A. Mackinnon (eds), *The Hawke Legacy*, Adelaide: Wakefield Press, pp. 180–97.

Polonski, V., 2018, 'Why AI can't solve everything', *The Conversation*, 25 May, <https://theconversation.com/why-ai-cant-solve-everything-97022>, accessed 1 June 2018.

Prain, V., Cox, P., Deed, C., Edwards, D., Farrelly, C., Keeffe, M., Lovejoy, V., Mow, L., Sellings, P. & Waldrip, B., 2015, *Personalised Learning in Open-Plan Schools*, Rotterdam: Sense Publishing.

Preston, B., 2013, *The social make-up of schools: A report prepared for the Australian Education Union*, South Melbourne: AEU, pp. 1–44.

Primack, B., Shensa, A., Sidani, J., Whaite, W., Lin, L., Rosen, D., Colditz, J., Radovic, A. & Miller, W., 2017, 'Social media use and perceived social isolation among young adults in the US', *American Journal of Preventive Medicine*, vol. 53, no. 1, pp. 1–8.

Pusey, M., 1991, *Economic Rationalism in Canberra: A Nation-Building State Changes Its Mind*, London: Cambridge University Press.

Pyne, C., 2012, *Achieving Teacher Quality: The Coalition's Approach*, address to the Sydney Institute, 16 July, <www.pyneonline.com.au/media-centre/speeches/sydney-institute-address-achieving-teacher-quality-the-coalitions-approach>, accessed 24 January 2019.

Pyne, C., 2014, *Launch of the Australian Government's Independent Public Schools initiative*, 3 February, Canberra: Media Centre for Ministers of the Department of Education and Training, <https://ministers.education.gov.au/pyne/launch-australian-governments-independent-public-schools-initiative>, accessed 30 March 2019.

Quay, J., 2013, 'Cloud schooling: Why we still need teachers in the internet age', *The Conversation*, 18 November, <https://theconversation.com/cloud-schooling-why-we-still-need-teachers-in-the-internet-age-19872>, accessed 30 May 2019.

Rand Corp., 2018, *Improving Teacher Effectiveness—Final Report*, Santa

Monica: Rand Corporation, <https://www.rand.org/pubs/research_reports/RR2242.html>, accessed 30 May 2019.
Ravitch, D., 2013, *Reign of Error: The Hoax of Privatization Movement and the Danger to America's Public Schools*, New York, NY: Alfred Knopf.
Ravitch, D., 2016, *The Death and Life of the Great American Schooling System: How Testing and Choice are Undermining Education*, 2nd edn, New York, NY: Basic Books.
Reich, R., 2018, *The Common Good*, New York, NY: Alfred Knopf.
Reid, A., 2004, *Towards a Culture of Inquiry in DECS*, Occasional Paper No. 1, Adelaide: Department of Education and Children's Services.
Reid, A., 2006, 'Key Competencies: A New Way Forward or More of the Same?', *Curriculum Matters*, vol. 2, pp. 43–62.
Reid, A., 2013a, 'Deepening the equity discourse', in A. Reid & L. Reynolds (eds), *Equity and Education: Exploring New Directions For Equity in Australian Education*, Sydney: Australian College of Educators, pp. 4–15.
Reid, A., 2013b, 'Renewing the public and the role of research in education', *Australian Educational Researcher,* vol. 40, no. 3, pp. 281–97.
Reid, A., 2016, *Building our Nation Through Public Education*, Melbourne: Australian Government Primary Principals' Association.
Reid, A., 2017, *Public Education in South Australia*, Adelaide: DECD.
Reid, A., Cranston, N., Keating, J. & Mulford, B., 2010, *Exploring the Public Purposes of Education in Australian Primary Schools*, Melbourne: Australian Government Primary Principals' Association.
Reid, A. & Price, D., 2018, *The Australian Curriculum: Promises, Problems and Possibilities*, Canberra: Australian Curriculum Studies Association.
Rifkin, J., 2011, *The Third Industrial Revolution: How Lateral Power Is Transforming Energy, the Economy and the World*, New York, NY: Palgrave Macmillan.
Rifkin, J., 2014, *The Zero Marginal Cost Society: The Internet of Things, the Collaborative Commons, and the Eclipse of Capitalism*, New York, NY: Palgrave Macmillan.
Rifkin, J., 2016, 'The 2016 world economic forum misfires with its fourth industrial revolution theme', *Huffington Post*, 14 January, <www.huffingtonpost.com/jeremy-rifkin/the-2016-world-economic-f_b_8975326.html>, accessed 5 April 2018.
Rizvi, F. & Lingard, B., 2010, *Globalizing Education Policy*, Oxford: Routledge.
Roberts-Mahoney, H., Means, A.J. & Garrison, M.J., 2016, 'Netflixing human capital development: Personalized learning technology and the corporatization of K–12 education', *Journal of Education Policy*, vol. 31, pp. 405–420.
Rowe, E., 2017, 'Fewer students are going to public secondary schools in Australia', *The Conversation*, 19 June, <https://theconversation.com/fewer-students-are-going-to-public-secondary-schools-in-australia-79425>, accessed 10 July 2019.
Rowe, E. & Lubienski, C., 2017, 'Shopping for schools or shopping for peers: Public schools and catchment area segregation', *Journal of Education Policy*, vol. 32, no. 3, pp. 340–56.

Rowe, E. & Perry, L., 2019, 'Private financing in urban public schools: inequalities in a stratified education marketplace', *Australian Educational Researcher*, <https://doi.org/10.1007/s13384-019-00328-0>, accessed 10 July 2019.

Rudd, K., 2009, 'The global financial crisis', *The Monthly*, February, <www.themonthly.com.au/issue/2009/february/1319602475/kevin-rudd/global-financial-crisis>, accessed 28 March 2019.

Runcie C. & Brooks, D., 2018, *Reclaiming Education: Renewing Schools and Universities in Contemporary Western Culture*, Revesby: Edwin Lowe.

Runciman, D., 2018, *How Democracy Ends*, London: Profile Books.

Russell, B., 1967, *The Autobiography of Bertrand Russell, Vol. 3: 1944–1969*, London: George Allen and Unwin.

Ryan, C., 2013, 'What is behind the decline of student achievement in Australia?', *Economics of Education Review*, vol. 37, pp. 226–39.

Sahlberg, P., 2012, 'How GERM is infecting schools around the world', *The Washington Post*, 29 June, <www.washingtonpost.com/blogs/answer-sheet/post/how-germ-is-infecting-schools-aroundtheworld/2012/06/29/gJQAVELZAW_blog.html?utm_term=.27f9a896ca0e>, accessed 1 April 2018.

Sahlberg, P., 2015, *Finnish lessons 2.0: What Can the World Learn From Educational Change in Finland?*, New York, NY: Teachers College Press.

Sample, I., 2017, 'Give robots an "ethical black box" to track and explain decisions, say scientists', *The Guardian*, 20 July, <www.theguardian.com/science/2017/jul/19/give-robots-an-ethical-black-box-to-track-and-explain-decisions-say-scientists>, accessed 9 April 2018.

Sandel, M., 2010, 'The lost art of democratic debate', *TED: Ideas Worth Spreading*, <www.ted.com/talks/michael_sandel_the_lost_art_of_democratic_debate?language=en>, accessed 18 October 2018.

Sandel, M., 2012, *What Money Can't Buy: The Moral Limits of Markets*, London: Allen Lane.

Sandlin, J.A., Burdick, J. & Norris, T., 2012, 'Erosion and Experience: Education for Democracy in a Consumer Society', *Review of Research in Education*, vol. 36, no. 1, pp. 139–68.

Savage, G., 2014, 'Independent public schools: A dangerous reform path', *The Conversation*, 4 February, <https://theconversation.com/independent-public-schools-a-dangerous-reform-path-22684>, accessed 20 March 2019.

Savola, A., 2017, 'Global inequality is on the rise—but at vastly different rates across the world', *The Conversation*, 14 December, <https://theconversation.com/global-inequality-is-on-the-rise-but-at-vastly-different-rates-across-the-world-88976>, accessed 30 May 2019.

Schleicher, A., 2018, *World Class: How to Build a 21st Century Schooling System*, Paris: OECD.

Schleicher, A., 2019, 'Why PISA is testing students' social and emotional skills', *The Sydney Morning Herald*, 18 May, <www.smh.com.au/education/why-pisa-is-testing-students-social-and-emotional-skills-20190426-p51hic.html>, accessed 28 May 2019.

Schneider, J., 2019, 'School's out: Charters were supposed to save public education. Why are Americans turning against them?', *Washington Post*, 30 May, <https://wapo.st/2EGFBeK>, accessed 2 June 2019.

Schneider, J. & Menefee-Libey, D., 2018, 'Why big bets on educational reform haven't fixed the US school system', *The Conversation*, 8 March, <https://theconversation.com/why-big-bets-on-educational-reform-havent-fixed-the-us-school-system-92327>, accessed 25 January 2019.

Schwab, J., 1962, 'The teaching of science as enquiry', in J. Schwab & P. Brandwan (eds), *The Teaching of Science*, Cambridge, MA: Harvard University Press.

Schwab, K., 2015, 'The fourth industrial revolution: What it means and how to respond', *Foreign Affairs*, 12 December, <www.foreignaffairs.com/articles/2015-12-12/fourth-industrial-revolution>, accessed 8 April 2018.

Schwab, K., 2016, *The Fourth Industrial Revolution*, New York, NY: Crown Business.

Scott, C., 2015, *The Futures of Learning 2: What Kind of Learning for the 21st century?* Paris: OECD.

Sellar, S., Thomson, G. & Rutkowski, D., 2017, *The Global Education Race: Taking the Measure of PISA and International Testing*, Edmonton: Brush Education.

Sen, A., 2001, *Development as Freedom*, 2nd edn, Oxford: Oxford University Press.

Sen, V., 2016, 'Towards customized privatization in public education in British Columbia: The provincial education plan and personalized learning', *Canadian Journal of Educational Administration and Policy*, no. 80, pp. 135–168.

Shanahan, M., 2009, 'Economic policy of the Hawke years', in G. Bloustein, B. Comber & A. Mackinnon (eds), *The Hawke Legacy*, Adelaide: Wakefield Press, pp. 167–179.

Shepherd, B., 2014, *What MySchool Tells Us About Schools Funding*, Melbourne: Australian Education Union.

Sloan, J., 2012, 'Why I don't give a Gonski for more school spending', *The Australian*, 28 August, <www.theaustralian.com.au/opinion/columnists/why-i-dont-give-a-gonski-for-more-school-spending/newsstory/7017c7b2fbd968a2b6c760b091c0e722?nk=7c175d1545f16dfa8a292422c61bec43-1548300714>, accessed 24 January 2019.

Smart, D., Scott, R., Murphy, K. & Dudley, J., 1986, 'The Hawke government and education 1983–1985', *Politics*, vol. 21, no. 1, pp. 63–81.

Snook, I., O'Neill, J., Clark, J., O'Neill, A-M. & Openshaw, R., 2009, 'Invisible learnings? A commentary on John Hattie's Book—"Visible learning: A synthesis of over 800 meta-analyses relating to achievement"', *New Zealand Journal of Educational Studies*, vol. 44, no. 1, pp. 93–106.

Sommer, K. & Boden, M., 2018, 'Why R2D2 could be your child's teacher sooner than you think', *The Conversation*, 17 October, <https://theconversation.com/why-r2d2-could-be-your-childs-teacher-sooner-than-you-think-103284>, accessed 30 May 2019.

Spady, W., 2014, *Bringing Heart and Soul to Education: Inspiring Approaches, Transformational Perspectives, Empowered Learning*, Boulder, CO: Mason Works Press.

Srivastava, P., 2015, 'Low-fee private schools and poor children: What do we really know?', *The Guardian*, 12 August, <www.theguardian.com/global-development-professionals-network/2015/aug/12/low-fee-private-schools-poverty-development-economist>, accessed 25 January 2019.

Srivastava, P., 2016, 'Questioning the global scaling-up of low-fee private schooling: The nexus between business, philanthropy, and PPPs', in A. Verger, C. Lubienski & G. Steiner-Khamsi (eds), *The World Yearbook of Education 2016: The Global Education Industry*, New York, NY: Routledge.

Srnicek, N. & Williams, A., 2015, *Inventing the Future: Postcapitalism and a World Without Work*, New York, NY: Verso.

Stein, J., 2018, 'Don't be too quick to dismiss "dying trades", those skills are still in demand', *The Conversation*, 6 December, <https://theconversation.com/dont-be-too-quick-to-dismiss-dying-trades-those-skills-are-still-in-demand-107894>, accessed 13 December 2018.

Steiner-Khamsi, G. (ed.), 2004, *The Global Politics of Educational Borrowing and Lending*, New York, NY: Teachers College Press.

Steiner-Khamsi, G., 2016, 'New directions in policy borrowing research', *Asia Pacific Education Review*, vol. 17, no. 3, pp. 381–90.

Sternberg, R.J., 2003, *Wisdom, Intelligence, and Creativity, Synthesized*, New York, NY: Cambridge University Press.

Stewart, W., 2013, 'Is PISA fundamentally flawed?', *Times Educational Supplement*, 26 July, <www.tes.com/news/long-read-does-pisa-really-tell-us-anything-useful-about-schools>, accessed 20 May 2018.

Stewart, W., 2014, 'More than a quarter of Shanghai pupils missed by international PISA rankings', *Times Education Supplement*, 6 March, <www.tes.co.uk/news/school-news/breaking-news/more-a-quartershanghai-pupils-missed-international-pisa-rankings>, accessed 30 March 2019.

Stokes, R., 2018, 'Let's end our neo-liberal school testing fixation', *Sydney Morning Herald*, 14 December, <www.smh.com.au/education/let-s-end-our-neo-liberal-school-testing-fixation-20181213-p50m3q.html>, accessed 18 January 2019.

Stroud, G., 2018, *Teacher: One Woman's Struggle to Keep the Heart in Teaching*, Crows Nest: Allen & Unwin.

Susaria, A., 2018, 'How artificial intelligence can detect—and create—fake news', *The Conversation*, 3 May, <https://theconversation.com/how-artificial-intelligence-can-detect-and-create-fake-news-95404>, accessed 7 May 2018.

Swan, W., 2017, 'The Hawke-Keating agenda was laborism, not neoliberalism, and is still a guiding light', *The Guardian*, 14 May, <www.theguardian.com/commentisfree/2017/may/14/the-hawke-keating-agenda-was-laborism-not-neoliberalism-and-is-still-a-guiding-light>, accessed 30 May 2019.

Tampio, N., 2019, 'How Gate's Foundation's push for "high-quality" curriculum will stifle teaching', *The Conversation*, 28 January, <https://theconversation.com/how-gates-foundations-push-for-high-quality-curriculum-will-stifle-teaching-110323>, accessed 30 May 2019.

Teese, R., 2011, *From Opportunity to Outcomes: The Changing Role of Public Schooling in Australia and National Funding Arrangements*, commissioned report, Melbourne: Centre for Research on Education Systems, pp. 1–75.

The Times Editorial Board, 2016, 'Gate's Foundation failures show philanthropists shouldn't be setting America's public school agenda', *Los Angeles Times*, 1 June, <www.latimes.com/opinion/editorials/la-ed-gates-education-20160601-snap-story.html>, accessed 25 January 2019.

Thompson, D., 2015, 'A world without work', *The Atlantic*, July/August, <www.theatlantic.com/magazine/archive/2015/07/world-without-work/395294/>, accessed 8 April 2018.

Thompson, G., Hogan, A. & Shield, P., 2017, *Commercialisation in Public Schooling (CIPS) Survey: Final Report*, Sydney: News South Wales Teachers Federation.

Thompson, G., Hogan, A. & Rahimi, M., 2019, 'Private funding in Australian public schools: A problem of equity', *Australian Educational Researcher* (In Press).

Thompson, G., Savage, G. & Lingard, R., 2015, 'Think tanks, edu-businesses and education policy: Issues of evidence, expertise and influence', *Australian Educational Researcher*, vol. 43, no. 1, <www.researchgate.net/publication/289519268_Introduction_Think_tanks_edu-businesses_and_education_policy_Issues_of_evidence_expertise_and_influence>, accessed 30 March 2019.

Thomson, S., De Bortoli, L. & Underwood, C., 2017, *PISA 2015: Reporting Australia's results*, Hawthorn: ACER, <https://research.acer.edu.au/ozpisa/22>, accessed 18 June 2018.

Thrupp, M., 2018, *The Search for Better Educational Standards: A cautionary tale*, Cham: Springer.

Ting, I., Liu, R. & Scott, N., 2018, 'Cutting the cost of the education revolution', *ABC News* [online], <www.abc.net.au/news/2018-11-22/counting-the-cost-of-the-education-revolution/10495756>, accessed 29 January 2019.

Tooley, J., 2009, *The Beautiful Tree: A Personal Journey Into How the World's Poorest People Are Educating Themselves*, Washington, DC: Cato Institute.

Tooley, J., 2018, 'A chain of low-cost private schools for England', *Policy*, vol. 34, no. 2, pp. 13–17.

Tovey, J., 2013, 'NAPLAN results used as entry criteria for private schools', *Sydney Morning Herald*, 12 May, <www.smh.com.au/education/naplan-results-used-as-entry-criteria-for-private-schools-20130511-2jemo.html>, accessed 30 May 2019.

Triffitt, M., 2018, 'Reforming our political system is not a quick fix', *The Conversation*, 11 September, <http://theconversation.com/reforming-our-political-system-is-not-a-quick-fix-heres-a-step-by-step-guide-to-how-to-do-it-102415>, accessed 1 December 2018.

Trilling, B. & Fadel, C., 2009, *21st Century Skills: Learning for Life in Our Time*, San Francisco, CA: Jossey-Bass.

Tyack, D. & Tobin, W., 1994, 'The grammar of schooling: Why has it been so hard to change?', *American Educational Research Journal*, vol. 31, no. 3, pp. 453–80.

UNICEF, 2018, 'An unfair start: Inequality in children's education in rich

countries', *Innocenti Report Card 15*, Florence: UNICEF Office of Research.
Urban, R., 2018, 'Classroom behaviour the key to future pay', *The Weekend Australian*, 19–20 May, p. 7.
Walker, M. & Unterhalter, E. (eds), 2007, *Amartya Sen's Capability Approach and Social Justice in Education*, New York, NY: Palgrave Macmillan.
Walsh, T., 2017a, *It's Alive: Artificial Intelligence From the Logic Piano to Killer Robot*, Melbourne: La Trobe University Press.
Walsh, T., 2017b, 'Will robots bring about the end of work?', *The Guardian*, 1 October, <www.theguardian.com/science/political-science/2017/oct/01/will-robots-bring-about-the-end-of-work>, accessed 9 April 2018.
Walsh, T., 2018, *2062: The World That AI Made*, Melbourne: Latrobe University Press.
Ward, H., 2017, 'PISA data may be incomparable, Schleicher admits', *Times Educational Supplement*, 24 March, <www.tes.com/news/exclusive-pisa-data-may-be-incomparable-schleicher-admits>, accessed 21 May 2018.
Washor, E. & Mojkowski, C., 2014, 'Student disengagement: It's deeper than you think', *Phi Delta Kappan*, vol. 95, no. 8, pp. 8–10.
Watkins, W. (ed.), 2012, *The Assault On Public Education: Confronting the Politics of Corporate School Reform*, New York, NY: Teachers College Press.
Watson, L. & Ryan, C., 2010, 'Choosers and losers: The impact of government subsidies on Australian secondary schools', *Australian Journal of Education*, vol. 54, no. 1, pp. 86–107.
Weale, S., 2015, '"It's a political failure": How Sweden's celebrated schools system fell into crisis', *The Guardian*, 10 June, <www.theguardian.com/world/2015/jun/10/sweden-schools-crisis-political-failure-education>, accessed 28 March 2019.
Wells, A., Fox, L. & Cordova-Cobo, C., 2016, *How Socially Diverse Schools and Classrooms Can Benefit All Students*, New York, NY: Century Foundation.
West, A., 2014, 'What Swedish free schools reveal about social segregation', *The Conversation*, 26 March, <https://theconversation.com/what-swedish-free-schools-reveal-about-social-segregation-24682>, accessed 25 January 2019.
West, D., 2018, *The Future of Work: Robots, AI and Automation*, New York, NY: Brookings Institution.
West-Burnham, J. & Coates, M., 2005, *Personalizing Learning: Transforming Education for Every Child*, Heatherton: Hawker Brownlow Education.
Whitby, G., 2013, *Educating Gen Wi-Fi: How to Make Schools Relevant for 21st Century Learners*, Sydney: HarperCollins.
White, F., Maunder, R. & Verrelli, S., 2018, 'How research is helping to reduce prejudice between people online', *The Conversation*, 13 November, <https://theconversation.com/how-research-is-helping-to-reduce-prejudice-between-people-online-106175>, accessed 4 December 2018.
Whitty, G. (ed.), 2016, *Research and Policy in Education: Evidence, Ideology and Impact*, London: University College London Press.
Whitty, G., Power, S. & Halpin, D., 1998, *Devolution and Choice in Education: The School, the State and the Market*, Buckingham: Open University Press.

References

Wiborg, S., 2014, 'The big winners from Sweden's for-profit "free" schools are companies not pupils', *The Conversation*, 9 September, <https://theconversation.com/the-big-winners-from-swedens-for-profit-free-schools-are-companies-not-pupils-29929>, accessed 25 January 2019.

Wilby, P., 2013, 'Professor James Tooley: A champion of low-cost schools or a dangerous man?', *The Guardian*, 12 November, <www.theguardian.com/education/2013/nov/12/professor-james-tooley-low-cost-schools>, accessed 20 February 2015.

Wilkinson, R. & Pickett, K., 2009, *The Spirit Level: Why More Equal Societies Almost Always Do Better*, London: Allen Lane.

Williams, R., 1985, 'The economic determinants of private schooling in Australia', *Economic Record*, vol. 61, pp. 622–628.

Williams, T., 2017, 'Aussie schoolchildren far noisier and rowdier in classroom than overseas students, report finds', *The Advertiser*, 14 March, <www.adelaidenow.com.au/news/south-australia/aussie-schoolchildren-far-noiser-and-rowdier-in-classroom-than-overseas-students-report-finds/news-story/c2deaa20a79e232bdf4b4e218a2cad9>, accessed 10 July 2019.

Williams, T., 2018, 'Education department plan to place SA schools with world's best systems within a decade', *The Advertiser*, 31 August, <www.adelaidenow.com.au/news/south-australia/education-department-plan-to-place-sa-schools-with-worlds-best-systems-within-a-decade/news-story/6309786f1f70edfe9b15b03519782851>, accessed 20 April 2019.

Wilson, E.O., 1998, *Consilience: The Unity of Knowledge*, New York, NY: Vintage.

Wilson, N., 1997, 'Educational standards and the problem of error', *Education Policy Analysis Archives*, vol. 6, no. 10, <https://epaa.asu.edu/ojs/article/view/577http://epaa.asu.edu/epaa/vol6n10/>, accessed 20 January 2019.

Wilson, N., 2007, 'A little less than valid: An essay review', *Education Review*, vol. 10, no. 5, <http://edrev.asu.edu/essays/v10n5index.html>, accessed 26 April 2019.

Wu, M. & Hornsby, D., 2014, 'Inappropriate uses of NAPLAN results', *Practically Primary*, vol. 19, no. 2, pp. 16–17, <https://search.informit.com.au/documentSummary;dn=320310592534323;res=IELHSS>,ISSN: 1324-5961>, accessed 18 January 2019.

Wylie, C., 2012, *Vital Connections: Why We Need More Than Self-Managing Schools*, Auckland: NZCER Press.

Wyn, J., Turnbull, M. & Grimshaw, L., 2014, *The Experience of Education: A Qualitative Study*, Sydney: Whitlam Institute, pp. 1–15.

Wyn, J., 2014, 'NAPLAN testing does more harm than good', *The Conversation*, 20 May, <https://theconversation.com/naplan-testing-does-more-harm-than-good-26923>, accessed 18 January 2019.

Young, M., 2008, *Bringing Knowledge Back In: From Social Constructivism to Social Realism in the Sociology of Education*, Milton Park: Routledge.

Young, M., 2014, 'Why start with the curriculum?', in M. Young & D. Lambert with C. Roberts & M. Roberts, *Knowledge and the Future School: Curriculum and Social Justice*, London: Bloomsbury, pp. 41–64.

Young, I.M., 2011, *Justice and the Politics of Difference*, Princeton, NJ: Princeton University Press.

Young, M. & Lambert, D. (eds), 2014, *Knowledge and the Future School: Curriculum and Social Justice*, Bloomsbury: London.

Zeng, M., 2018, 'China's Social Credit system outs its people under pressure to be model citizens', *The Conversation*, 24 January, <https://theconversation.com/chinas-social-credit-system-puts-its-people-under-pressure-to-be-model-citizens-89963>, accessed 9 April 2018.

Zhao, Y., 2014, *Who's Afraid of the Big Bad Dragon: Why China Has the Best (and Worst) Education System in the World*, San Francisco, CA: Jossey-Bass.

Zipin, L., 2017, 'Pursuing a problematic-based curriculum approach for the sake of social justice', *Journal of Education*, vol. 69, pp. 67–92.

Zuboff, S., 2019, *The Age of Surveillance Capitalism: The Fight For a Human Future at the New Frontier of Power*, London: Profile Books.

Zygnier, D., 2019, 'Public schools actually outperform private schools and with less money', *The Conversation*, 30 April, <https://theconversation.com/public-schools-actually-outperform-private-schools-and-with-less-money-113914>, accessed 26 May 2019.

Index

'21st-century learning' xvi, 241–2, 253

Abbott, Tony 11
Abbott Government funding model 65–6
accountability 99, 100
  alternative approach 297
  importance of 39–40, 79–80, 296
  neo-liberalism view 296
  testing and xv, 40–1, 296
  top-down xi
'achievement gap' 28, 33, 134
  causes of, understanding 34
Adelaide Declaration of 1999 171
Africa, school autonomy 119
after-hours cram schools 85
Amazon 214
American Statistical Association 147
Amplify 140–1
artificial intelligence (AI) xvi, 162, 164, 170, 195
  'AI solutionism' 214
  biases in 222
  developments in 197–8
  ethical dilemmas 217–18
  humanity and 221
  private ownership of 214
  'weak AI' 201
Australian Brain Initiative 252
Australian Competition and Consumer Commission (ACCC) 13
Australian Council for Educational Research (ACER) 80, 95, 96

Australian Council of Social Services (ACOSS) 12–13
Australian Curriculum *see also* changing the curriculum; curriculum
  components 231–7, 253
  disadvantage, addressing 239–41
  disciplinary learning 231, 232
  general capabilities learning 233, 241–7
  interdisciplinary learning 232, 234–5
  meta-learning 233, 235–6, 247–8, 252
  official for compulsory years 229
Australian Curriculum and Assessment Authority (ACARA) 24, 41, 142
  Index of Socio-Educational Advantage (ICSEA) 69, 73
  interdisciplinary learning, facilitation 239
Australian Secondary Principals' Association (ASPA) xii
Average Government School Recurrent Costs (AGSRC) 61, 62

'best practice' xi, 25, 273, 299
Biesta, Gert 168, 247
Biggs, John 248
Bill and Melinda Gates Foundation (BMGF) 145–8
biotechnology xvi, 170, 220
Birmingham, Simon 66, 96
Bonner, Chris 30
Boyer lectures 138

capabilities *see* general capabilities learning
'capacities for social practice' 175
Catching Up: Learning from the best school systems in Asia 83
   contradictory messages 112–13
   methodology, inadequacy of 107–8, 110–12
   PISA results, acceptance and use of 107, 108–9
   process of writing 106
   reaction to 104–6
Catholic schools 66, 69, 70, 73
Centre for Independent Studies 262, 264
Centre for Research on Educational Outcomes (CREDO) 124, 125
changing the curriculum 237–52
   disadvantage, addressing 239–41
   disciplinary/interdisciplinary binary 237–9
   general capabilities learning 241–4
   silver bullets, adoption of 250
China, 'social credit' 213
Christodoulou, Daisy 155, 243
Cobbold, Trevor 69
collaboration 23, 43, 116, 286
commercialisation of education 23, 24, 76–7, 282
'customer', students as 24, 38, 282
Common Core curriculum standards 147–8
common good xxiii, 18, 24, 78, 178, 224, 281
   commitment to 217
   education for 282
   nurturing disposition for 281
   public education and 282–6
   values comprising 178
competition xv, 21, 22, 34
   neoliberalism 4, 295–6
compulsory public education 16, 17
Connell, Raewyn 47
consultants, external xvi, 20–1, 46–7, 103–4
corporate influences
   managerialism 20, 42, 76–7
   non-educators, of 130–1, 137–8
creativity 246
cultural diversity
   benefits to a school 285
   curriculum catering for 239–41
culture of research and inquiry 273–4
   inquiry-based learning 262–3, 277–80

curriculum *see also* Australian Curriculum; changing the curriculum
   broad, belief in 18
   components of 231–7, 253
   contemporary curriculum xxv, 231–7, 252–3
   contextualising 273
   equity in 284
   global homogenisation 85
   'hidden curriculum' 272
   innovation x, xiii
   narrowing 41
   'reforms' 44
   transplanting 86

data 33, 79, 211–13
   use in policy development xvi, 79, 90–2
Dawkins, John 19–20
decision-making
   democracy in 284
   educators voice, exclusion 181, 294–5, 299
   evidence and 299
   proposed model for *see* six-step decision-making process
   traditional approach, issues 181
democracy
   big tech companies, power of 214, 217
   capacities needed 215–18
   civic and political engagement 216
   common good 217
   democratic education system 284–5
   discerning propaganda 216
   elections, hyper-targeting 210–11
   fourth industrial revolution and 210–15
   Freedom House reports 215
   hashtag democracy 213
   knowledge of 216
   metadata 213
   public sphere, fragmentation 212–13
   surveillance systems 213
Denniss, Richard 13–14
Department of Employment, Education and Training 20
Desmond-Hellmann, Sue 148
'devolution' 22, 44
digital age 193
digital learning xvi, 141
direct instruction model 266
disability, students with 37, 73

Index

Disadvantaged Schools Program (DSP) 18, 19
disadvantaged students
  curriculum, catering for 239–41
  public schools, attending 31, 61, 64, 67, 70, 77
disciplinary-based learning 231, 232
  inter-disciplinary and 237–9
Donnelly, Dr Kevin 117, 260
  critique of school autonomy stance 118–27
Dweck, Carol 249, 250

Eacott, Scott 117
'edubusinesses' 103, 142
education
  decision-making *see* decision-making
  economic purposes of 20, 21
  government departments 20–1, 42
  human right, as 283
  knowledge base 45, 46
  nation-building project, as 17
  neoliberalism and 15, 19–24, 48–9, 289–90, 295–300
  pre-neoliberalism, overview 16–19
  principles *see* values and principles of education
  purposes *see* purposes of education
  role of ix, 48
  values *see* values and principles of education
Education Council 170, 301
education market xxi, 21–2, 42, 59, 75–6, 129
Education Resources Index (ERI) 61–2
educators *see also* non-educators; teachers
  learning from teaching 274
  policy, role in shaping xiii, 302–3
  political engagement 302–3
  role of ix–x, 302
employment
  automation 201, 202, 204
  clusters of work 203
  fourth industrial revolution and 199–207
  machine learning 205–6
  post-work society 206, 207
  redistribution 222–3
  robots 201, 202, 222
  structure of 202
  work conditions 204
  work-related capacities 208–9
entitlement, principle of 56, 59–62, 77

equity 18, 21, 33, 35, 64, 169, 175, 297
  curriculum promoting 284
  entitlement and 61–3
  neo-liberalism view 297
  US charter schools 126–8

Facebook 211, 212, 214
Fadel, Charles 248
fake news 212, 214
Federation 16
Finkel, Alan 238
Finland 83, 84–5
for-profit schools 38, 117
Foundation for Young Australians 203
four Rs 154–5, 155–164
  main tenets of 165
fourth industrial revolution
  case study 190–2, 225–6, 293
  convergence of technologies 196
  democracy, implications for 210–15
  digital awareness, capacity for 224–5
  employment, implications for *see* employment
  ethical dilemmas 214–15, 217–18, 224
  individuals, impact on 218–22
  knowledge capacities 208–9
  life-long learning capacities 208–9
  meaning of term 192–6
  political capacities 209
  social capacities 209
  thinking capacities 209
  work-related capacities 208–9
Fraser Government funding model 58–9
free market xx, 4, 6, 8, 39
Friedman, Milton *Capitalism and Freedom* 5–6
funding of schools
  Abbott Government 65–6
  Commonwealth contribution 17, 68
  complexity 56
  disparity in 29, 67, 75
  entitlement, according to 56, 59–60, 77
  Fraser Government 58–9
  Gillard Government 64–5
  high-SES and low-SES 29
  Howard Government 62
  mechanisms 57
  Morrison Government 67
  needs-based 19, 56, 60, 61
  per capita arguments 60
  private schools 55, 57
  resource disparity 29

schooling resource standard (SRS) 64, 69
SES model 62–3, 65
state-aid debate 57
states constitutional responsibility 16, 17, 68
Whitlam Government 58, 68
futures approach xvi, xvii, 49–50 *see also* new educational narrative

Garrett, Peter 105, 106
gender imbalance in leadership roles 18
general capabilities learning 233, 241–2
   Australian Curriculum, in 242–7
   capabilities to function 244
   Gonski Review 242, 246
   meaning of specific 245
   purpose of 243
Gillard, Julia 22, 63, 106, 134, 137
   Klein agenda, borrowing of 134–7
Gillard Government
   Australian Education Bill 2013 81
   funding model 64–5
Global Financial Crisis (GFC) 9–11, 13
global curriculum homogenisation 85–6
global education reform movement (GERM) xv–xvi, xvii, 15, 264
   Australia, in 15
globalisation xvi, 19, 170
Gonski Review 63–5, 73, 105
   Gonski 2.0 66–7, 172, 265, 266–7, 269
Google 212, 214
Grattan Institute 67, 103

Harari, Yuval 197–8, 206, 220
Harvey, David 4
Hattie, Professor John 250–1
   Visible Learning 157–9
Hawke Government 7–8, 19, 60
Hayek, Friedrich *The Road to Serfdom* 5
high-SES students, drift to private sector 72
Ho, Christina 31
Hong Kong 83, 86, 88, 89, 95, 106, 107, 110
Howard Government 8–9, 21, 62
human capital 19

independent public schools (IPS) 37–9, 116
India, school autonomy 119

Indigenous students 28
   public schools, in 73
   Year 12 29
inequality of income and wealth 12–13
innovation, culture of 287
inquiry-based learning 262–3, 273–4
   conditions for 279–80
   dangers 279
   model 277–8
   potential outcomes 278–9
   public representation of 263–4
interdisciplinary learning 232, 234–5
   discipline-based learning and 237–9
International Monetary Fund (IMF) 6, 12
internet
   collective commons, as 210
   dark side 196
   predictive assistance 218–19, 220
   promise of 210
Internet of Things 195, 197, 219

Jackson, Philip 272
Jensen, Dr Ben 104, 105, 106
Jerrim, John 86

Karmel Report (1973) 55
Kemp, Les x, xii–xiii
'key performance indicators' xi, 76
Keynesian economic policy 6, 8
Klein, Joel 131–4, 140–1
   education agenda 131–8
Kreiner, Professor Svend 87

LBOTE background students 31–2
learning *see also* meta-learning
   concept of, understanding 247
   constructivism 256
   inquiry-based learning 262–4
   instructivism 256
   learning to learn 160, 247–8
local community involvement 38–9, 54, 123, 127, 146, 286
Loveless, Tom 88–9
low-SES students 28, 30–1
   public schools, in 37, 72–3

machine learning xvi, 162, 170, 205
McKinsey and Company xvi, xvii–xx, 104, 132, 262, 263–4
Mcloughlin, Claire 120
managerial model 20, 42, 76–7, 275, 276–7

Index

Melbourne Declaration on Educational Goals for Young Australians 170–3, 300
Menzies Government 55
meta-learning 233, 235–6, 247–8, 252
metacognition 249
metadata xvi, 183, 213
Microsoft 214
mindset theory 250–2
Mitra, Professor Sugata 162–4
Morrison Government funding model 67
Murdoch, Rupert 140–1
  Golden Age of Freedom speeches 138–9
My School website 22, 31, 134

'naming and shaming' xv, 34, 296
National Assessment Plan—Literacy and Numeracy (NAPLAN) xii, xviii, 22, 28, 40, 49, 99, 134
  accountability and 40–1
  damage caused by 42
  introduction 22
  low-SES students 28
  methodology, criticisms 41
  My School website 22
  NAPLAN preparation 41
  use of 41
National Assessment Program (NAP) 29
National Education Policy Center (US) 268
need, principle of 57
neoliberalism xx–xxi, xxii
  Australia, in 7–11, 153–4
  dominance 13, 24, 25
  education, in 19–24, 48–9, 153–4, 180, 289–90, 295–300
  effects of 11–15, 28–48
  government and 4, 6
  key elements 13
  language of 24
  nature of 4–5
  origins 5–7
  pervasiveness 15
  rhetoric 14
  school autonomy and 114–18
new educational narrative
  accountability 296–7
  collaborative culture 286
  common good 281–7
  community-based 286
  culture of research and inquiry 273–4
  decision-making 299
  democratic system 284–5
  educators role in 302–3
  elements 187–8, 290–2
  equity 297
  futures-focused 187, 188, 292, 295
  innovation, culture of 287
  requirements to establish 300–4
  socially just culture 283–4
  supporting conditions 271–2
New Schools Policy 21, 62
New Zealand Partnership schools 121–2
News Corporation 140–1
news cycle, 24-hour 213, 217
non-educators 130–1, 137–8
  Murdoch 138–41
  philanthrocapitalism *see* philanthrocapitalism
  policy-influencers, as 145, 148–9

Organisation for Economic Co-operation and Development (OECD) xvi, xvii, 13, 23
  PISA test *see* Program for International Student Assessment (PISA)

Participation and Equity Program (PEP) 19
Pearson 23–4, 120, 142
pedagogy
  approach, choice of 254–5, 258, 260, 269, 270
  assessment 259
  didactic pedagogy xxiv, 238
  framework, proposed 256–61
  inquiry-based learning 262–4
  organisational models 259
  outcomes 254
  personalised learning *see* personalised learning
  standardisation and 264–5
  teaching principles 255–6
  teaching strategies 258–9
  technology and 261
  view of learning 256, 258
performance pay for teachers 35, 82, 135
personalised learning 161, 268–9
  approaches 266
  'customised privatization' 268
  Gonski 2.0 version 265, 266–7, 269
philanthrocapitalism 143, 144, 149
  accountability and 149, 150

Bill and Melinda Gates Foundation (BMGF) 145–8
  nature of 143, 144
  policy-influencers, as 145, 148–9
philanthropy 149–50
  Gonski Review recommendations 143–4
  philanthrocapitalism *see* philanthrocapitalism
  Schools Plus 144, 150
  traditional 143
policy, education
  alternative to neoliberalism 49, 295
  change, need for xiv, 289
  Commonwealth Government involvement 19
  decision-making *see* decision-making
  edubusinesses and 103
  educators, involvement 302–3
  evidence-based policy xvi, 25, 47, 101, 113–14, 299
  flexibility, need for 181
  four Rs approaches 154–5
  impact xi
  neoliberalism and 15, 19–24, 48–9, 289–90, 295–300
  societal trends and 176, 181–3, 225, 293–4
  transplanting of *see* transplanting education policy
  work imposition caused by 44
policy networks xxiv, 106, 130
Preston, Barbara 72
principals
  entrepreneurs, as 42–3
  fixed-term tenure 43
private schools 57
  commonwealth funding, percentage 68
  expansion of 21–2
  fees charged 70
  funding 55, 57–68
  government privileging 53
  income of 69
  numbers attending 30, 36, 54, 70
  per capita funding arguments 60
  reasons for choosing 70–1
privatisation of education 23, 35, 37, 75–7, 282–3, 295–6
  technology companies and 267–8
process for a futures-focused education 187, 188, 292, 295
  developing new 301

Program for International Student Assessment (PISA) xvi, xvii, xviii, 23, 49, 99
  2015 results, reactions 82
  accountability and 40–1, 100
  additional questionnaires 81, 92
  Australian focus on 81–2
  conducting of tests, variations 88–9
  criticisms of 87–9
  cultural neutrality 85, 88
  data produced 91–2
  disciplinary climate data 92–7
  inquiry-based learning and 263–4
  lowest SES, students from 28–9
  media reporting of results 82, 89, 96–8
  methodology 87–9
  narrowness of focus 83, 84–6, 98
  OECD response to criticism 99–100
  overview 80–1, 99–101
  Policies and Practices for Successful Schools 91
  subjects tested 80, 81, 84
  unquestioning acceptance of 82, 83, 91–2
Progress in International Reading Literacy Study (PIRLS) xviii
pseudo-scientific studies 45–8, 83
Public Education Foundation 28
public schools
  common good, for 282, 283–4
  decline in attendance 30, 36, 53, 70
  'devolution' 22
  disability, students with 37, 73
  disadvantaged students, numbers 31, 61, 64, 67, 70, 77
  establishment 16
  fragmentation of 73–4
  Indigenous students 37, 73
  integrative function 39
  low-SES student numbers 37, 72–3
  major educational provider, as 19
  privatisation *see* privatisation of education
  public purpose 39
  remote area students 28 , 73
  resourcing xxiv
  safety net, as 36, 53, 63, 282
  secondary schools 53–4
  selective 73
  social mix 54, 74
  special purpose 73
purposes of education 187, 290
  absence of explicit 167–8

benefits of 175
bipartisan agreement about 300–1
democratic 173
economic 173
individual 173–4
Melbourne Declaration, in 171, 300
proposed 173–8
social and cultural 174
who determines 168–9
Pyne, Christopher 105

Rasch model 87–8
Ravitch, Dianne 126, 127, 137, 138
Reagan, Ronald 6, 8
reboot 157–9, 165
Reclaiming Education 155
reframe 159–62, 165
Reich, Robert 178, 281
remote area students 28, 73
replace 162–4, 165
research 20
    consultants and edubusinesses, by 103
    culture of research and inquiry 273–4
    marginalisation of 47–8
    methods, debate as to 45–6
    standardised tests, based on 25, 46
residualising public education 35–6, 55, 72–5
resources, redistribution 34
revert 155–7, 165
Rifkin, Jeremy 193–5, 196, 205
robotics xvi, 162, 164, 201, 202
'robust justice' 34
Rudd, Kevin 'The Global Financial Crisis' 11
Rudd Government 9, 22
Rudd–Gillard Governments 63

Schleicher, Andreas 89, 91–2
scholarships 71
school autonomy
    concept of, differing 113–16, 128
    evidence about 117
    forms of 118
    Indian and African versions 119
    neoliberalism and 114–18
    New Zealand Partnership schools 121–2
    Swedish version 122–3
    US charter schools 123–8
school choice xv, xxi, 21, 39, 286, 295–6
    rationale 59–60

schools
    cultural diversity, benefits 285–6
    end of school outcomes 30
    institutions, importance as 176
    obsolescence 163, 176
    social function of 176
Schools Commission 20
Schools Plus 144, 150
Schwab, Professor Klaus 195–6
secondary education 16, 17
    public schools 53–4
segregation of school system 54, 74, 77, 286
    ethnicity 31–2, 74
    low-SES and high-SES students 30–1
    US charter schools 127
Seven Myths About Education 155
Shanghai 88–9, 104, 112
Singapore 83, 85, 86, 95, 106, 108, 112
six-step decision-making process 182–4, 293, 301
    focus of each step 185
    individual schools, application 185–6
    system-wide application 185, 186
Sloan, Judith 105
Snowden affair 213
social and cultural purpose of education 174
social justice 11, 18, 283–4
social media 212
    data from, use of 211, 218–19
    elections, use in 211
    hashtag democracy 213
    negative impacts 219
    silos of sameness 212, 217
societal trends and 170, 176, 181–3, 293–4
    educational implications 182
    examples of 182–3
    ongoing examination 189–90
South Australian case study xvii–xx
South Korea 83, 85, 86, 89, 106, 108
standardisation xv–xvii, xix–xx, 51, 98, 265
    alternative *see* new education narrative
    challenges to xxiii, 188
    characteristics of agenda xix–xx, 15
    dominance of xxii, 295
    impact xvii, xxi, 3, 28, 280
    origins xx, 19–24
standardised testing 22, 25, 33, 98, 296
    limitations of 46
    PISA *see* Program for International Student Assessment (PISA)
    validity and reliability 296

STEM 234
Stiglitz, Joseph xxiii
Stokes, Rob 42
stratification of education xxi, 30, 33, 55, 286
Strengthening Australia's Schools 20
Stroud, Gabbie *Teacher* 44
student agency, fostering 285
student assessment
   futures-focused approach 298
   norm-referenced 298
   purpose of 259, 298
   reference point made against 259
student engagement 84, 85
student:teacher ratios 71
student wellbeing 85
Summit 267–8
surveillance
   global 213, 217
   surveillance capitalism 219
Sweden, school autonomy 122–3

Teach for Australia 135
teachers
   administrative workload xi, 44
   collegial relationships xiii
   de-professionalising 44, 137
   effectiveness, evaluating 147
   fixed period positions 43
   new entrants leaving profession 45
   performance pay 35, 82
   practiced-based knowledge 299
   trust in the professionalism of 18
   voice in decision-making 47, 181, 299
teaching *see also* learning; pedagogy
   approaches and models 258
   assessment 259
   'good teaching' 33
   principles 255–6, 257
   strategies 258–9
'teaching to the test' 35, 41
techno-humanism 220–1
technology 141 *see also* fourth industrial revolution
   big companies, power of 214
   common good 225
   ethical dilemmas 214–15, 217–18, 224
   hole-in-the-wall project 162–4
   pedagogy and 261

personalised learning and 161
predictive assistance 218–19, 220
testing regimes *see* standardised testing
Thatcher, Margaret 6, 8
think tanks 103, 130
Third Way ideology 7, 8
Times Educational Supplement 87, 157
Tooley, James 119–20
transplanting education policy 131–7, 273
Trends in Mathematics and Science Study (TIMSS) xviii
'trickle-down economics' xxiii, 11–12
Turnbull Government funding model 66
Twitter 212, 213

United Nations Children's Emergency Fund (UNICEF) 28
universalism, principle of 56–7
university 16
US charter schools 123–8
   equity and 126–8
   falling support for 128
   overview 123
   racial segregation 127
   student learning outcomes 124–5
   variations 123–4

values and principles of education 177–81, 188, 291
   bipartisan agreement about 300–1
   common good 178
   examples which may form basis of education 179–80, 291

Walsh, Toby 197, 198, 205
welfare recipients 9
welfare state 5, 19
Whitby, Greg 141, 161–2
Whitlam Government 55, 57
   funding model 58, 68
'world-class' education xvii–xx
World War 2 17
Wylie, Dr Cathy 121–2

year levels, removing 265
Young, Michael 156

Zhao, Yong 85, 86
Zuboff, Shoshana 219
Zuckerberg, Mark 145, 267

For Product Safety Concerns and Information please contact our EU representative GPSR@taylorandfrancis.com
Taylor & Francis Verlag GmbH, Kaufingerstraße 24, 80331 München, Germany

www.ingramcontent.com/pod-product-compliance
Lightning Source LLC
Chambersburg PA
CBHW061423300426
44114CB00014B/1507